INVENTING REALITY

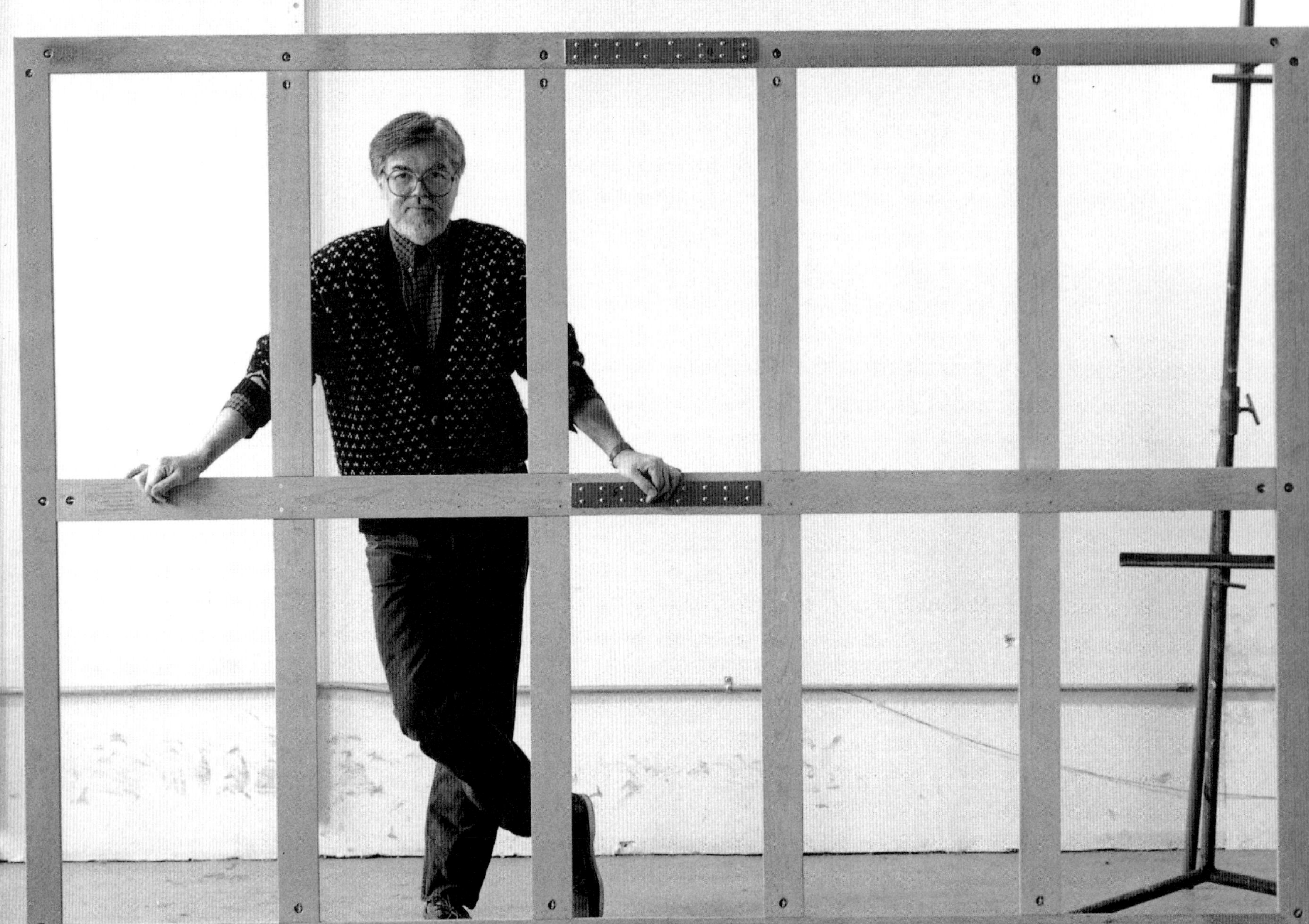

INVENTING REALITY

The Paintings of John Moore

by Therese Dolan

Hudson Hills Press, New York

First Edition

Published in the United States by Hudson Hills Press, Inc., Suite 1308, 230 Fifth Avenue, New York, NY 10001-7704.

Distributed in the United States, its territories and possessions, Canada, Mexico, and Central and South America by National Book Network.
Distributed in the United Kingdom, Eire, and Europe by Art Books International Ltd.
Exclusive representation in Asia, Australia, and New Zealand by EM International.

Editor and Publisher: Paul Anbinder

Copy Editor: Karen Siatras

Editorial Assistant: Faye Chiu

Proofreader: Lydia Edwards

Designer: Sisco & Evans Ltd., New York

Composition: Angela Taormina

Manufactured in Japan by Toppan Printing Company.

Frontispiece: John Moore in his Boston studio, 1994

Library of Congress Cataloguing-in-Publication Data

Dolan, Therese, 1946–
Inventing reality : the paintings of John Moore / Therese Dolan. – 1st ed.
p. cm.
Includes bibliographical references and index.
ISBN 1-55595-134-1 (alk. paper)
1. Moore, John, 1944– —Criticism and interpretation.
I. Title.
ND237.M684D66 1996
759.13—dc20

96-17760
CIP

CONTENTS

PLATES

Works indicated with an asterisk (*) are reproduced in color.

ACKNOWLEDGMENTS

I am grateful to Temple University and especially to Dean Rochelle Toner of Tyler School of Art for a study leave awarded fall semester 1993. Dean Toner has been a constant source of encouragement throughout the writing of this book.

Maxine S. Turek encouraged me to write when I was very young and shared her love of art to nurture my own. Dorothy Liggett awakened me to the love of the mind and sees to it that this continues.

Stuart Feld, Frank Del Deo, and especially Betty Cuningham, of Hirschl & Adler Gallery in New York, have been crucial in facilitating the completion of this book. Their generosity has been significant. Lawrence Di Carlo at Fischbach Gallery was helpful in locating early work.

Sandra Moore deserves a special debt of gratitude. Her insights, her knowledge of the chronology of her husband's work, and especially her support have made this project a true pleasure. John Arthur encouraged the idea of a book on Moore from its very earliest stages. His pioneering work in the field of contemporary American realism gave me a needed context for my research. Frank H. Goodyear, Jr.'s seminal exhibit *Contemporary American Realism since 1960* first got me interested in the movement. His generosity in reading portions of the manuscript is gratefully acknowledged.

Conversations with studio faculty at Temple University—Frank Bramblett, Daniel Dallmann, and Susan Moore—often clarified issues and provided welcome insights. My colleagues Charles Schmidt, Gerald Silk, and Martin Werner took on the more onerous task of reading the manuscript at various stages. Cynthia Lawrence was helpful with the cityscape chapter and with her constant encouragement of this project, while David Lawrence supplied an unforgettable interpretation of one of Moore's paintings. Frank Galuszka of the University of the Arts also read portions of the manuscript at a crucial stage in its development. I thank all of the above for their time and suggestions, which helped in the revisions. I am also grateful to Professors Mark Sullivan of Villanova University and Steven Z. Levine of Bryn Mawr College for inviting me to read portions of the manuscript in public lectures that brought forth good questions. In the end, I wrote the book that I needed to write, and the decisions on how to see the paintings ultimately were my own. I hold none of these generous people responsible for any shortcomings that may exist. It is my hope that others will take up the challenge and write about how they interpret Moore's work, knowing that we will always agree that this is important American painting and that it richly deserves critical attention.

From the time I approached John Moore about wanting to write on his art, he has been a model of modesty, tact, patience, and generosity. He has made every step of the way a pleasure by his willingness to supply ever more material, answer questions, check the manuscript, and attend to the often tedious details involved in getting a work such as this into production. The quality of his work inspired me at the same time that it provided such profound aesthetic pleasure that it was with genuine reluctance that I wrote the last entry. I look forward to volume two!

To borrow a phrase from Victor Borge, I would like to thank my parents for making this book possible, and my children for making it necessary.

After writing so many words to complete this book, I find myself at a loss to express adequately my gratitude to Gunter R. Haase, M.D. Not only did he provide a room with a view in his home in which this book was written and an amusing beagle to keep me company during the hours it took to compose it, but most importantly he continuously gave the love and support that sustained me throughout the project. It is to him, in gratitude for so much, that I dedicate this work.

INTRODUCTION

THE 1960s ART SCENE in America witnessed the demise of modernist abstraction and a greater tolerance toward a diversity of stylistic expression. During the 1950s abstraction seemed to exclude recognizable imagery, despite the fact that artists such as Arshile Gorky and Willem de Kooning continued to employ a loose type of figuration. Gesture and mark making came to be valued as more truthful to painting than any adherence to natural appearances, to the point that, as Irving Sandler bluntly remarked, "abstract artists, unless they were obviously *retardataire,* derivative, or decorative, never had to worry about their art being minor, but purely figurative artists always did."[1] When the energy associated with abstraction began to flag and the freedom it promised seemed more like a shackle, several artists who had worked in a gestural style made inroads against the hostile climate surrounding representational imagery sustained by critics such as Clement Greenberg and artists such as Ad Reinhardt. Painters began considering formalist abstraction as an option rather than a mandate and sought to restore a fully embodied pictorial illusionism to the canvas. They felt the need to record the objects of their everyday life, their contemporaries, and their surroundings in images that verified reality and realized a physical presence in the picture plane. This attitude toward the visible world eventually acquired the name of new realism and, after an initial period of critical confusion, became visually as well as aesthetically distinct from the ironic blandness of pop art and the sharp focus of photorealism.

Favorable reviews from Lawrence Campbell, Sidney Tillim, Hilton Kramer, and Lawrence Alloway, along with analytical articles by realist artists such as Fairfield Porter and Philip Pearlstein, signaled a growing support for the emerging realist movement. Porter met head-on Greenberg's refusal to acknowledge the validity of a realist style by contending that the insistence that "you cannot paint the figure today is like an architectural critic saying that you cannot use ornament."[2] Although continuity with earlier traditions of picture making remained an issue, the new realists sought to challenge past practices on a variety of representational and conceptual levels. References to modernist art in the return to realism were often more frequent than to those of previous eras. Love of the medium was no longer found to be incompatible with the love of visual reality as artists challenged themselves to render what they saw and what they felt with equal intensity. What had been stylistically marginalized during the heyday of modernist abstraction gradually became accepted as innovative and pictorially valid to the point that in 1968, when Linda Nochlin asked if it was possible for a realist to be new at all in the second half of the twentieth century, she answered her own question with a resounding yes that took the form of an exhibition called *Realism Now.*[3]

Since the late 1960s John Moore's still lifes, cityscapes, and industrial scenes have been acknowledged for their part in the innovations of realist painting in America. From the time of his first New York show of still lifes and figure paintings in 1969, Moore has consistently investigated his everyday surroundings in works that address issues of vision and style, questioning how the perceptual record of things can serve in the pictorial construction of the visual field. His paintings engage the traditions of both recent and older art, acknowledging the past while posing questions about fresh possibilities of expression. How we see and what we see, how we are conditioned by our cultural surroundings, and how the past influences the present are some of the concerns Moore addresses in his canvases and watercolors. Art critics of the late sixties and early seventies looked at Moore's work as evidence that formalist abstraction was not the only viable manner of expression open to avant-garde artists in late-twentieth-century America.[4] Throughout the seventies and eighties Moore participated in many of the major exhibitions that helped to define the critical issues of contemporary American realism.[5] His numerous solo exhibitions during this same period and the recognition they received confirmed his place in the mainstream of this movement.

Born and raised in St. Louis, Missouri, Moore received his B.F.A. from Washington University in 1966, then took his M.F.A. at Yale, graduating with the Ely Harwood Schless Memorial Prize in 1968. For twenty years he taught at Temple University's Tyler School of Art in Philadelphia. In 1988 he moved to Boston University, where he assumed the primary responsibility for the graduate program in painting. He has twice received the Childe Hassam Award from the American Academy and Institute of Arts and Letters. In 1982 and 1990 he received Visual Arts Fellowships in painting from the National Endowment for the Arts. His career has been one of steady growth in quality, accomplished without the circus atmosphere that so often accompanied art stars of the seventies and eighties. Moore's focus has always been on achieving the fullest potential of his talent. The critical notice that he has received has been measured and sensible rather than sensational.

In 1969 the artist and critic Scott Burton answered what he perceived as a "crisis in attenuation" in abstract painting with a show he organized at Fischbach Gallery in New York titled *Direct Representation.* Claiming that a new credibility of appearance could accommodate a wide range of sensibilities and intentions, he contentiously claimed that "straight figuration" was at that point "the only major mode now available to painting adequate for the expression of the fullest individuality."[6] He acknowledged that the venture into illusionism after the long break of abstraction was risky, but he confidently predicted that the quality of the painting represented in the show would prevent any lapse into a retrograde academic phase in contemporary art. As an example, he pointed to John Moore's traditional subjects and what he characterized as Moore's neo-classicist European taste refreshingly updated by his generalizing of forms to accentuate their abstract shapes. Art such as Moore's retained its consciousness of modernism's strategies, yet sought to expand upon its aesthetic potential rather than merely repeating it or reducing it to a prosaic formula.

The show caught the attention of several critics, among them Lawrence Alloway, Cindy Nemser, Peter Schjeldahl, and Robert Pincus-Witten, who used their reviews to address the issue of representational painting and its role in the art of the late sixties.[7] Schjeldahl agreed with Burton that abstraction had little more to give the art world because of its fetish of originality, and he expected that the new realists would reinvigorate easel painting.[8] Schjeldahl's forecast came at a time when painting's preeminence had been seriously questioned by the deliberate temporality of performance art, process art, and earth works of the sixties. The ephemeral, the serial, and the conceptual openly challenged the uniqueness of easel painting as a worthy art object. Schjeldahl noted Moore's deliberate simplification of his subject matter and his avoidance of any gimmickry of "style," predicting that Moore would be heard from again. Pincus-Witten took issue with Burton's insistence that direct representation offered the only significant avenue to the expression of individuality, but on the whole he endorsed the show and found Moore's canvases "impressive in a solid and uncompromising way."[9] Cindy Nemser viewed new realism as a synthesis of the lessons of art history with an allegiance to modernist principles, feeling "the stirrings of hope" when she looked at Moore's work.[10]

These reviews had to be encouraging to an artist in his late twenties who had graduated only the year before from Yale's graduate painting program and had been hired by David Pease to teach at Temple University's Tyler School of Art in suburban Philadelphia. Committed at this early stage to representational painting, Moore initiated a course titled Direct Painting that approached art on a straightforward perceptual basis. His work continued to attract favorable critical notice, and in 1972 Fischbach gave him his first solo exhibition. As the art scene became more responsive to representational painting, Moore was frequently invited to participate in shows that attempted to situate realism within the pluralist art scene of the seventies and eighties. Critics often found his early work difficult to classify, calling him a metaphysical naturalist, a perceptual realist, a magic realist, a minimal realist, and an artist who seemed to reinvent realist art from scratch.[11] Despite quibbles over labels, critics consistently lauded the promise and conviction in his still lifes and interiors, finding his visual asceticism refreshingly honest.

Moore began painting still lifes in 1967, during his last year of graduate school at Yale, following the examples of Lennart Anderson, William Bailey, and Jack Beal. Experiments with abstraction had proven frustrating as his love for detail impelled him to materialize light, shape, and form rather than diffuse them into generalized strokes. He came to believe that he did not know how to paint, that he was faking it, and that he needed to start from scratch. Still life gave him something concrete to paint, allowing him the control he felt he needed to comprehend thoroughly the elements of visual design and prompting him to study the achievements of earlier masters of the genre. With the discipline of description he found a way to begin to correlate what he saw with how he wanted it to be seen. Strongly influenced by his colleague Italo Scanga's emphasis on the forms of things rather than their utilitarian function, and attracted to the shapes and colors of the "uncommon common things" his wife Sandy collected, Moore dedicated himself to the still-life genre and quickly gained recognition for the quality of his work.

Still life offered Moore the opportunity to focus intently on issues of perception without the presence of the live model, which he found to be distracting. It provided him with complex visual problems of light, perspective, and form that sustained his interest. He often painted still lifes in series, investigating subtle differences in light, color, volume, and perspective, discovering that each new work suggested other questions and different solutions. Moore's still lifes investigate the sensate world to draw feeling out of geometry, to highlight the cognitive aspects of viewing art. They provide a viable realist alternative to reductive abstraction while eliciting strength from the same visual imperatives as non-objective art. Moore's alertness to the tension implicit in an overall surface, combined with the realistic depiction of objects, results in a compelling contemporary challenge to the traditions of both abstraction and naturalism. His objects, while never shedding their representational identity, contribute strongly to the abstract nature of the painting.

Moore's shift in focus in the late 1970s from still lifes to cityscapes marked not only a variation in artistic motif but a changed attitude toward subject matter. At that time Moore became keenly interested in recording the urban views of North Philadelphia and the fading neighborhoods of Tioga and Kensington. "North Philadelphia, with its nineteenth century factories and row houses, not only provided visual surprises that I could never dream up in my studio," Moore commented, "but was a record of a world of work that I wanted to recognize or acknowledge in my painting."[12]

Years of painting still lifes had taught Moore how to control his subject; through them he trained his eye to observe ever more complex detail and his hand to record the intricacies of shape and space under different conditions of light. Once these skills were mastered, however, he found that formalist problems could not adequately sustain his interest. The tabletops and the activity taking place there no longer seemed significant enough for him as matter for painting. Turning his gaze to his immediate surroundings—to urban buildings and congested city spaces, to the quiet middle-class streets and modest homes of his suburban neighborhood, and to the industrial sites recorded by the precisionists—Moore discovered sources of subject matter that not only stimulated his visual interest but, more significantly, satisfied a strong desire to record a way of life that he was experiencing directly. He came to think of his paintings as "workingscapes" that recorded the environment of the anonymous laborers and common people whose passage through life is all too often deemed insignificant by an elitist culture.

Moore often prefers to picture the city at moments when the light is caught and held in a mood that is transformative and affecting. Early morning and late afternoon light provide strong contrasts and rich color modulations, while dusk sets luminescence against ambiguity, transfiguring spatial distinctions into enigmatic encounters. The viewer is invited to gaze at areas of the city that light has converted from the ordinary into the exceptional. Moore often ennobles the architecture of the underclass, ordering the city's confusion without hiding its indignities. He manipulates the urban fabric, culling images from various locales to accord architecture a heightened status, opening up a dialogue between geometric form and descriptive detail. Maintaining a balance between the evocative and the informative, Moore combines his concern for the materiality of the cityscape with a care for the emotive effects of light. He establishes a relationship between the grandeur of the realist style and the factual referents of what he paints, thereby indicating that the complexity of the city is social as well as visual.

Moore's paintings are a function of his cumulative knowledge of a place over time. He feels free to change the elements of a site until it conveys an experience and satisfies his sense of what makes a good painting. When he moved away from still life to the cityscape, he was initially overwhelmed by the complexity of detail that made it so different from his studio arrangements. Watercolor studies executed on site provided information when he returned to the studio to paint, but he began to supplement these with slides and photographs so that the final work was most often drawn from oil studies, watercolors, photographs, slides, and on-site notations. His use of photographic material had nothing to do, however, with the procedures of photorealism, which was popular at the time these works were painted. He had, and has, no desire to make the painting surface replicate the glossy finish of the photo, nor is he interested in recording a site in obsessively accurate detail. His use of multiple sources makes subject matter more accessible to him, allowing him to graft an evocative element from one site onto another or to explore aspects that resonate with layers of time, change, and experience that he seeks in his work. This method provides him with the freedom to take liberties in composition that he feels would not be possible working in a more literal mode. His interest is in distilling the sense of a site rather than capturing every chip in every brick. Moore's procedure has as much to do with memory as with observation, and for this reason his city views tend to be combinations of various sites.

Moore's cityscapes often include industrial neighborhoods where older factories and row houses huddle together on land that shows by its depletion or decay how economic investors have taken their fill and then moved on to more lucrative exploits elsewhere. Industrial architecture has always interested Moore. Retrospective exhibitions on Charles Demuth and Ralston Crawford in the 1980s prompted him to visit Coatesville, Pennsylvania, where these precisionists had found their subject matter. He then embarked on a series of paintings that reconsidered these industrial scenes from the vantage point of the late twentieth century. Once seen as testimonials to cultural advancement, these sites are now probed by Moore as records of a social and economic vision that underpinned modernist aspirations and are called into question in the declining years of the twentieth century.

Moore's industrial paintings deal with these sites not so much for their topographical exactitude—although he discovered that many of the sites had physically changed minimally over the intervening years—but chose them because they allowed him to rethink the precisionist traditions of art and to analyze what those images promised and what has actually been achieved. Moore's descriptions constitute subtle critiques of politics and economy, relying for their legibility on their similarities to and differences from their iconographical heritage. He trusted that he could portray his images in such a way that their tangible characteristics would ultimately shed light on the ethical and cultural implications encoded in their structures.

The evolution from the spartan austerity of Moore's earliest still lifes to the profuse but tightly controlled detail of his most recent cityscapes and industrial views is dramatic. He has evolved from the position of an entrenched modernist primarily concerned with formal issues and realist theory in his early still lifes to that of a social analyst embracing bold daylight and moody nocturnal effects within oddly evocative sites. Through the skillful manipulation of spatial perspectives and his focus on detail, the common becomes compelling, intensifying the experience of the everyday. The increased ambition of his move toward greater visual complexity in his painting speaks of a sense of urgency to tell more and more about society as it edges toward the end of the century.

"THERE'S A STYLE that consists in not making a big fuss about things," the realist artist Rackstraw Downes wrote. "The artist may present himself as diffident or off-hand, while working his intensity into stating the facts in a way that doesn't draw attention to itself."[13] This statement describes well the procedure of the realist whose aim is to portray the world in a naturalistic style that abjures the loaded brush or the expressionistic gesture. To describe the uniqueness of the everyday, to reveal the complexity of the ordinary, became the purpose of many realist artists seeking an alternative to the high-pitched emotion of action painting or the cerebral reductivism of minimalism.

Like the novels of Raymond Chandler and John Updike, Moore's art investigates the experience of the lower middle class—Formica tabletops and molded plastic chairs, simple homes and roads, factories and storage sheds—seeking to communicate something about the social facts of these sites and objects in twentieth-century culture. Robert Pinsky, a poet whose work Moore deeply admires, once remarked: "I've found myself responding to how evocative certain physical objects are, and how independent of us they are at the same time that we invest or discern feeling in them. But in my work, this often involves knowing the physical being of objects through the smell of humanity. I feel interested in getting the social aroma or aura of physical details."[14] Like Pinsky, Moore desires to be an honest witness to the physical sense of a certain part of the world he came from and that formed him.

Moore's contemporary realism takes on meaning by its relationship to and difference from modernist abstraction and the realisms of the past. By maintaining an active tension between surface design and spatial recession, he invokes modernism and tradition, transforming both by charging them with a contemporary idiom that intensifies their interaction. He throws both terms into question by their overlap and interpenetration. Moore is not out to dissolve cubism into a rarefied realism, overlay painterly marks onto stark precisionist factory facades, or update Hopperesque loneliness in order to squeeze out a more timely angst. By their visual and iconographic complexity, his images work against being reduced to a formula or trapped by readily available explanations. His paintings encourage us to see in a manner that is determined by visual reference to a historically rich tradition of painting with eyes and minds that are the products of a modernist heritage. Each of the following chapters will study Moore's paintings and watercolors, setting them in their thematic and historical context to show what he drew from older traditions, how he responded to the art of his own time, and how his unique vision of late-twentieth-century America has enriched contemporary art.

INVENTING REALITY

Chapter 1

Mute Eloquence

STILL LIFES AND INTERIOR VIEWS

ARTISTS WHO RENDERED the recognizable world set in illusionistic space in the late sixties and early seventies earned themselves labels such as "the inhumanists"[15] from critics who often scorned realism as hopelessly old-fashioned, a failure of nerve, or a temporary lapse during a season that had no new aesthetic revolution to offer.[16] For a contemporary artist to paint a still life seemed a step back to the conservative traditions of previous centuries. The twentieth century saw the object dissected and analyzed in cubism, exploded by energetic forces in futurism, lampooned in dada, psychoanalyzed in surrealism, until it seemed to disappear in skeins of color on abstract expressionist canvases. When it re-emerged on pop canvases, the object functioned as a sign, flattened and emblematic. To engage the object in its plenitude, to place it back into perspectival space, and to investigate its surface properties in the final decades of the twentieth century struck many as aesthetically reactionary. One critic reviewing the Whitney Museum's *22 Realists* show in 1970 complained that other technologies captured illusions better than painting could, and dismissed realists "who try to pretend as if Daguerre never lived" as sentimental idealists.[17]

Nevertheless, the new realism remained more than a minor blip on the stylistic scene and came to be considered in its own right rather than as the straw man in a polemic against the failures of abstraction.[18] If the return to the figure in painting marked a shift to postmodernism, the appearance of the still life on the canvases of a number of artists signaled a renewed interest in craftsmanship and naturalism. Many realists turned to the object as a subject for formal investigation. Artists such as William Bailey, Paul Wonner, Janet Fish, and Audrey Flack found their way to realism by means of the still life because of its affinity to abstraction in formal problems such as spatial tension and color relationships. Freed from the problems of the psychology of the figure or the vagaries of weather in landscape, artists investigated the physical presence of objects, which they often arranged with a touch as personal and expressive as the abstract mark. The treatment of the object broadened outward from the replication of commercialized logos and the rows of foodstuffs that constituted the familiar repertoire of pop art, with its references to mass media. Paul Weisenfeld's coffee services set on polished wood, Gabriel Laderman's earthenware vessels on wooden tables in front of rough-hewn walls, Stephen Posen's wrapped objects, or Carolyn Brady's elegantly set tables spoke more about individual preferences than about a desire to achieve a common look dedicated to a group aesthetic.

While some artists avoided narrative or symbolic meaning, others such as Audrey Flack and Jack Beal embraced it wholeheartedly in emulation of the *vanitas* tradition. In order to avoid being retrograde, the realist still life had in some way to challenge the genre if it intended to pay more than just lip service to tradition. Ever since the cubists made guitars and newspapers crucial objects in a major stylistic statement about form and René Magritte convinced us that a picture of a pipe was not a pipe, artists have realized that the still-life object possesses the potential to move out of the confines of its historically low status to occupy a central position in an art of high seriousness. By choosing to focus on what José Ortega y Gasset has called "the mute things that surround us most closely,"[19] artists such as John Moore have displayed a passion for examining their surroundings and depicting them in a representational style.

Before turning to still life in graduate school at Yale, Moore had experimented with abstractions from nature. The still life retained the sense of the landscape for him but afforded him a firmer control of his subject, providing him with a direct, legible image through which he could study complex problems of space, light, and color. He investigated still life for its potential to help him re-establish contact with the visible world. His interest centered on the relationships between objects and the spaces surrounding them, on what they could say about cultural life and artistic style in the wake of abstraction, and on how they allowed him to contemplate the complexities of representation in an era that was critically attuned to questioning sensed phenomena.

Moore's earliest work in still life consisted of a series of quietly absorbing depictions of household objects on tables. *Cylinders* (pl. 1) and *Yellow Table* (pl. 2) are notable for their stark plasticity and clarity of form combined with an elusive sense of mystery. In *Spring* (pl. 3) a cattail and some dried flower buds extend into space over the edge of the table, occupying the role that the knife traditionally played in earlier still lifes. The colors are quiet and restrained, allowing for a concentration on the subtle play of gray light on the wall and white cloth. The tour de force of paint handling in a range of whitenesses, and

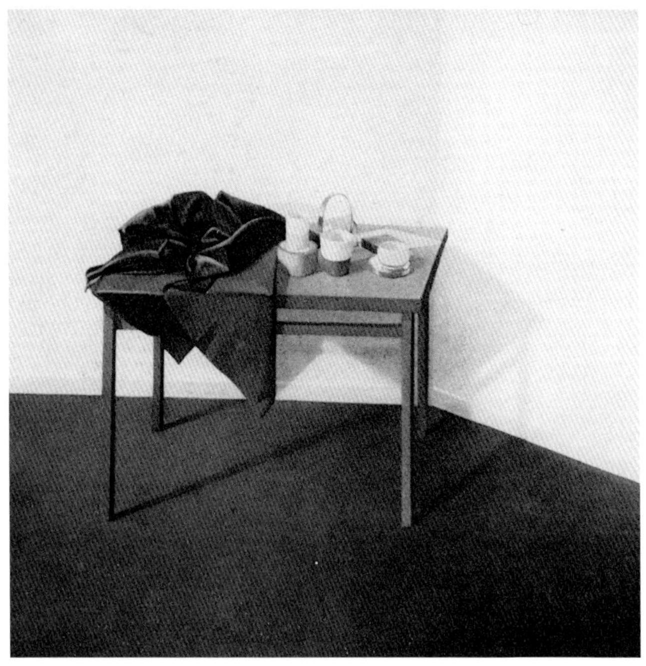

1

CYLINDERS, 1969

Oil on canvas, 60 × 72 in.
Collection of the artist.

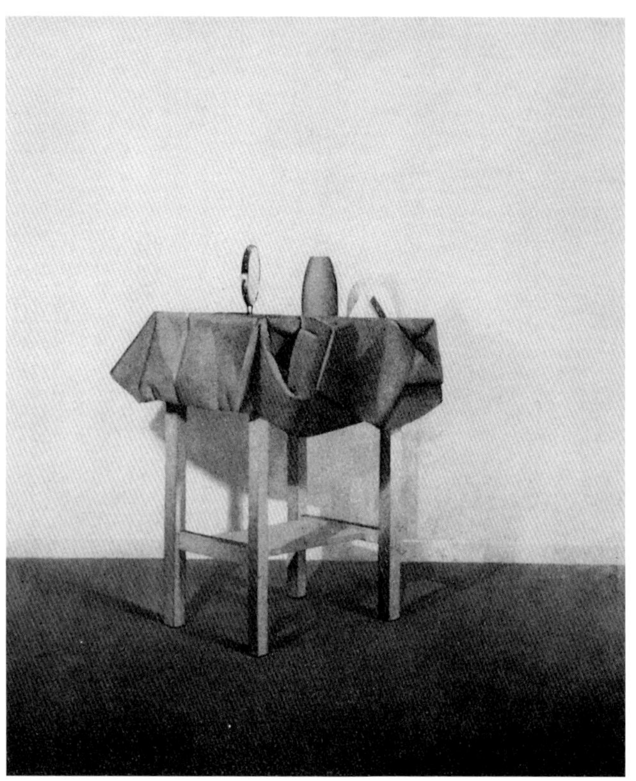

2

YELLOW TABLE, 1970

Oil on canvas, 60 × 52 in.
Private collection

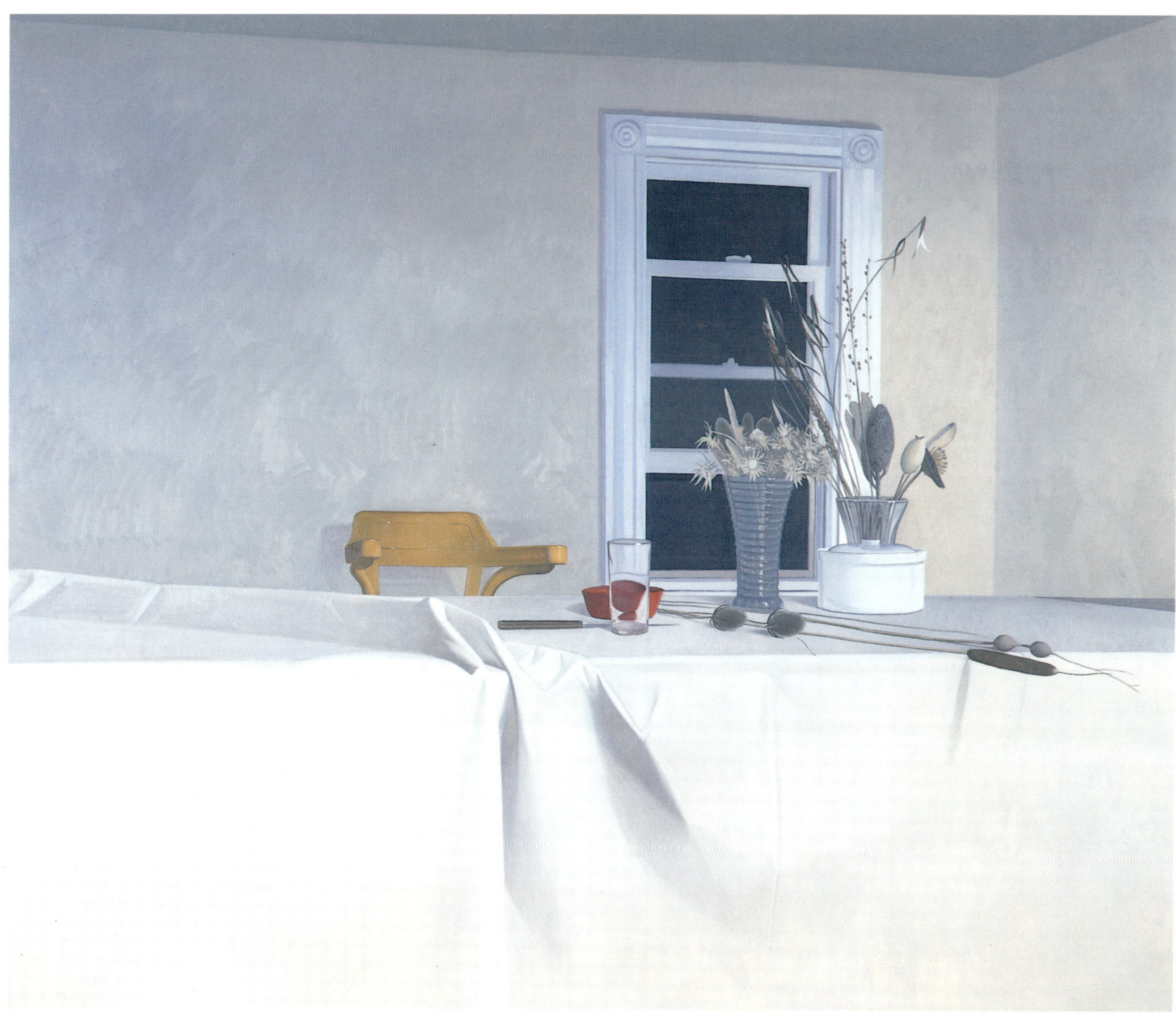

3 SPRING, 1972

Oil on canvas, 75 × 90 in.
Museum of Art, Rhode Island School of Design, Providence, Albert Pilavin Memorial Collection of American Art.

especially the sharply delineated cloth, recall a famous icon of early American art, Raphaelle Peale's *After the Bath* (fig. 1). Like Peale, Moore achieves a mastery of abstract design and convincing illusion with the simple subject of a white expanse of fabric, while also recalling the role that Philadelphia played in the early history of still life.[20] Yet Moore's references were not always to the still-life tradition. In this painting Moore has arranged the objects on the table in imitation of the compositional grouping found in Théodore Géricault's *Raft of the Medusa*, as if in illustration of William Carlos Williams's observation:

> *All poems can be represented by*
> *Still lifes not to say*
> *Watercolors The violence of*
> *the Iliad lends itself to an arrangement*
> *of narcissi in a jar. . . .* [21]

Moore chose to portray simple household objects in *Summer* (pl. 4), but like the seventeenth-century Spanish still-life masters he endowed them with a sense of poetic reverie and quiet intensity. The austere simplicity of the objects arranged frontally, combined with the blackness of the square window, evokes the ascetic dignity that informed the solemn larders of Juan Sanchez-Cotán. The arrangement of lemons, the centered wicker basket, and the vase of flowers to the right provide a loose quotation of and variation on Francisco de Zurbarán's *Lemons, Oranges, and a Rose* (fig. 2).

Moore's references to old-master art do not deny his paintings their modernity, however. As Laurie Anderson astutely noted, the windows in *Summer* are strongly reminiscent of Marcel Duchamp's *Fresh Widow* (fig. 3) as they block the outside view in a counterplay on the notion of the Renaissance window providing a view of a believable reality.[22] The shadow on the lower wall on the left reflects the objects on the table, but it also softly imitates landscape and architecture in a subtle visual pun on the inside/outside motif suggested by the blackened window.

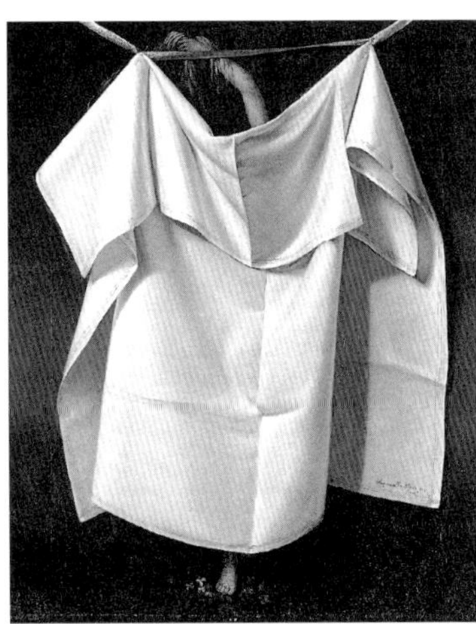

Figure 1. Raphaelle Peale, *Venus Rising from the Sea—A Deception (After the Bath)*, ca. 1882, oil on canvas, 29¼ × 24⅛ in. Nelson-Atkins Museum of Art, Kansas City, Missouri, Nelson Trust purchase.

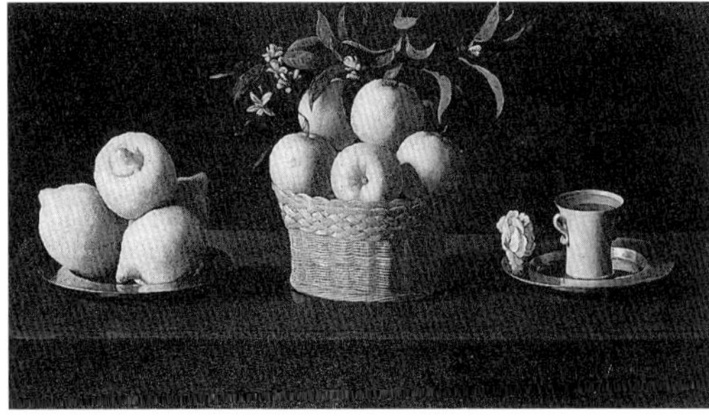

Figure 2. Francisco de Zurbarán, *Still Life with Lemons, Oranges, and a Rose*, 1633, oil on canvas, 24½ × 43⅛ in. Norton Simon Foundation, Pasadena, California.

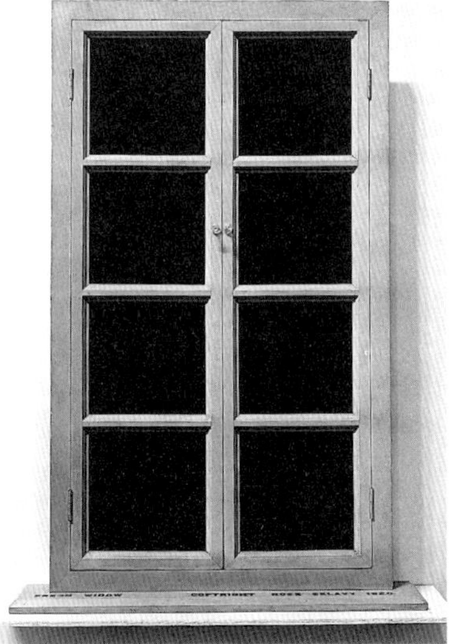

Figure 3. Marcel Duchamp, *Fresh Widow*, 1920, miniature French window, painted wood frame, and eight panes of glass covered with black leather, 30½ × 17⅝ in. on wood sill, ¾ × 21 × 4 in. Museum of Modern Art, New York, Katherine S. Dreier Bequest.

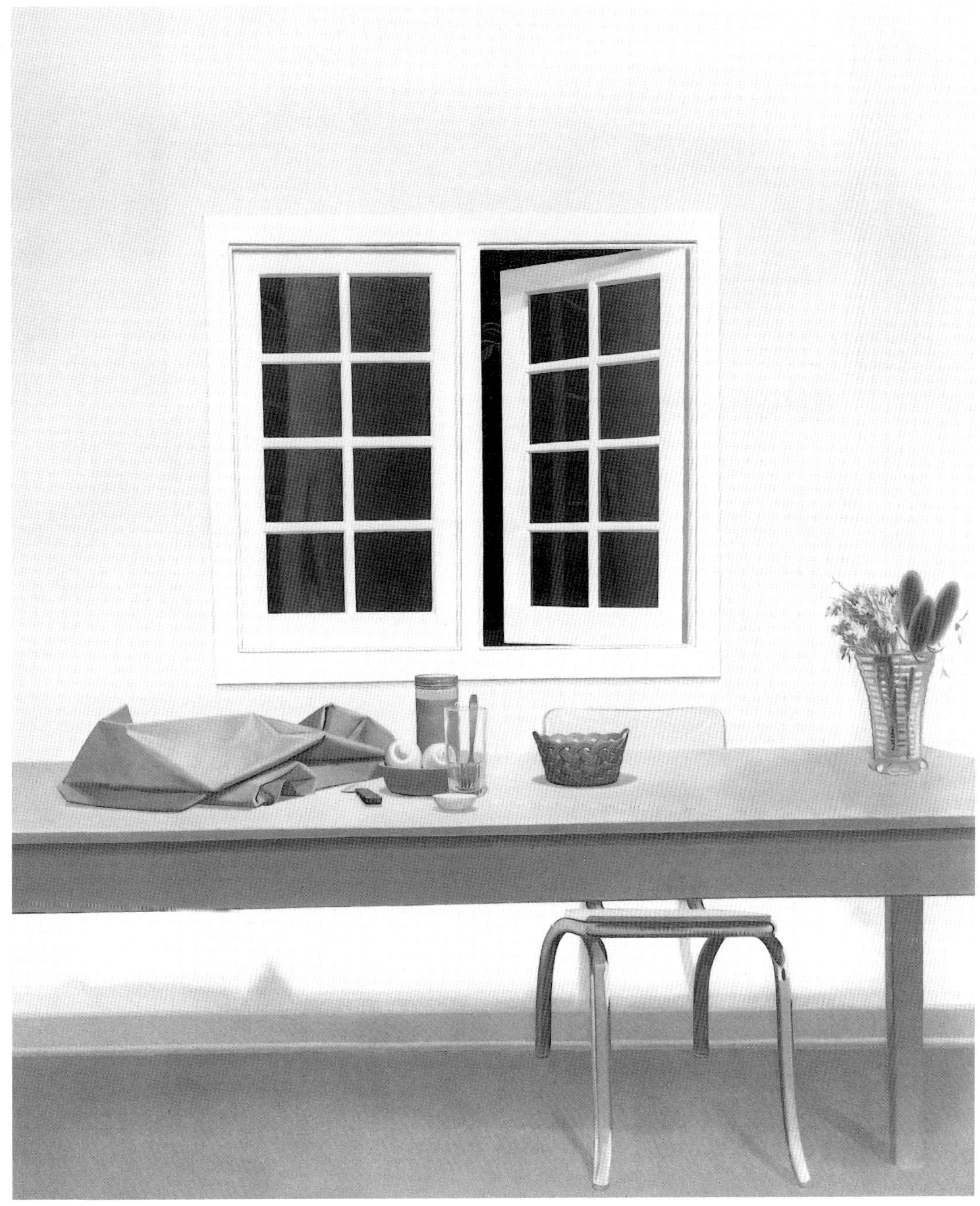

4 SUMMER, 1972

Oil on canvas, 89 3/4 × 75 1/8 in.
Pennsylvania Academy of the Fine Arts, Philadelphia.
Gift of the American Academy of Arts and Letters
(Childe Hassam Fund).

Moore's series of still lifes on tables has an enigmatic quality that verges on the surreal. Although the objects and the setting remain ordinary, the abstract handling of shapes through his suppression of detail and the visual emphasis on essential forms create an air of mystery throughout the series. By keeping the casual everyday sense of place in this initial series of still lifes to a minimum, Moore alerts the viewer to a specialized sense of realism where the act of perception intensifies the object beyond the normal. The isolation of the objects against starkly plain walls produces an almost hypnotic effect as the eye focuses intently on the shapes and the intervals between them. Moore renders each object with such intense concern for its individuality that it ceases to suggest a functional use and surrenders to the realm of the purely aesthetic.

Moore's tables and their contents are only as precise as they need to be in order to convince the viewer of their shape and weight in space. Nothing unessential is allowed to intrude in these works that are almost monastic in their insistence on a meditative stillness. The objects and their setting have an aura of the symbolic about them, a seriousness of the emblematic. The paintings invite not a quick glance of recognition but a slowed reflection on the intrinsic pictorial values of design. The brushstroke remains dedicated to the task of defining form rather than calling attention to any painterly gesture or modernist mark making. Wallace Stevens wrote, "To get at the thing/Without gestures is to get at it as/Idea."[23] Moore's unpretentious canvases, his graceful simplifications, seem concentrated on an identical goal.

Double windows open onto a night scene in *Tiger Lilies* (pl. 5). Beneath the window some papers, a white vase containing tiger lilies, and a television sit on a low black chest with scroll legs. To the left and slightly in front of the table is an A-shaped stand with sunglasses and boxes placed on top of a black-and-white polka-dot cloth. Squares and rectangles calibrate the space of the painting with a measured regularity. The ascetic color scheme of repeated blacks and whites is broken only by the orange of the flowers in the center of the painting, an organic note in a composition of almost Mondrianesque severity of shape and color, and a tip of the hat to fellow realist Alex Katz, who frequently painted large decorative canvases of tiger lilies at the time. A mirror reflecting only the blankness of the opposite wall hangs to the right. As a white square, it answers to the black glass squares of the windows and the television set. Each article is precisely drawn and is intrinsically felt in its physicality. This evocative presence gives the objects the sense of having been newly born into the taut space of the room they so pristinely occupy.

There is an absoluteness to this painting in its insistence on the square and on the polarities of black and white, relieved only by the oneiric tiger lilies. The objects are placed in such a way as to rivet the eye to their presence. The blank mirror, slightly askew on the wall, almost parodies Kazimir Malevich's *White on White.* The black face of the television and the black window panes coincide with this same artist's *Black Square.* If Malevich took refuge in the square to free himself from the burden of the object, Moore's process is the opposite here as he seeks to anchor his objects in a credible space. But Moore shares with Malevich a passion for the expressivity of geometrical relations and the organization of dynamic tensions of shape.

Moore's inclusion of a mirror and a window in the painting leads to a consideration of issues of perception and representation that were so integral to the critical discussions of new realism at the time. Because the windows open onto a night scene, they ambiguously conceal and expose the view. Like an updated allegory on vision, objects specifically concerned with sight are inventoried in the painting: windows, mirror, television screen, and sunglasses. Yet each of these things fails to perform its usual visual function in this instance: the windows open onto a darkened view, the mirror reflects only blankness, the television set is turned off, and the sunglasses are useless at night. Detached from their normal use, these objects exist for contemplation alone, heightened beyond their routine function as if elected for a moment to symbolize their essence. Frontally displayed and devoid of any decoration not essential to their telling, the objects in *Tiger Lilies* act as interchanges between presentation and representation in a setting whose spareness enhances their purpose.

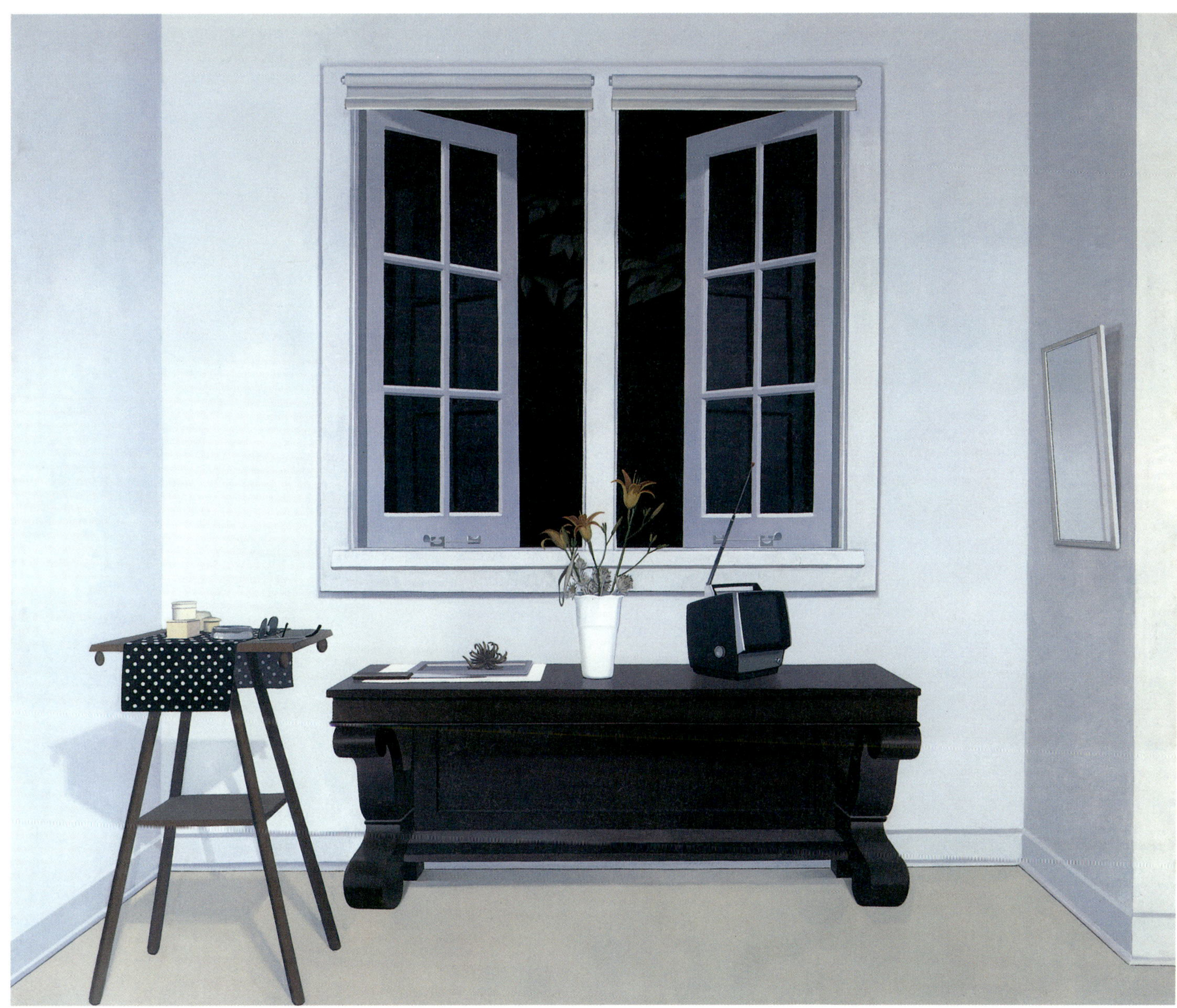

5 TIGER LILIES, 1973

Oil on canvas, 75 × 90 in.
AT&T Corporate Collection.

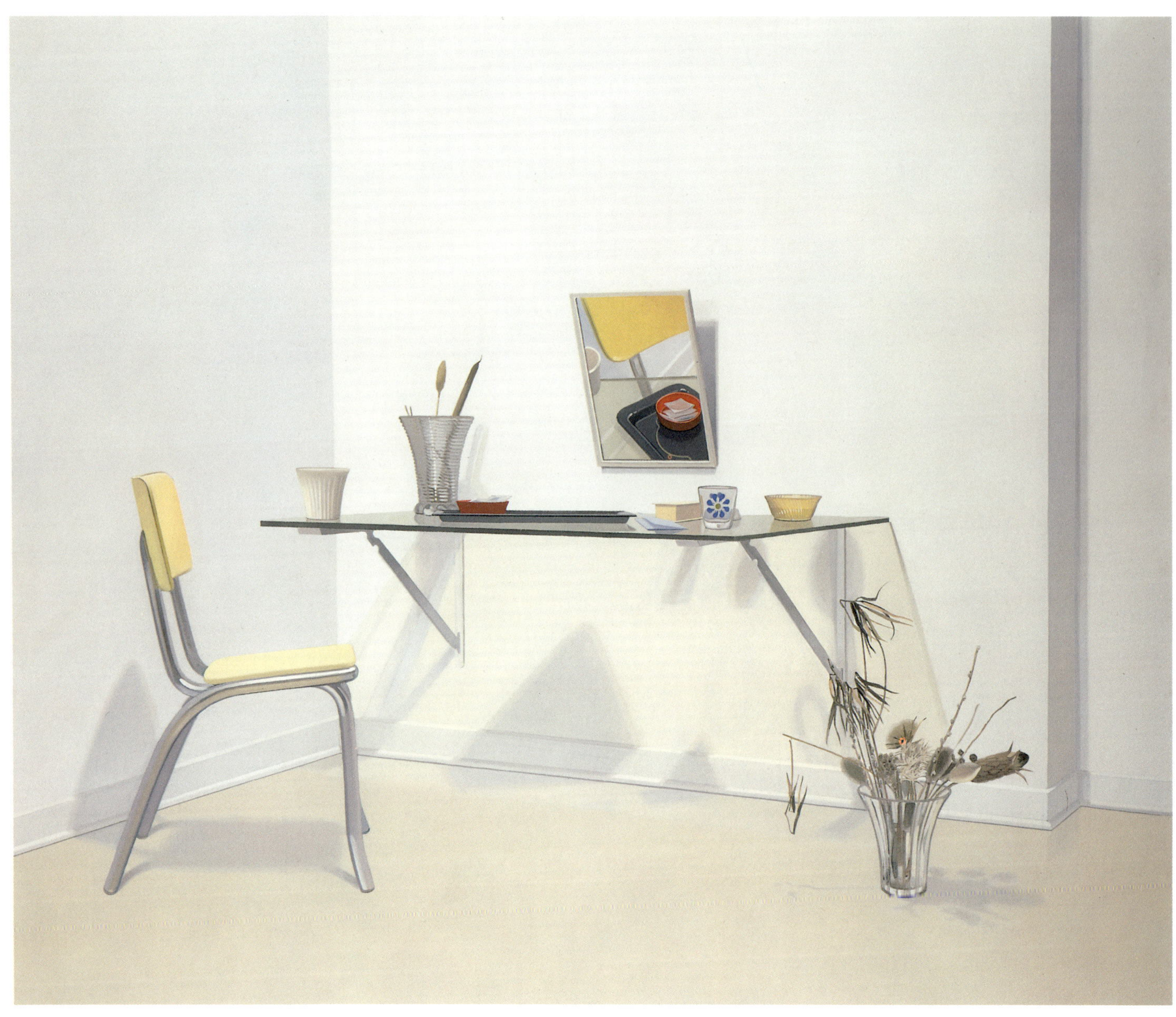

6 THE GLASS TABLE, 1973

Oil on canvas, 75 × 90 in.
Arizona State University Art Museum, Tempe.

Moore's attention to common artifacts and the bare interiors in which they are placed speaks of the period in which these paintings were created. The prosaic nature of the objects, their impersonality and lack of expressive gesture, situate them in the post–pop art milieu of the late sixties and early seventies. The undecorated rooms, the emphasis on the planarity of table supports, and the geometry of the windows ally the artist with a minimalist sensibility.

While working on a still-life painting in his studio, Moore became engrossed in the play of light through a glass shelf on a back wall. The shelf was under a skylight, and Moore gradually took notice of the shadows cast by objects under shifting conditions of light. The painting that resulted, *The Glass Table* (pl. 6), did not differ greatly in subject from his previous still lifes of tables in corners. What did change, however, was his increased interest in transparency, translucency, and the role of natural light. The starkness of his earlier work gives way to a muted bluish-gray atmosphere that permeates the canvas and softens the edges of objects. The structure of the work is still a prerequisite, but it is now subordinated to the overall effect of the subtleties of half tones and softly colored shadows contrasting with the strong primary colors of the yellow chair, the black tray, and the red bowl. The chair in the painting is life size, and everything was painted from ten feet away. Moore was so intent upon testing his perception that he refused to move closer to the objects to check details. He chose the motif because it was a concrete thing from a specific time and place in normal life rather than art life.

This painting marked an important moment for Moore. He felt it was the first work that was truly his own and not the result of another artist's ideas or style. His apprenticeship completed, he felt ready to explore his own individuality and to develop his own pictorial problems and solutions. The painting brought with it an increased awareness of the complexity of observed phenomena and a keener interest on Moore's part in the role of perception and artifice in representational painting.

In two related works of the same year, *The Black Tray* (pl. 7) and *Palm Trees* (pl. 8), Moore moves closer to the table and views it from above. By de-emphasizing evidence of the supporting brackets attached to the wall, Moore converts the shelf into a floating transparent glass square. The shadows cast by the objects softly emerge as ethereal abstractions on the wall and the floor, ghostly echoes of pure shape. Moore backs away from the tight close-up on objects that is common to traditional and much contemporary still life, allowing the objects to breathe in the shallow depth of the room. His interest centers on how transparencies and reflections affect our experience of three-dimensional form; how, for example, a clear glass dish is read on top of a glass shelf against a neutral white wall under sunlight.

In each of these paintings the most solid object in the work appears to be the precise reflection in the rectangular mirror. In *The Glass Table* the mirror flattens the distance between the snack tray on the table and the chair placed at an angle to it. The reflection conflates the two objects into a visual pun in which the tray seems to be resting directly on the seat of the chair or paradoxically appears to be the seat itself. The mirror in *The Black Tray* doubles the strongest and most solid color accents of red and black in the painting into a flat decorative pattern, accentuating opacity against transparency, while in *Palm Trees* it effectively isolates and concentrates the round and square forms that constitute the dominant shapes in the canvas. The everyday objects in these paintings set apart in the mirror assume an enhanced intensity that they do not possess on the table. The viewer becomes more conscious of them as abstract pattern without losing sight of their physical presence as real objects. They fluctuate between the real and the unreal, between the common and the uncommon, their shapes well attuned to the minimalist sensibility of the times.

But the mirror plays a larger role here than just a reflecting surface. It calls into question the nature of realism and the canvas as a fictional surface. Since the time of Plato's discussion of the mirror and its relationship to painting in his tenth book of *The Republic,* the mirror has been used to comment on the artifice of art and to question what is real. In these paintings the mirror introduces the idea of cubism by its spatial reflection of the objects, tipped up and forward so that front, back, and depth are seen simultaneously in the same painting. The three-dimensional space of the room is compressed into two-dimensional flatness by the mirror reflection. What is whole and entire on the table becomes partial and abstract

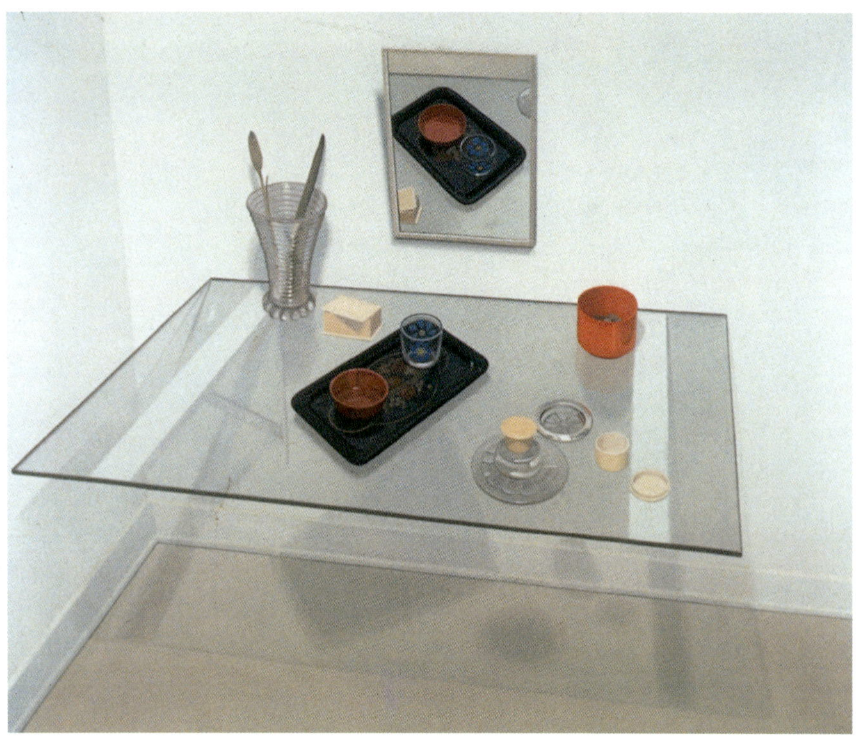

7

THE BLACK TRAY, 1973

Oil on canvas, 40 × 50 in.
Private collection.

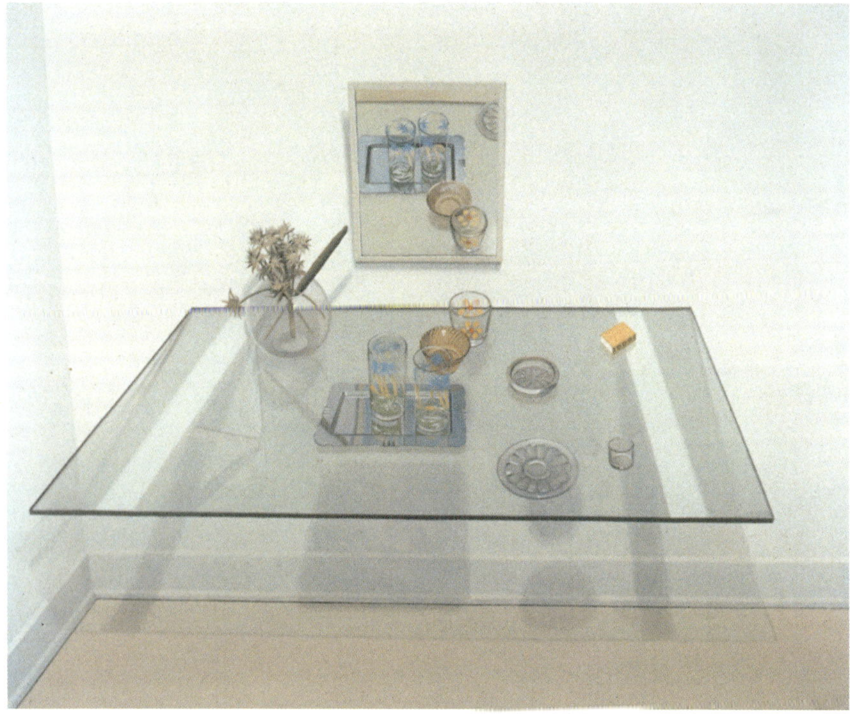

8

PALM TREES, 1973

Oil on canvas, 40 × 50 in.
Private collection.

in a mirror that hangs in a space that could easily accommodate—or be—a painting. By invoking cubism Moore maintains a reciprocal tension between the flatness of the picture plane essential to modernism and the plasticity of form characteristic of realism.

The mirror also comments in its own way on truth and ambiguity in realist art. Leonardo da Vinci recommended the mirror as the true test of realism in art, and artists throughout history, from Van Eyck to Manet, from Picasso to Pearlstein, have included references to mirrors in their art. What Moore has shown us in his use of mirrors is how unstable the definition of reality is, how it changes under different lights, various perspectives, and altered points of view. The mirror imparts ambiguity to a painting that would otherwise be a straightforward depiction of visual fact. It comments on the process of realist art itself: it bodies forth objects that are recognizable but whose physical model is elsewhere. It offers a translation of things in the world but re-creates them on a two-dimensional surface. Thus Moore makes us aware that realism is not simply the preeminence of content over form, but an interrelationship of abstract elements with natural objects described in a credible space.

Moore's purpose is to enrich through illusion, not to deceive the viewer. The willed tension between realism and abstraction evident in Moore's handling of form, along with the importance of the cubist still life in his artistic formation, are acknowledged here in a simplified setting. Moore was interested in contrasting images seen flatly with those seen in three-dimensional space. When he first saw Diego Velázquez's *Las Meniñas* at the Prado in Spain in 1970, he was fascinated by the way the great Spanish realist had painted tiny granules of dust on the mirror to keep it from being a hole in the background. Moore thus painted dust on the glass shelves and mirrors in these works to achieve a similar visual effect and also, like Velázquez, to use the mirror as a vehicle for invoking the complexities of representation.

The Glass Table, The Black Tray, and *Palm Trees* can also serve as updated versions of the metaphysics of painting. The glass table and shelves function simultaneously as a flat surface and as a framed field for the still-life elements strewn across their surface. The objects cast shadows that float in disembodied reproduction beneath the transparent planes, while the mirror above crops a section of the arrangement into an enclosed reflective illusion. Plato's famous discourse on mimesis in book ten of *The Republic* involves the ideal or real form, the image or the appearance of the ideal that he defines in terms of the shadow world, and the painted image that Plato declares as an imitation of an imitation that is twice removed from reality. Moore's paintings offer a visual analogy of the tripartite Platonic levels of pictorial reality and imitation. His work seems to operate at the level once described by Wallace Stevens as "the flux/between the thing as idea and the idea as thing."[24]

Modernist critics such as Clement Greenberg upheld a ban on the mimetic re-creation of a three-dimensional reality because it would deflect attention from the honesty of the medium, which was seen to be the true essence of art. A decentralized decorative surface reinforced the unity of the art work and permitted no literary narrative, implied or actual, to intrude upon the purity of the work. Many new realist painters began to challenge these proscriptions by applying the scale of abstract expressionism and the intellectual rigor of minimalism to their canvases, thereby asserting that the representation of the visual world could be as aesthetically progressive and visually challenging as nonobjective forms of art. Much of contemporary realist art work intended to be radical in its newness rather than retrograde in its references.

As the representational function of art came to be reappraised, several realist artists began to include mirrors or mirrored surfaces in their canvases. Sylvia Plimack Mangold depicted parquet floors in mirrors placed in corners; Janet Fish placed glass tumblers on mirrored surfaces to study the multiple refractions and reflections of light; Audrey Flack allowed the mirror to intensify the kaleidoscopic aspect of her still lifes and to comment on them as part of the *vanitas* tradition; Philip Pearlstein energized limbs at angles in mirrors in radical croppings of his nudes. Richard Estes and Don Eddy simulated aspects of the city in the reflective chrome and plate glass of their storefronts and window displays. Each of these artists—and the list is by no means exhaustive—investigated realist rendering as a means to modernist inquiry. All of them, Moore included, introduced ambiguity and intricacy in their works by means of reflections. They challenged the viewer to decode the real from the illusionistic and to question empirical observations as truthful and absolute. If Moore's transparent shelves with mirrors avoid the lushness of the glass-filled still lifes of Janet Fish and the personal narratives of Audrey Flack's works of the same period, they are no less replete with artistic and personal meaning. The random placement of objects scattered casually across the glass surfaces of Moore's paintings works to assert the dynamics of shape and space against the planar geometry of the setting. Thoroughly committed to representation, Moore demonstrates that realism need not necessarily be antithetical to abstraction. With these works he reached a new level of suppleness and ease in his handling of form and a firmer sense of his own individuality.

Moore continued his investigations of transparency, light, and shadow in a series of watercolors titled *Flower Glass* (pl. 9). In *Flower Glass* (pl. 10) he depicted a paper cup, glasses, a small ceramic pitcher, a green tray, and a petal-shaped plastic pocket calendar, viewing them from above with no horizon line to anchor the composition in traditional space. As in Paul Gauguin's 1888 *Still Life with Three Puppies* (fig. 4), the objects are viewed as elements of pattern and design strongly influenced by a Japanese aesthetic. But unlike the post-impressionist, Moore is not interested in arbitrary distortions of size or in suppressing the depth of the field in an absolute two-dimensionality. By focusing on how two different sources of light create various shadow patterns cast from solid and translucent forms, Moore allows the shadows to stabilize the objects so that they appear sculptural and do not float, unanchored, in space. At the same time, they help to define the plane of the table and to accentuate its flatness. The pictorial field is never crowded, allowing each object to breathe in its own space and mark out its individuality. The abstract nature of the objects emerges from the act of perceiving the rhythm of the placements, the geometry of the shapes, and from the control of detail. With an exquisite visual tact, Moore reconciles traditional illusionism with modernist style.

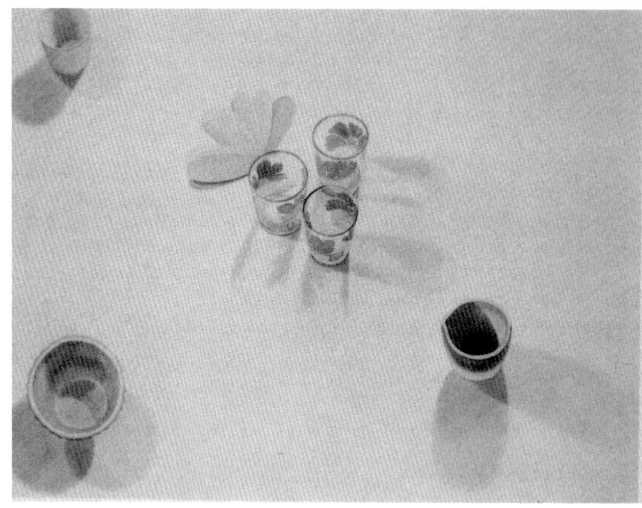

9

FLOWER GLASS, 1974

Watercolor on paper, $22^{1}/_{2} \times 30$ in.
Private collection.

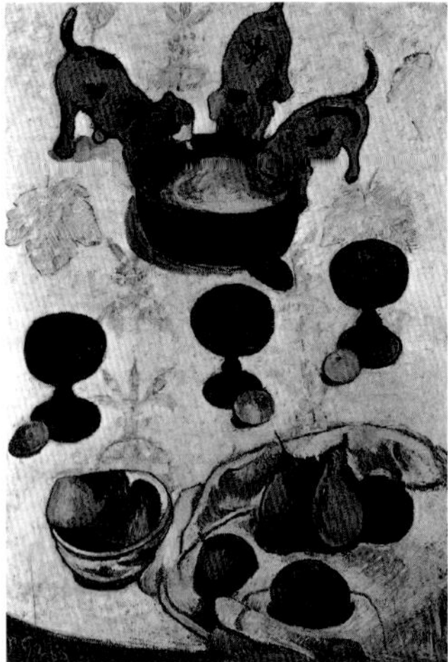

Figure 4. Paul Gauguin, *Still Life with Three Puppies*, 1888, oil on wood, $36^{1}/_{8} \times 24^{5}/_{8}$ in. Museum of Modern Art, New York, Mrs. Simon Guggenheim Fund.

Like Pliny's bird flying over Zeuxis's painting, we are placed above the carefully depicted objects. By plunging the eye downward and eliminating any anchoring horizon line in these watercolors, Moore deliberately reduces the foreshortening of perspective, forcing the viewer to focus on the silhouettes of the objects and the delicacy of their shadows. Each light container possesses its own integrity as a distinct shape, yet its definition is simultaneously enhanced by its relationship to the other objects in the work and the edges of the support.

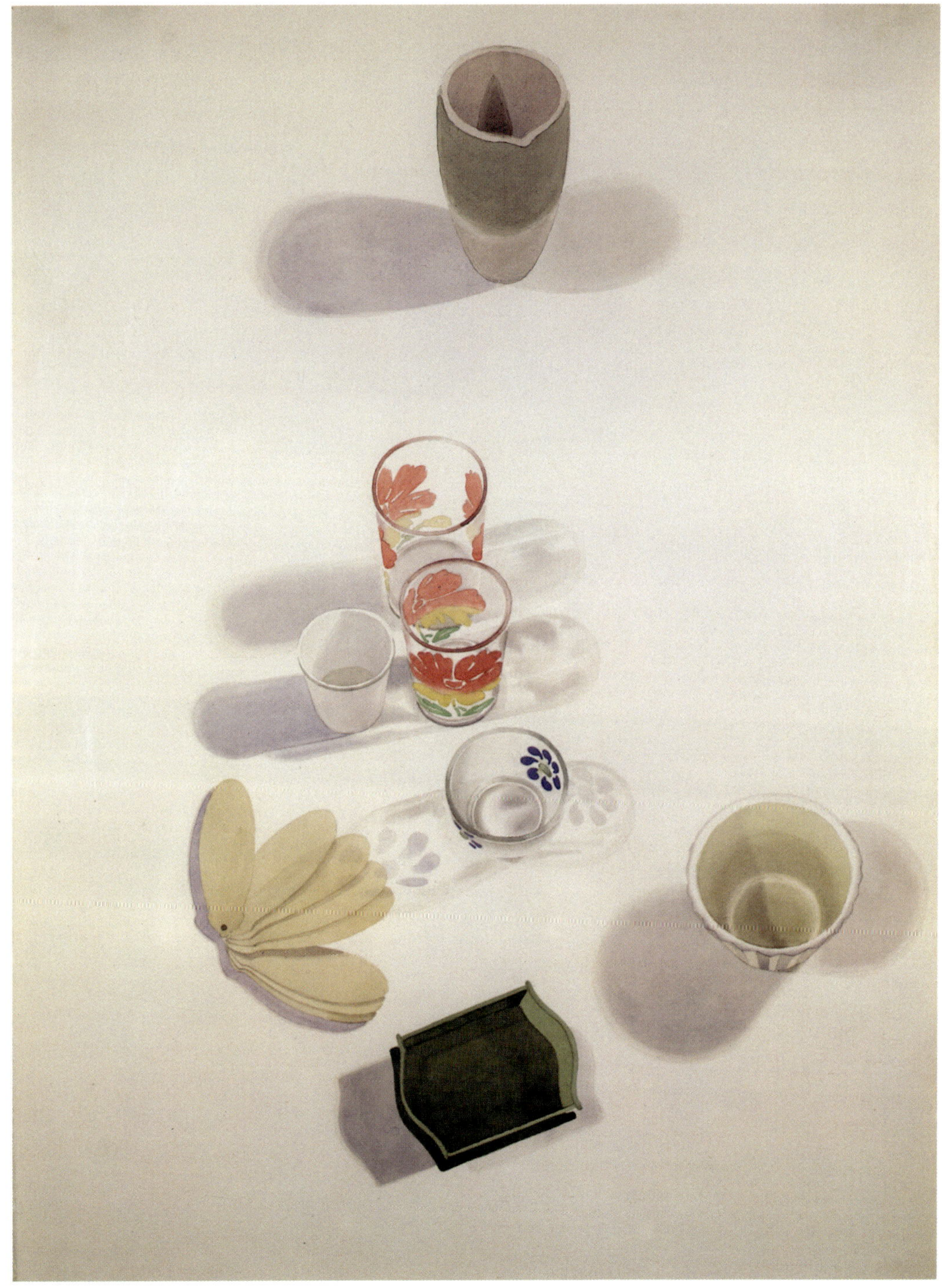

10 FLOWER GLASS, 1974

Watercolor on paper, 30 × 22½ in.
Museum of Fine Arts, Boston.

Moore's sensitivity to how the containers take light and enclose it, distort it, magnify it, spread it, and color it, keeps these compositions from degenerating into formulaic designs. He invites the viewer to compare the transparency of glass with the translucency of a paper cup and to contrast these with the opacity of ceramic and plastic. Suppressing the context of a room or a support on which they rest allows a consideration of these objects as shape and form, removed as they are from their implied function in everyday use. Indeed, the glasses are empty and the vases and trays contain only their physical mold, accentuating their function as elements of a surface pattern and containers of light. In their scattered arrangement across the field of whiteness of the watercolor page, the objects speak more directly to the syncopated rhythms of abstract design, attaining an almost oriental delicacy by their placement. Moore thus alerts vision to a sense of its own powers and pleasures.

The objects Moore paints are prosaic and familiar to a twentieth-century sensibility, the flower glasses being obvious commodities from dime stores and supermarkets. Moore's interest in the common artifacts of daily life differs, however, from pop art's celebration of the banal image borrowed from the commercial realm. Moore never aimed in his work at the deadpan literalness that characterized pop, and if he chose mass-produced objects of everyday use such as the flower glasses, it was never for the purpose of ironic distancing and depersonalization, but for their contemporaneity in a context of the traditions of still life. If Willem Kalf's *Nautilus Cup* can speak of seventeenth-century Holland and Jean-Baptiste Siméon Chardin's humble crockery of eighteenth-century France, so also Moore's common glasses are distinctly of their own age and of a certain social class. In their own amusing and kitschy way, they add subtle visual wit to the watercolor as they remind us how often glasses filled with flowers served as subjects for great still lifes of the past to the present from Boschaert the Elder through Auguste Renoir and Janet Fish. The decoration on the glasses declares itself openly as illusionist application flatly applied and, along with the petal-shaped leaves of the plastic pocket calendar, comments self-reflexively on the artist's task of translating nature into art.

The Open Window (pl. 11) and *Red Snapper* (pl. 12) mark an advance in Moore's ambition to describe the tension between artifice and reality that is basic to much of his work in the still-life genre. By employing the tabletop composition, one of the most prevalent motifs in the history of still-life paintings, Moore allied his art with its heritage while drawing attention to the intrinsic differences that challenge and advance that tradition. Moore's still lifes are never just technical exercises, but are instead profound inquiries into the nature of art and its relation to reality.

One of the charges most frequently leveled at contemporary realists was that of being academic in their imitation of the art of the past. While Moore's work inevitably invokes other visual sources, he retains a strong individuality by his intense relationship to historical tradition and the freshness of vision that he brings to it. As Carol Zemel has noted, *Red Snapper* inevitably calls to mind Henri Matisse's *Harmony in Red* by its use of the floral decorative cloth. She also perceives a relationship to Vermeer's paintings where daily life quietly unfolds in a corner setting that suggests a reality beyond the painted space.[25] One can also detect an allusion to cubism in the upended space in the mirrors in both works.

The mirrors in these two paintings can be seen to function as a kind of realist reprise of Georges Braque's nail in his 1910 *Violin and Palette* (fig. 5). Braque's inclusion of a trompe l'oeil nail in the midst of the floating analytic fragments of form in his canvas reinforced the cubist doctrine that art is essentially a world of artifice. The shadow cast by the nail suggests that the canvas is a flat surface attached to a wall, but more importantly, it also asserts that the shifting abstracted planes of the violin and pitcher are no less real than the illusionistic nail: both belong to the fiction of art. While Braque brought the semi-abstract shifting planes to the foreground in a compressed space and kept his reference to the traditional plasticity of the nail to a minimum, Moore as a realist works from the opposite side of the history of modernist illusionism. His mirrors present a condensed, flattened image of the three-dimensional objects in the rooms. Cubist artists provided realist clues such as watch chains and violin scrolls to identify the subject in their presentational paintings of multiple viewpoints. Moore, by means of his mirrors and floral cloths, invokes the vocabulary of fauvism and cubism to identify his modernist concerns. He preserves the solidity of objects in the shallow three-dimensional space of his paintings, but remains acutely aware of the autonomy of the picture plane by portraying in both paintings at least one large smooth area of flat decorative surface. Although slightly moved back in space in *Red Snapper,* the cloth retains its insistence on planarity by continuing across the entire horizontal surface of the canvas. In *Open Window* the wooden chest spans the length of the painting, echoing the rectilinearity of the window and the shelf above it.

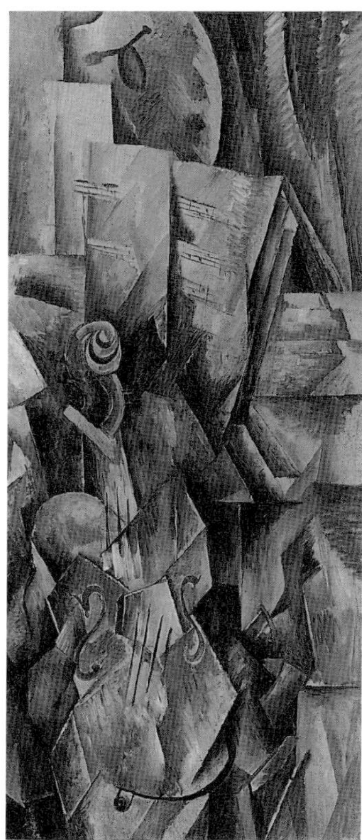

Figure 5. Georges Braque, *Violin and Palette,* 1910, oil on canvas, 36⅛ × 16⅞ in. Solomon R. Guggenheim Museum, New York.

Braque's analytical cubist work claimed that the purely structural elements and their formal relationships supplanted the representational function of painting, and that the object is reconstructed in the imagination of the viewer in a manner that ultimately cancels out the need for exacting realism. The mirrors and cloths in Moore's paintings also maneuver the viewer between art life and real life, between the two-dimensional fact of the painted canvas and the three-dimensional forms of the objects depicted. Braque's nail reminds the viewer that a work of art can invoke external reality, but it also possesses an internal reality of its own. Moore's interior still lifes reinforce this modernist lesson with subtle visual plays on cubist *passage* by the "real" flowers in the clear vase in *Red Snapper* whose petals fall onto the "false" flowers on the cloth in a visually apt pun on the animate and inanimate. A single floral bud decorates the empty vase to the left of the clear vase, as if part of the decoration of the cloth had whimsically crept up on it. Moore's realist interiors appear to be exact replicas of reality, yet the viewer is challenged to test their various levels of re-creation on the surface of the canvas and in the implied depth of the space.

Moore's repertoire of repeated objects allows him to revise his variables so that each new canvas represents another opportunity to deal with complex aesthetic problems related to past movements. His questioning of perceptual reality's difference from art's reality, of truth and falsehood in art, is

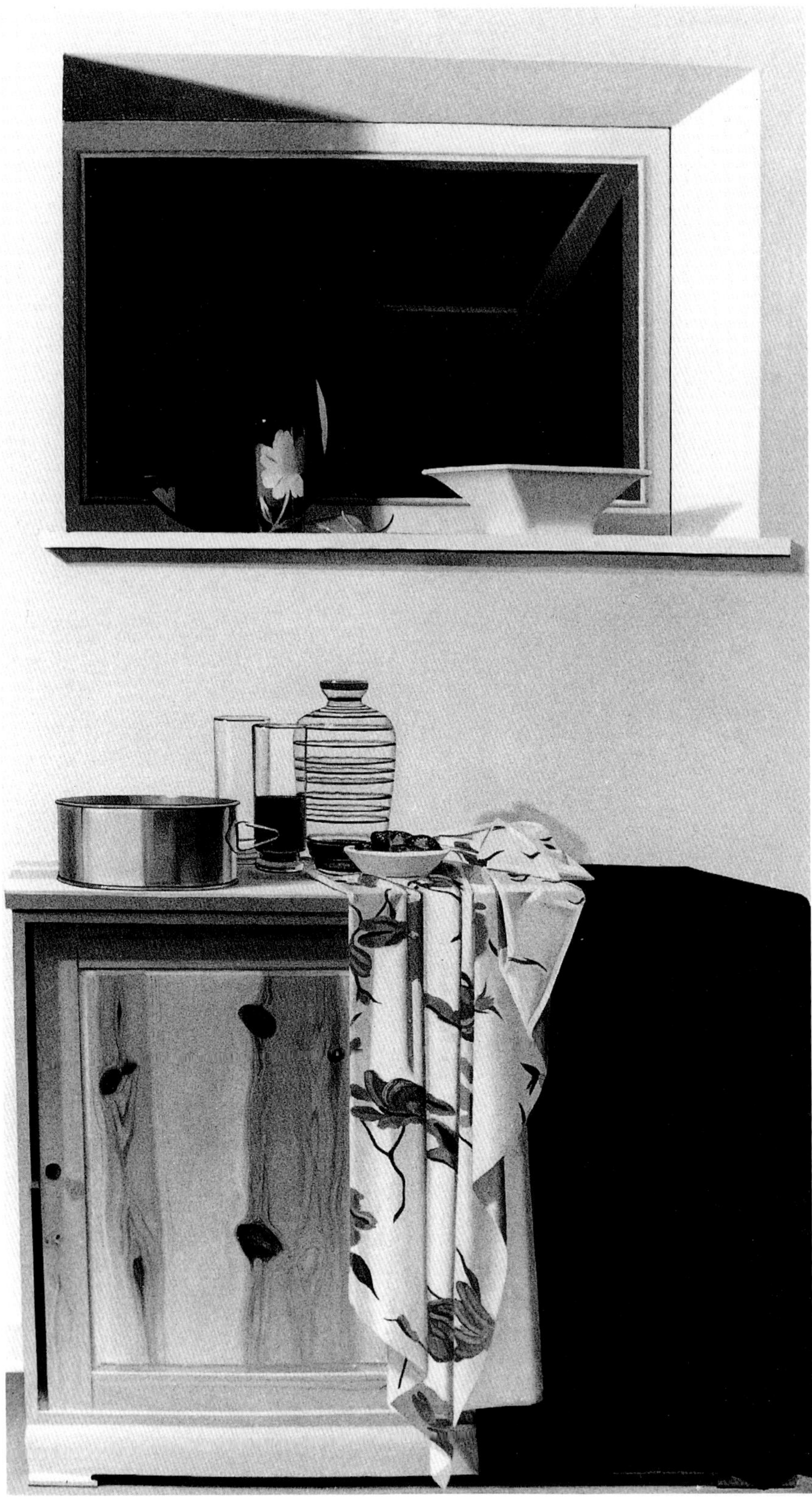

11

OPEN WINDOW, 1975

Oil on canvas, 70 × 44 in.
Private collection.

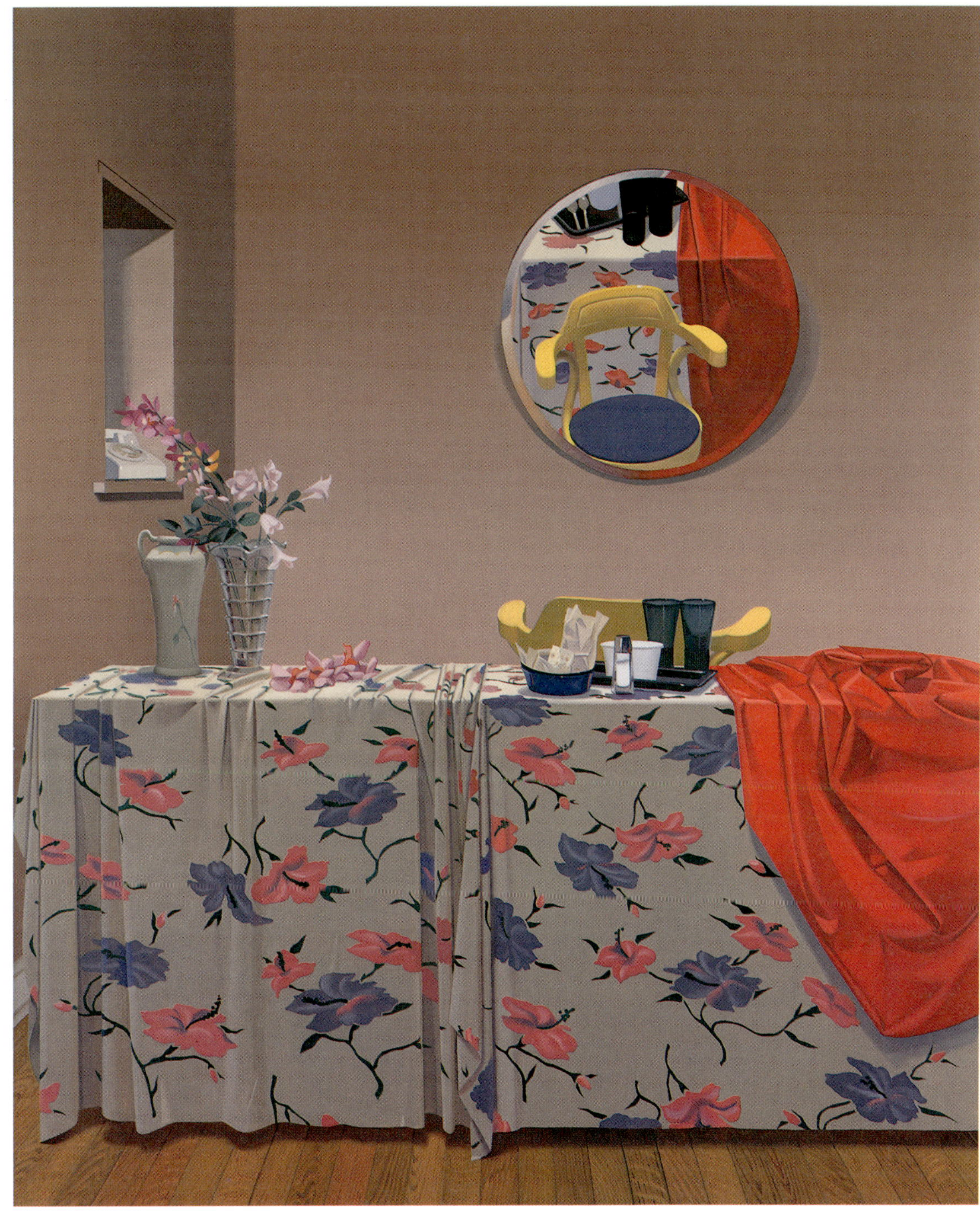

12 RED SNAPPER, 1975

Oil on canvas, 90 × 75 in.
Sandra Moore.

cued by the inclusion in the mirror image of a pair of spoons and the seat of the chair in *Red Snapper,* objects that the viewer can see only with the aid of the mirror. By this Moore can suggest that realist art is involved in the re-creation not only of what the artist sees in the world, but also what he knows of it; that the visual and the intellectual are both integral to the full realization of the image, and that the charge leveled against realists from the time of Gustave Courbet onward of mindless copying is clearly a misnomer. The mirror produces an image of an image but does not double exactly the scene before the viewer. By adding new objects in its surface, it suggests that realist painting is not merely conventional. As an image of only part of the painting, the mirror possesses a logic of its own, a selective vision like that of the realist artist who, by the act of painting, isolates a scene for representation. The mirror alerts the viewer to the fallacy of mistaking factual precision for the whole truth of the painting. It offers a slice of life of the room and is incomprehensible without the larger context of the space where the objects reside. Realism, so often wrongly disparaged as a styleless style, an art that conceals art, and a mindless mirroring of mundane visual elements, achieves an enhanced significance in contemporary discourse by its interrelations with past styles and current aesthetic predispositions.

The oval seat of the yellow chair reflected in the mirror in *Red Snapper* can evoke memories of Picasso's *Still Life with Chair Caning* and the aesthetic questions posed by the cubist collage in relation to realist illusion. If the cubists challenged themselves to create canvases indicating spatial relationships that were no longer dependent on Renaissance perspective systems, Moore in these canvases similarly involved himself with the paradoxes and ambiguities of abstraction and reality. The coexistence of cubism and realist referents in the same canvas calls attention to the tensions between surface and image, imagination and truth, that sustained the modernist discourse with its roots in cubist practice. Realist art need not be seen as the antithesis of abstraction, but as a further opportunity to expand the language of art.

One can inventory with assurance the common objects Moore paints, such as the salt shaker and the soda cracker in *Red Snapper,* painted with all the detailed realism of a William Harnett. These items are familiar and accessible, yet the strange indeterminacy of the setting—midway between home and studio—leads away from the denotation of objects to the connotation of feeling. Moore's decontextualization of the room suspends it between nature and use. His narrative relates to the art world rather than the real world and, as Carol Zemel astutely commented, there is no real "necessity" or even logic for such a place beyond the artist's invention.[26] By creating a tension between the familiar objects of daily use and the strangeness of their setting, Moore lets the painting function both as an artful arrangement and as a description of actuality. The unnatural juxtapositions of chair, wall, and table that Moore depicts in these and his earlier works coerce the viewer to think about the different sensations of space in real life and in art life. The viewing point in *Red Snapper* is just slightly to the right of the image rather than centralized, a subtle dislocation that inhibits physical access and strengthens the decorative surface of the canvas. The freedom from the projection of traditional space announced by cubist art is restated in Moore's realism as a freedom from the need to portray an easily describable setting.

The Open Window represents an increase in complexity of detail and pattern in Moore's work. At the time he made this painting he was exhibiting at Fischbach Gallery in New York with Sylvia Plimack Mangold, who was making her series of paintings of mirrors set in corners to reflect the patterns of wood floors. Moore's response to Mangold's art is found in the knotty-pine chest of this painting. Moore depicts a red-and-blue striped vase and a flowered tablecloth whose liveliness balances and somewhat softens the geometry of the rest of the objects in the canvas. The mirror on the windowsill reminds us that, despite the exacting economy with which he has portrayed texture and surface in this work, his art is more than sleight-of-hand trickery. Placed in a darkened window, the mirror seems strangely transparent as it appears to absorb the outside darkness like the windowpane rather than to reflect the brightness of the room as it normally should. While the small portion of the reflected glass and white edge are understandable in its round surface, the blackness is not. We see things "through a glass, darkly" in Moore's realism, and he reminds us by the mirror and the window that painting for him is more than a simple recording of lifelike particulars on a surface. If his paintings show an increase in incremental detail in their intensified realism, they are no less about the abstraction of reality than they are an objective description of it, and they suggest that the process of a realist artist is more subjective than it might appear at first glance.

Moore continued to explore the ambiguous nature of illusion and reality in paintings where vintage glassware is viewed through display cases. *Montrose* (pl. 13) and *Downtown* (pl. 14) present containers and trays on glass shelves that occupy the lower portion of the canvas while the upper section in each painting contains a window overlooking an urban scene. The narrow vertical shape of the canvas recalls Gothic panels, reinforcing the sensation that these objects exist as iconic vessels for light and ritual and that their carefully selected placement has an aura of the sacramental about it. The stark artificial lighting imbues the objects with a visual sharpness that isolates them from everyday use and lends them an air of heightened significance. The clustered arrangement and emphasis on the variations of roundness in the objects counter the orderly horizontal edges of the glass shelves and window frame.

The urban space shown through the window in *Montrose* almost suggests a rectangular still life as it is related to the objects by a similarity in color that tends to eliminate the implied distance between the foreground and the vista. The pale blue strips of reflections of the window frame sit flatly on the surface of the canvas at the same time that they describe the light bouncing off the glass vitrine and marble window well. Tangible but weightless, they function as both form and description, leading the eye up the surface of the vertical canvas by their varied repetition around the window and wittily reproducing a small portion of the outdoor scene as if in a mirror. Thus realist exactitude is firmly synchronized with abstract intention. The urban vista also secures the contemporaneity of the work in terms of place and style. If the glassware draws one back to earlier decades of its making, the architecture roots the viewer in the here and now, analogizing in a sense the circuit of references inherent in Moore's realist art, with its still-life origins in previous eras but its stylistic intentions squarely in the present. Cityscape and still life are conceptually united in this work by being man-made objects viewed through glass.

Montrose and *Downtown* compel the viewer to employ two directional gazes that seem to conflict with each other, as it is impossible to look out of the window and down at the display case at the same time. This physical difficulty signals the conflict inherent in the realist debate about the disparity between real life and art life that the window in these works, as in his others, invokes. The windows in these paintings echo the vertical shape of the canvas. The objects below the window are displayed in vitrines, a synonym for a window taken from the French. By conflating the two, Moore compels the viewer to think about the issue of representation and presentation, about the differences between what a painting depicts and what it can be said to display in terms of its own making.[27]

The window has operated as an analogy for the spectacle of vision and for the fictive nature of painting since the early Renaissance, when Leon Battista Alberti declared the painting to be a window onto an imaginary world. Modernist art gradually declared itself free from the illusions of this Albertian window until minimalism proclaimed the square to be nonreferential, an object in itself. Moore's work plays simultaneously with the notion of illusion and the idea of painting as an object. Like the First Style of Romano-Campanian wall painters who mimicked precious marble and other materials with cheap plaster and paint,[28] Moore delights in the conscious deception of lifting the marbleized pattern from a piece of household Formica. Artifice finds further resonance in the crafted artifacts displayed in the vitrine. Like Moore's canvases, they resolutely present themselves as art objects, as things in themselves, removed from function and clearly on display.

The discrepancy of visual focus, the teasing disruption between the view of the world outside and the sight of the objects nesting securely in their cases, illustrates the separation in Moore's work of the illusionist intent from the formalist purpose, of the functional role of the objects from their conceptual basis. The visual dynamics of the painting require the dual function of looking out and looking in, a physical duplication of the act of viewing and its intellectual counterpart of contemplation.

There is an inverted parallelism about these two paintings that is like a fugue in its orchestrated differences and counterpoints. In *Downtown* Moore sets the objects against a plain rose-colored interior wall with a nighttime view seen through a window darkened by purple shadow. With *Montrose* the exterior scene is one of daytime, while the black marble walls suggest that night has come inside. The quiet upper portion

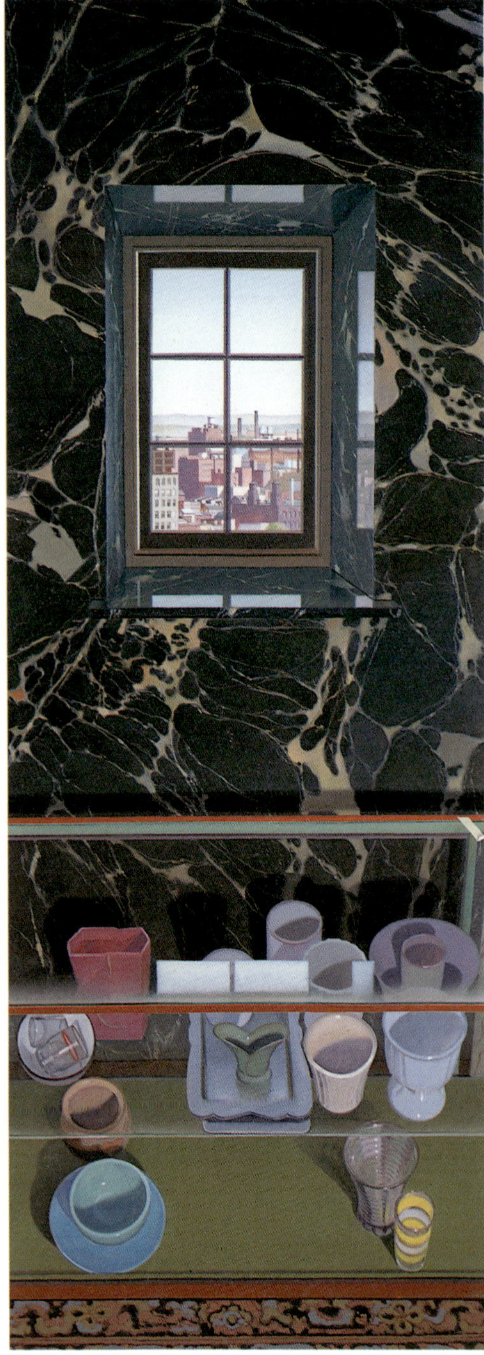

13

MONTROSE, 1979–82

Oil on canvas, 96 × 36 in.
Collection of Castellani Art Museum, Niagara University, New York. Gift of Dr. and Mrs. Armand J. Castellani.

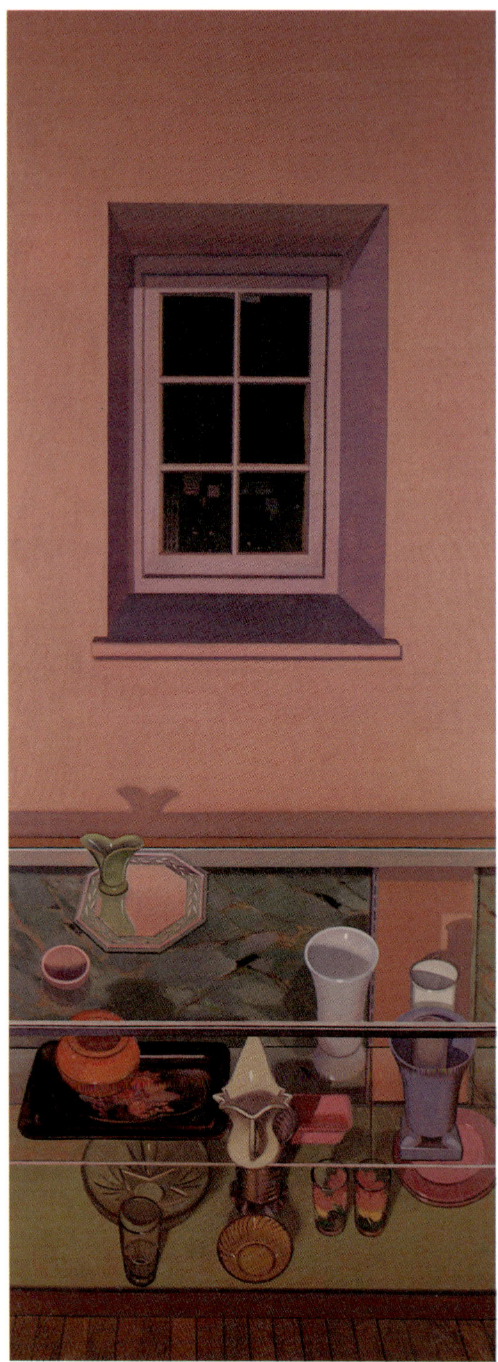

14

DOWNTOWN, 1980

Oil on canvas, 96 × 36 in.
Dr. and Mrs. Armand J. Castellani.

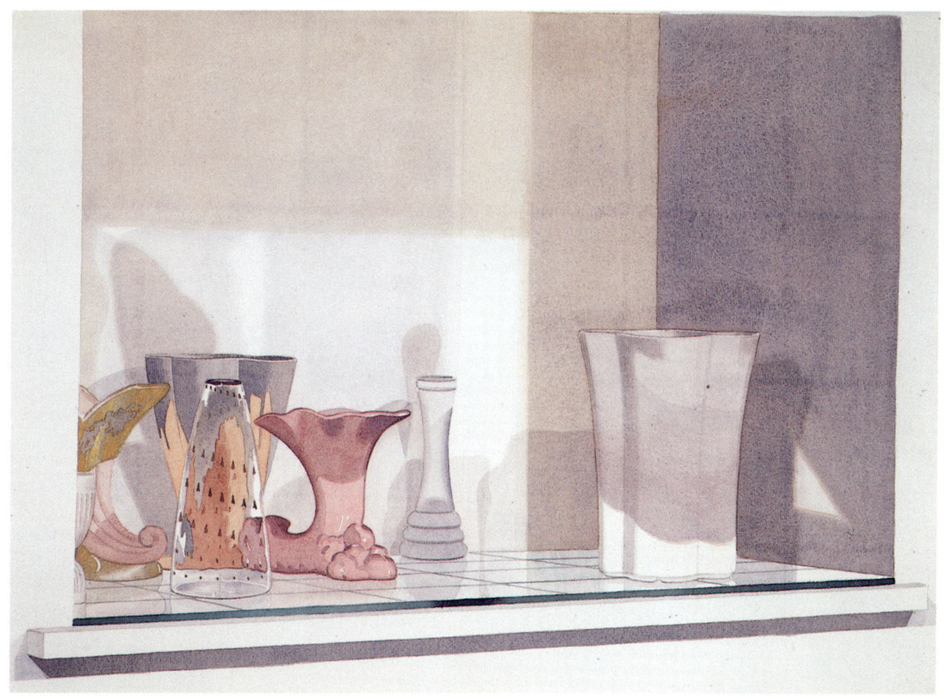

15

NIGHT LIGHT (6TH ORDER), 1980

Watercolor on paper, 22½ × 30 in.
Private collection.

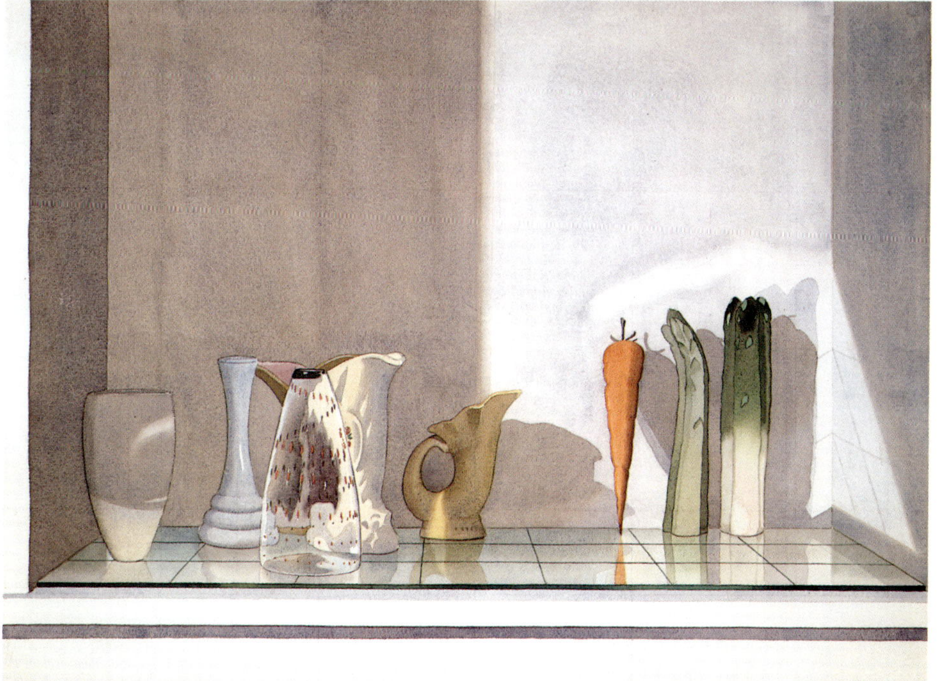

16

NIGHT LIGHT (8TH ORDER), 1980

Watercolor on paper, 22½ × 30 in.
Private collection.

of *Downtown* contrasts with the lively detailing of the cut glass, mirrored tray, colorful lacquerware, and marble backdrop of the lower half, whereas in *Montrose* the visual energy is confined to the upper walls and the lower border of carpet, leaving the objects displayed with a minimum of ornamentation over a plain green surface. While attentive to the textures and shapes of his objects, Moore never loses the whole by allowing the eye to get absorbed in a single interesting part. *Downtown* has a visual affinity to an Adolph Gottlieb "Burst" painting with its binary opposition of a serene upper section hovering over a more calligraphically embellished lower field, which frees the eye to move between the two areas of the canvas. In *Montrose* the placement and the shapes of the objects, the baroque patterning of the marble, and the decorative fret of the carpet that almost seems to sit on the picture plane, keep the eye roving over the surface of the canvas. Moore's still lifes are not still.

A series of watercolors painted in 1980 and titled *Night Light* (pls. 15 and 16) indicate a change in Moore's usual content. Glassware, vintage china, and plastic produce sit on mirrored surfaces in a shallow alcove lit by artificial light. The objects are more animated in shape, hence less geometrically oriented, than his previous glassware. More vivid in personality and complex in ornament, they are no less stately for their attention to detail.

Dramatic shadows thrown up behind the objects, combined with lavender and gray recessed corners, impart a twilight cast that justifies the title of the series. A new sense of romanticism informing these works distinguishes them from Moore's previous, more cerebral works in the still-life genre. These quaint vessels and fake vegetables, unnoticeable perhaps on a thrift-shop table, have been reassembled by Moore like a cast of characters in a silent drama that is accentuated by the stagelike setting and theatrical illumination. The separation of the feminine-shaped vessels to the left from the upright vegetables to the right in *Night Light #8* could almost be a still-life version of Edgar Degas's *Young Spartans Exercising* (fig. 6).

The *Night Light* series testifies to the power that issues of light and shadow, transparency and opacity had for Moore throughout his investigation of the still-life genre. The watercolors involve the eye in comparing gradients of light as it passes through, over, and between glass vessels whose idiosyncratic shapes throw speckled skeins of shadows and phantomic replicas of themselves against the recessed walls of the alcove. Moore's containers in these works look more handcrafted and less manufactured than his previous still-life objects, which helps to account for the heightened expressivity and increased sense of tactility that are present in these images. This is manifestly art about art, and the *Night Light* series constituted the most romantic work of Moore's career to that point. In moving from the cerebral to the emotive connoted in the richly inflected contours and sumptuousness of the shadows, Moore introduced a new sensuousness in his work that opened his still lifes to a broader sensibility.

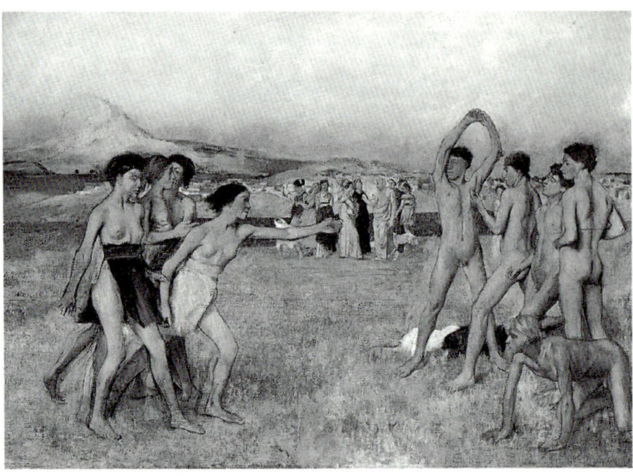

Figure 6. Hilaire-Germain-Edgar Degas, *Young Spartans Exercising*, c. 1860–62, oil on canvas, 44 7/8 × 61 in. Trustees of the National Gallery, London.

The arrangement of objects in Moore's still lifes never has the air of casual disorder that is so frequently a component of the tabletop still life from Pieter Claesz. through Chardin and the impressionists up to the contemporary works of Louisa Matthiasdottir and Carolyn Brady. One feels keenly the sense of placement of each object in Moore's still lifes, convinced that these configurations represent something achieved rather than a record of something happened upon by chance. This can be seen to assist Moore in his intensive questioning of the deceptions of art and the contribution of spatial illusion to sustaining the fiction of the real.

Gray Marble (pl. 17) presents a container and artificial vegetables in a high, shallow alcove. The repeated perpendiculars of the edges of the alcove, the division between the light and dark sides, the erect handle of the container and its shadow, and the upright vegetables restate the vertical proportions of

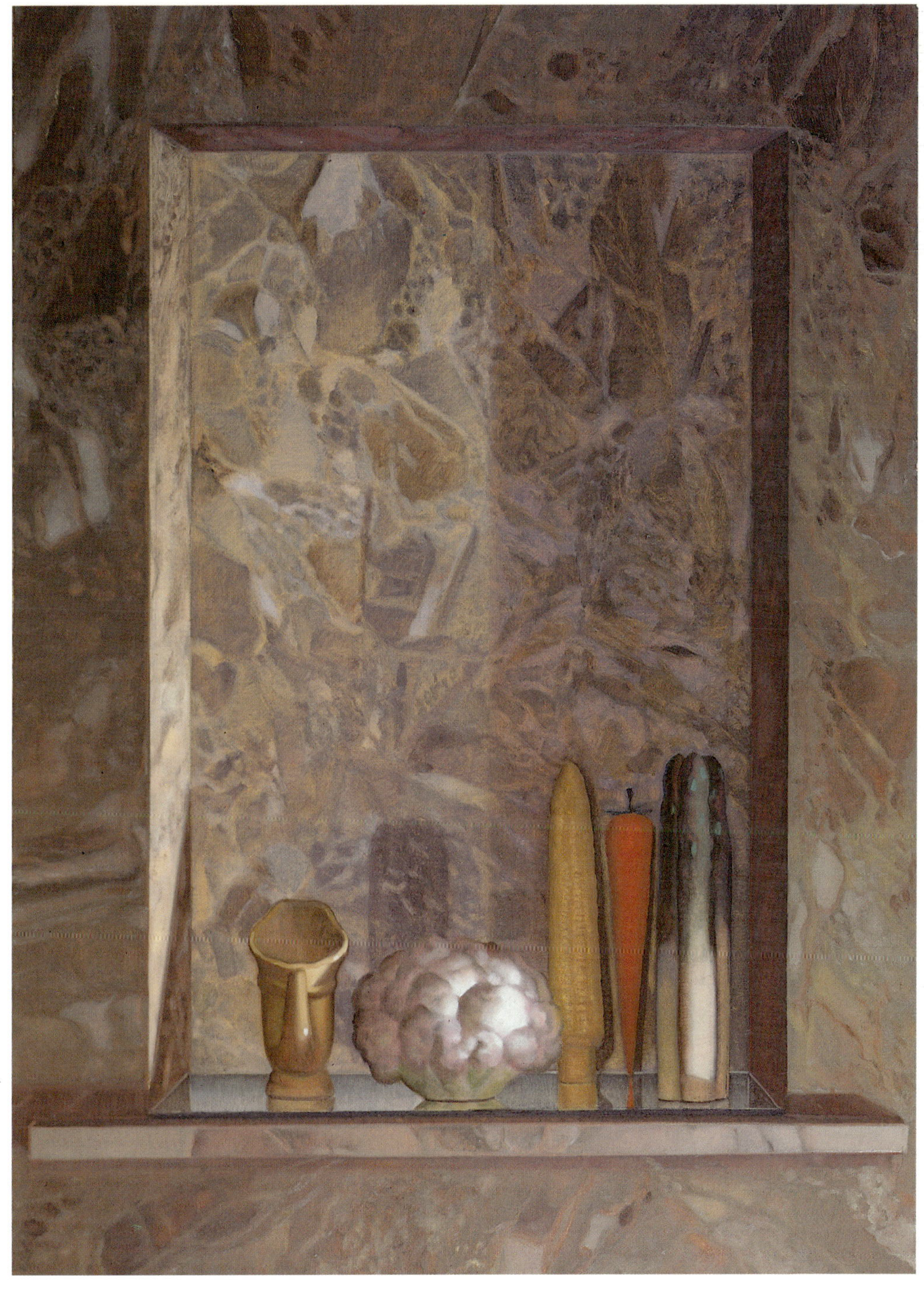

17 GRAY MARBLE, 1981

Oil on canvas, 29 × 40 in.
Private collection.

the canvas and generate a stately rhythm that anchors the objects in their opulent marble setting. Reminiscent of saints in their niches, the still-life objects seem like the majestic figures of Piero della Francesca as they shed their common origins and take their place in an austerely beautiful procession across the ledge of the support. Like Wallace Stevens's "ancientist saint ablaze with ancientist truth,"[29] the objects are presented as if placed on a secular altar lit by a mystical light.

Moore's Catholic upbringing may be pertinent to this image from several points of view. As an altar boy, his duty was to position the sacramental vessels, linens, and sacred scriptures in highly specific ceremonial positions. Belief in the Eucharist entails the transubstantiation of common elements of bread and wine into the body and blood of Christ, just as these ordinary artifacts are transformed from their lowly status as decorative craft into the higher order of art. The liturgy of the Mass aims at defamiliarizing contact with the physical substances, conferring a sacramental nature that transports them into the realm of the spiritual. During the consecration the priest presents the elements in such a way as to induce an intensity of perception and focus in order to convince the viewer/believer that the bread and wine are no longer of this world. Initially presented as food, the elements come to represent a truth that transcends their physicality, which has now become symbolic. The formality of the ritualized gestures assures an aesthetic distancing that aims to induce reverence and awe. Moore's registration of the still-life elements in *Gray Marble* is not far from this transformative process as one gradually senses another world existing within the painting. As with the Eucharist in the Mass, the material artifacts are the objects in the picture, but the subject is elsewhere, displaced here by art to a higher realm that, despite its secularism in this instance, retains a sense of the sacred. Each object stands alone, with minimal overlap, as if it were elected to represent the quintessential type of container and comestible, or as if it had been ceremoniously selected to fulfill some role higher than its normal use. A metaphysical hush seems to hover over the objects, removing them from their everyday connotation and converting them into figures of extraordinary eloquence. Their stillness, frontality, and hieraticism amplify the concentration and rarefaction of the image.

Despite the fastidious attention to detail—the fissured surface of the cauliflower, the individual kernels on the ear of corn, the continuous mottling of the marble—Moore never seems weighted down by the particularities of description. Nor does he lose his balance by letting detail dictate the painting, allowing technical facility to become the true subject of the work, the image a mere excuse. The distinctive features of surface elaboration sustain rather than dominate him and are harnessed for the expression of the entire work. Textures are suggested but tactility is suppressed by a delicate blurring of edges, as if incense hovered over the scene. Moore's work is a telling more than a showing of things; it is about the process of conceiving and picturing reality, and then communicating something important about the special quality of these processes. Moore uses common objects to speak of personal worlds of mystery and wonder.

By placing a container and artificial vegetables in unfamiliar settings, Moore increases the difficulty and length of perception as the viewer questions the plausibility of the situation. The cup contains no liquid, the waxen produce is factory produced and not nature's bounty. These are objects for display, not consumption, and no bird flown astray from Zeuxis's grapes would ever be tempted to peck at the produce in this painting. Despite the interior setting, Moore makes no attempt to refer to a recognizable table scene or a convivial gathering. By avoiding the suggestion of daily routine, Moore removes the objects from function and directs them toward aesthetic perception. As in the still lifes of Cotán, there is no appeal to taste or smell in these works. The objects are placed for balance and rhythmic spacing, not for sensory indulgence.

Moore's use of artificial produce provides a witty postmodern gloss on the various forms of still life, from the seventeenth-century Dutch banquet scenes with views into landscapes by artists such as Jan de Heem and Abraham van Beyern to the use of perishable objects that were allegorized in the *vanitas* tradition. One cannot peel his wax carrot, nor will decay brownly speckle the immaculate surface of his cauliflower. The transitory perfection and value of worldly possessions that often constituted the subject of pre-modern still life is gently lampooned to demonstrate that art is no longer solely about the imitation of nature.

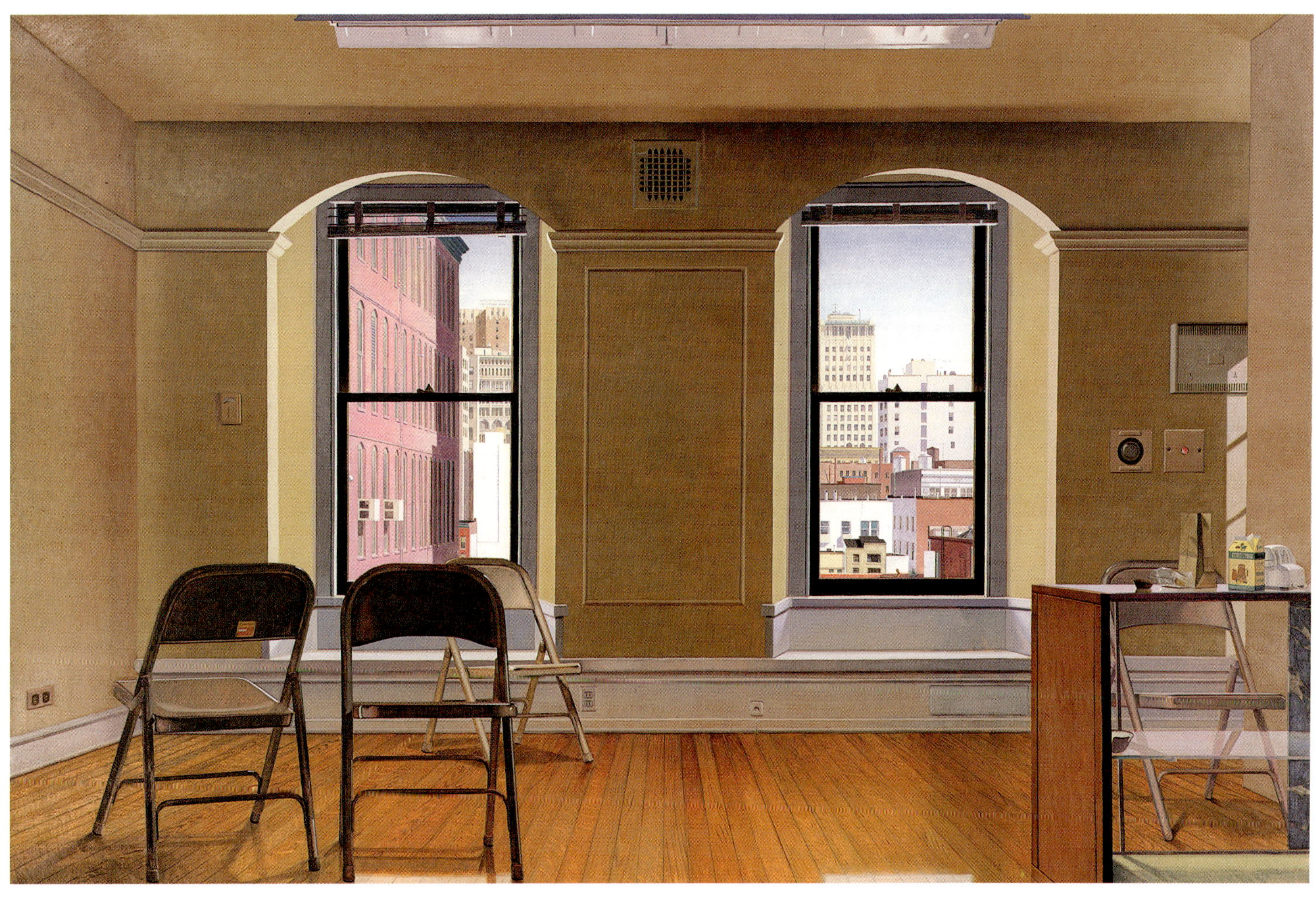

18 THURSDAY, 1980

Oil on canvas, 92 x 141 in.
Metropolitan Museum of Art, New York.

Moore often arranged his still lifes in quiet interiors. The unoccupied room scarcely appeared in art before the romantic movement, when Caspar David Friedrich and Eugène Delacroix began to explore its potential for emotive space. In the twentieth century Edward Hopper and Charles Sheeler, two painters Moore keenly admires, composed paintings of rooms where the only subject is the reflection of light on a bare floor or spare Shaker furniture. The order and clarity of Moore's still lifes are extended to an interior view in *Thursday* (pl. 18). A large painting, it depicts the interior of a loft that is sparsely furnished with a few metal folding chairs randomly scattered across a plain hardwood floor. A table in the lower-right-hand corner, with the remnants of a brown-bag lunch and a telephone on top of it, anchors the right side of the composition. Two large arched windows provide a view of an urban landscape beneath a hazy blue sky.

Moore achieves a classical serenity through his use of variations on the square. The horizontality of the canvas is strongly repeated from the top to the bottom of the canvas by shapes such as the overhead light, the wall moldings, and the deep floor molding of the baseboard. It continues in the seats of the metal chairs hyphenated across the picture plane, ending with the two horizontal reflections of light on the floor at the bottom edge of the canvas. These horizontals are then inverted and re-echoed by the cadenced vertical lines of the corners of the room. All of this symmetry and geometric regularity is gently humanized by the restful flex of the arch over the alcove window, which is reinforced by the repeated curves of the tops of the folding chairs.

The spare serenity of the room, with its space devoted to form and feeling, is classical in tone. The repetition and variation of the geometrical elements achieve the dignified monumentality and stateliness of a Brunelleschi facade. Muted shades of mauve, gray, brown, and green deftly applied in imperceptible strokes contribute to the quiet atmosphere of the room. Moore alternates areas of intense detail in the urban vista with the unadorned plainness of the walls and wooden floor. The laterally extended foreground of the floor converges into a blank rectangle at the very center of the canvas. This keeps our eyes from plunging into a deep perspectival panorama, as if to remind us that we are looking at—not through—the canvas.

Unlike the lonely interiors of Edward Hopper, Moore's *Thursday* speaks about privacy, not privation. The room is uncluttered, not empty. There is an almost pristine purity in the calibration of space, freed from the burden of superfluous decoration. The spareness of the room is soothing rather than alienating. Human presence is implied through the still-life elements; the iced-tea container, the brown bag, and the white phone suggest simple needs and desires, the unadorned metal chairs a casual informality and unpretentiousness. Moore creates a clear and convincing image out of routine reality and everyday things. He embraces the large scale of abstract expressionist painting, but substitutes a realistic detailing for the heroic gestural brushstroke, achieving a significance that is visual rather than heroic or dramatic.

This is a room in which nothing much happens, but a great deal is felt. If there is an absence of narrative and action, there is the presence of art. The beautifully articulated spatial order of the work imparts a sense of permanence that confounds the informal disorder of the chairs. Moore's examination of the interior is not strictly about objects or textures, but about atmosphere and a sense of place. The restraint of the drawing, combined with the abstractness of the spatial relations, contributes to the mood of quiet reserve that penetrates every aspect of the room. The hushed quality of light, the spare simplicity of the setting, and the serene notation of the time of day bring Vermeer to mind, while the urban architecture and modern styling of the furniture keep the work firmly anchored in the present. The understated color, the patient inventory of detail, the almost musical sense of intervals between objects and spaces, culminate in a work that eloquently combines the denotation of specific place with the connotation of harmonious tranquility.

Moore moves closer to the window in *Night Studio* (pl. 19), where he paints the view from the darkened interior of his studio overlooking the area around Boston University. He provides an incredible amount of detail in a night painting that nominally sets out to eliminate descriptive particulars by muting them beneath a surface of closely related tones and hues. The head-on view of the windowed wall provides a structured pictorial grid that echoes the shape of the canvas and holds firm the vagaries of indistinct shapes faintly perceived through the glass. The eye gradually adjusts to the darkness

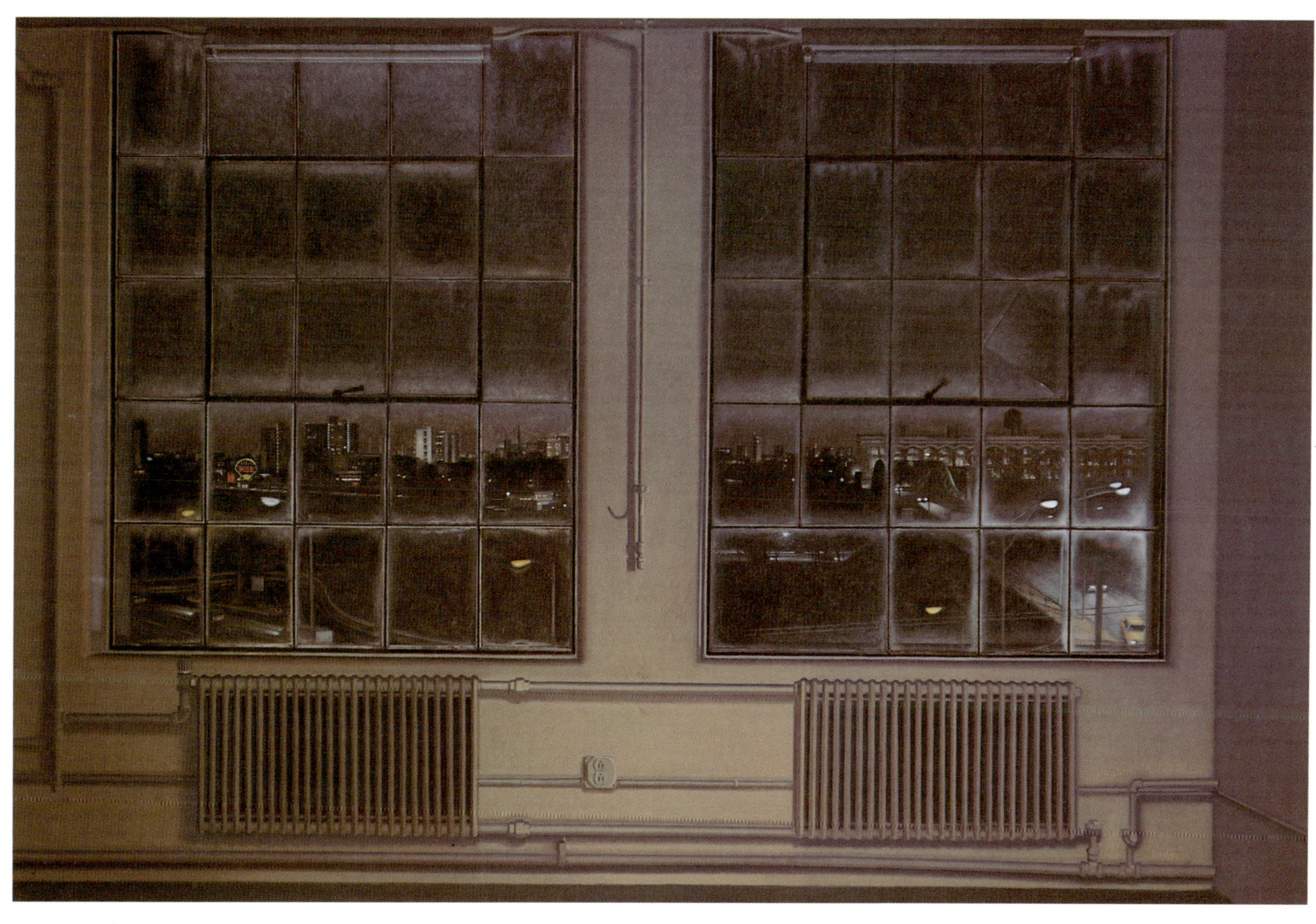

19 NIGHT STUDIO, 1988–89

Oil on canvas, 60 × 90 in.
Colby College Museum of Art, Waterville, Maine.

in the painting, as it would in real life, and is drawn to the different effects of nocturnal illumination from buildings, cars, neon advertisements, and streetlamps.

Silent and meditative, Moore's *Night Studio* is a virtuoso performance of tenebristic effects. The upper portion of the painting contains what appears to be a paired insert of windows, black squares outlined within larger black squares, inscribed against the night sky. This area, as subtle, abstract, and capable of holding the surface as a late Ad Reinhardt abstraction, invites prolonged attention as it emerges from the darkness to hold its own as a rich field of nuanced color. Beneath this section the city lights in the lower two registers of windows quietly animate the darkness and invite our attention, asking to be read slowly across the horizontal expanse. The rhythm of the radiator ribs across the lower section of the wall reinforces the classical symmetry of the work, flattening the space and accentuating the surface to enhance the two-dimensional modernist design of the canvas, thus keeping the eye from too deep a plunge outside.

Moore has taken the grid, with its characteristic lack of hierarchy, its modernist notion of the loss of a center, and wedded its inscription on the surface of the canvas with the depiction of a physical place. This interdependence of abstraction and realism is thereby kept fresh and supportive of Moore's aesthetic purpose. The rectilinear order of the painting with its repetition of the square keeps the surface elements in austere control while the overall darkness of the subject is vibrant with a luxuriant paint handling and multiple gradations of light. The upper windows reflecting only the night sky are as much alive with the visual incidence of pigmented color permutations as the lower windows are with their glinting indications of city life. Moore achieves a heightened awareness of formal purity but pursues it in the natural world.

The room takes on an iconic presence whose pervasive sensibility, like that of *Thursday*, is one of the stillness of a moment arrested for contemplation. Moore's exquisite attention to balance and to purity of design enhances the introspective demeanor of the room. In Psalm 18 we read, "He has made of darkness his secret place." Moore's *Night Studio* with its hushed tranquillity achieves a resonant hermeticism and suggests a spiritual encounter that is meditative and ethereal without recourse to traditional religious imagery. He achieves this aura of solemnity by his attentiveness to the intimacies of subtle light and atmospheric effects, unified through the tonal harmony of the entire work. He has created a space that seems designed for devotion and introspection, a retreat from the distracting details of daytime life. This interior provides serenity through a structure so perfectly attuned to the harmonies of formal beauty that the painting emanates a power of its own, quite apart from its representational content as a view through a darkened window. This black beauty of a painting achieves a visual sensation akin to that described poetically by Octavio Paz in his "San Idelfonso Nocturne":

> *In my window night*
> *invents another night*
> *another space:*
> *carnival convulsed*
> *in a square yard of blackness.*[30]

In *The Birds, 3/4, the Moon* (pl. 20) Moore gathered together assorted technical objects from a storeroom located in the same building as his Boston studio and arranged them on a window sill overlooking a wintry tree with birds on its uppermost branches against an urban view. The studio setting is the same as in *Night Studio,* but the early-morning view is a combination of snapshots of buildings in Barcelona taken by the artist during a visit in 1990. The tree with the birds in its bare branches was suggested by André Kertesz photographs. Brought together from divergent sources, the painting has a convincing naturalness that looks as if it truly existed and had been carefully and lovingly recorded. A deep shadow covers the lower half of the graceful facade of the building on the left, with the upper portion serving as a sunlit backdrop for the dark visual note of the birds whose organic shapes could be read as a double image for the absent leaves. The moon about to disappear in the morning sky keys the time of day and contributes its pale accent to the sense of chill of the clear winter morning.

Although drawn from diverse geographic and artistic sources, *The Birds, 3/4, the Moon* is above all a testimony to Moore's great love of Joan Miró and is, in essence, a still life and cityscape version of *The Farm* (fig. 7). Moore admires Miró's painting for its precise description of the landscape and its rich detail. He finds in Miró's early work an intimacy with the farm, a deep and abiding familiarity with its tools, animals, machinery, and daily routine. Miró's intense scrutiny allows each object to retain its individuality. His work abandons

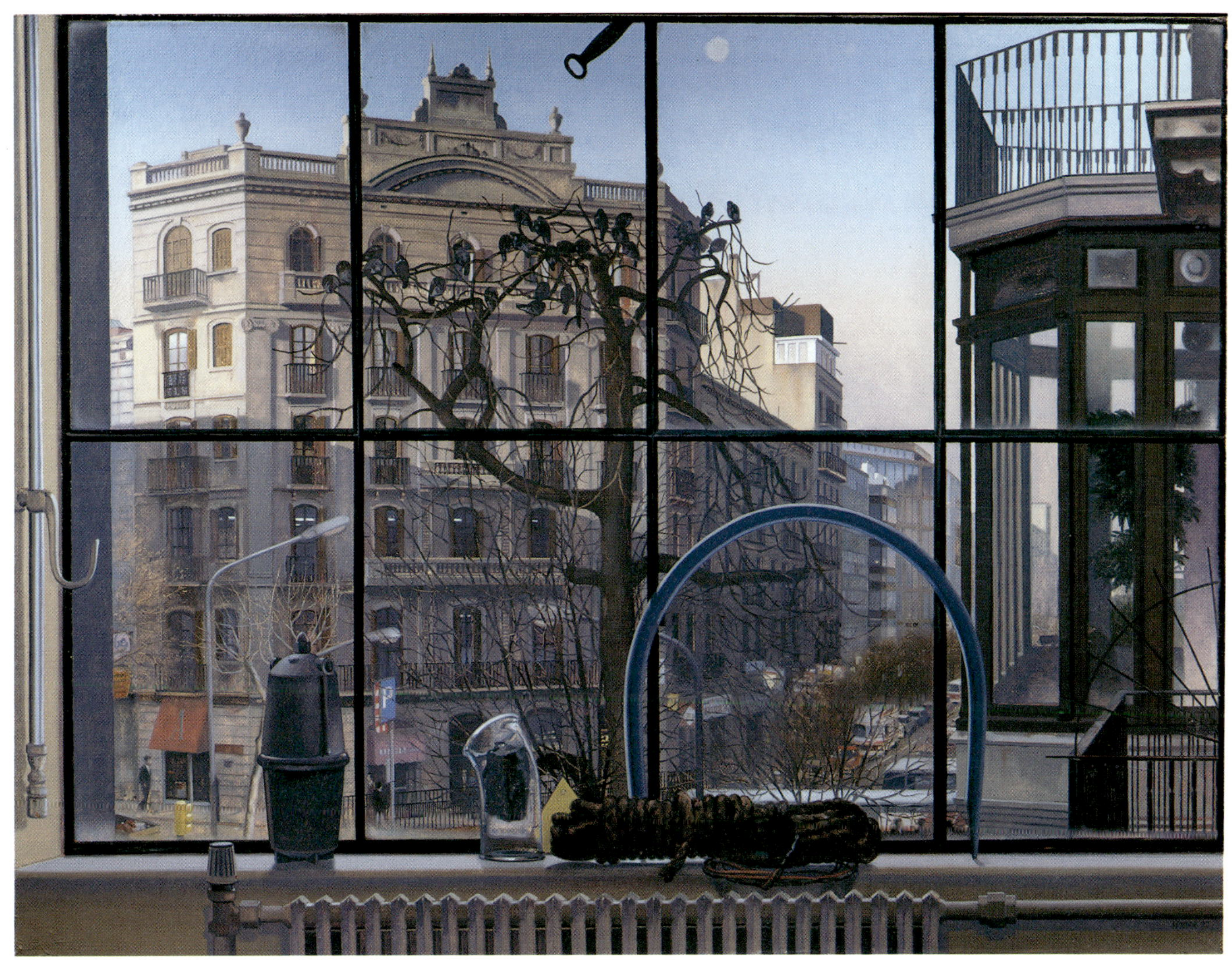

20 THE BIRDS, 3/4, THE MOON, 1993

Oil on canvas, 36 × 48 in.
Courtesy of the artist.

hierarchical distinctions to secure every aspect of the farm as integral to its fullest expression. Moore's still life in front of a cityscape likewise aims for an inclusivity of detail linked with a desire to portray things in such a way as to appreciate their individuality. He feels an affinity with Miró's compulsion to inventory all aspects that can communicate the essential character of a place in its quotidian existence. Miró's *Farm* was a prophetic work that announced many of the symbols that would recur through the rest of his art; Moore's *The Birds, 3/4, the Moon* is a synoptic piece that combines the still life with the cityscape, two of the major genres he has successfully explored in his career.

Miró wrote, "We must do things that will hold up against the classics."[31] Moore's still lifes, with their intense scrutiny of aesthetic issues, their often witty dialogue with old-master and contemporary art, attempt to do just that. With its Boston locale, Barcelona buildings, Kertesz tree, and memory of Miró, *The Birds, 3/4, the Moon* is, to borrow a phrase from Wallace Stevens, a "supreme fiction" that stands up to the best art and fulfills the poet's words:

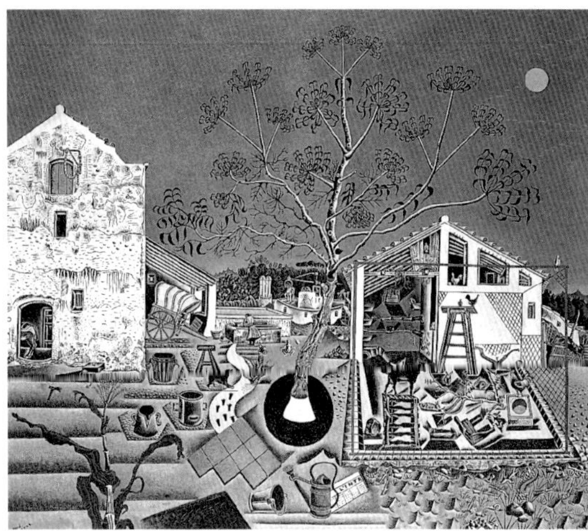

Figure 7. Joan Miró, *The Farm,* 1921–22, oil on canvas, 48¾ × 55⅝ in. National Gallery of Art, Washington, D.C., Gift of Mary Hemingway.

The freshness of transformation is
the freshness of a world. It is our own,
It is ourselves, the freshness of ourselves,
And that necessity and that presentation
Are rubbings of a glass in which we peer.[32]

FROM THEIR BEGINNING, Moore's still lifes and interior views have been marked by a private sensibility. His paintings take place in silent interiors with common objects unobtrusively placed to achieve a quiet monumentality or in front of urban vistas largely devoid of human activity. With their emphasis, for the most part, on the enigmatic rather than the dramatic, Moore's still lifes and interiors investigate formal beauty and the essence of art. The restraint in handling, the avoidance of texture, and the emphasis on geometry all contribute to a sense of pictorial equilibrium where objects are portrayed for their optical and physical sensations rather than for their functional use in everyday life. Moore searches out the intrinsic values of art, shunning the political commentary and gestural expressiveness of much contemporary work in order to concentrate on representational issues. The various moods created by his still lifes—contemplative and austere in the early table-top works such as *Summer* and *Tiger Lilies,* playful and robust in *Red Snapper* and *Montrose*, witty and complex in *Flower Glass* and *Downtown,* romantic and majestic in *Gray Marble*—all reveal themselves slowly and intimately, avoiding the rhetorical excesses of neo-expressionism or the cool, mechanical detachment of photorealism and minimalism.

Moore's still lifes are highly objective but deeply personal, rooted in the physical world yet spiritually inflected. His art involves complexities of thought and a deep potential for aesthetic analysis beneath a deceptively simple arrangement of forms. There is no appeal to sensual appetite in his work, no vestiges of eating or drinking, no active sense of physical participation. Moore's still lifes arouse perceptual rather than tactile pleasures, soliciting aesthetic emotions. The careful placement of objects in his still-life setups is calculated to sustain the relational aspects of perception, as he is intensely interested in the idea that how we see is as important as what we see. Moore's objects placed on tables in isolated corners, lined in display cases, set on ledges, tucked in shallow marble niches, or overlooking urban vistas are deliberately staged for the viewer. Vigilance replaces sensual indulgence as the dominant optical strategy in works finely crafted to secure the structural integrity of the support and to keep the premise of representation as presentation fresh and engaging.

Self-containment, measure, stability, and restraint characterize Moore's still lifes, aided by his immaculate surfaces. His preference for formal symmetries, structured balance, and an ordered harmony of design informs the emotive geometry of his canvases and watercolors with logic and lucidity. The mirrors, windows, and transparent surfaces he uses serve as devices to keep the rhetorical issues of realism vividly present. The reflections that are broken into flat fragments on the surface of the mirror signal alternative ways of imaging reality in the contemporary era made possible since cubism declared the status of the real to be a system of signs. The window reminds us of the tension between the picture plane as a material support and as a surface offering a perspectival illusion.

The recurring objects in Moore's still lifes allowed him to search for different visual pleasures among his presentations. The still life is considered the least spontaneous genre of painting because the artist exerts absolute control by selecting and positioning the articles to be painted. Moore's vases, cups, containers, and trays are like musical notes in a score arranged to evoke different sensations and harmonies by their interrelationships of color, shape, and spatial extensions. Moore composed classically, always conscious of a structural harmony and a geometric lucidity in his work, but never allowed an enervated sense of "tastefulness" to compromise his work. Technical skill is never allowed to become mere facility at rendering precise illusionist objects. Avoiding the gestural and painterly brushstroke, Moore dedicated his ability to the discovery of the tactile at the service of the conceptual. From the still-life objects on the tables of his earliest works that were involved with private domestic space, he gradually evolved to enlarging the window until it took over the surface of the canvas and led him to the public domain of the city. For this native Missourian, seeing is not only believing; it is comprehending the complexities of perception. It is also an acknowledgment that art originates as much in the mind as it does in the visible world. Moore's precise spatial dialectics—detached, puritan, spare, and matter-of-fact—are distinctly American in sensibility and demonstrate the continuing power of still life to inspire significant work.

Chapter 2

“Site-Seeing”

CITYSCAPES AND CITY MARGINS

DURING THE SUMMER of 1976 Moore regularly took a train from suburban Jenkintown, Pennsylvania, to the main campus at Temple University on Philadelphia's North Broad Street. He passed from the playgrounds and backyards of suburbia through the rows of jammed-up trains and acres of tracks that led to the nineteenth-century factory neighborhoods bordering Temple's campus. "I imagined what it would be like to live and work in those places, about the lawn furniture, why the lights were on in a specific building, about footpaths worn in the grass (shortcuts to where?), about odd appurtenances on rooftops; about what seemed sinister or strange about these places."[33] His curiosity about these physical facts and particular things prompted him to turn from the studio arrangements of still life to the cityscape.

City imagery has been a vital source of inspiration to artists in the modern and contemporary age. From the time Charles Baudelaire called for its depiction in his *Salon* of 1846 as part of the heroism of modern life, painters, novelists, poets, and musicians have sought to embody the city's moods and meanings. The city symbolized the new age, opportunity, and progress, as well as discontinuity, fragmentation, and change. The urban arena, shaped by human hands, in turn formed its inhabitants in a variety of ways that have sought expression in art. The Ash Can artists, Edward Hopper, Charles Sheeler, and Walker Evans are among a few notable twentieth-century artists who trained their sights on the city and sought to incorporate in their work some characteristic aspect of the metropolis that would embody their sense of the age in which they lived.

The city's enduring fascination continued even into abstraction with Willem de Kooning, Franz Kline, and Mark Tobey, whose dynamic strokes and energetic hieroglyphs connoted urban dynamism and motion in such works as *Gotham News, Wanamaker Block,* and *Broadway.* As Donald Kuspit observed, the "seeming instability of the modern urban world is a sign of its fertility, its revolutionary creativity."[34] The postmodern age recognized that a significant shift in the ethos and economy of the city had occurred, and thus sought a different style to articulate these transpositions. Artists such as Don Eddy, Richard Estes, and Robert Cottingham portrayed the city as a site of hectic economic activity restlessly refracted and reflected in the chrome and glitter of commercial displays, while Red Grooms and Robert Birmelin featured the inhabitants of the city and described their effect on the politics and sociology of the urban milieu.

In choosing to paint the city, the artist gives physical form to ideas about society and self, shaping perceptions in a manner that attempts to lend visual coherence to a particularized urban experience. John Moore's realist canvases of city life translate his views on urbanism into images that invoke older traditions of art but are executed in a style that sharpens awareness of the contemporary condition. A precept of realism has been the necessity to be of one's time, and this has required of the artist not a superficial image copied at random but a conscious replication of some aspect of life grasped in depth that can address issues more profound than technical virtuosity. Moore's account of the metropolis questions the traditions of city painting, demonstrates how the spatial inflects the social, and discloses how detail can transcribe the heterogeneity of urban experience while simultaneously clarifying its visual energy. Always more than a descriptive paraphrase of the urban arena, Moore's cityscapes offer a critical analysis of its social and historical conditions.

Moore's views go well beyond an aggregation of buildings. His fascination with urban architecture is not merely an interest in replicating a definable setting. His profound commitment to the distinctive presence of the city seeks to understand it as a place and a moral order. Moore works to discover something about the forces that shape urban culture, allowing the viewer to experience the realities of city life perceived through its varied buildings and highways. He remains alert to those aspects of city life that make it essentially American.

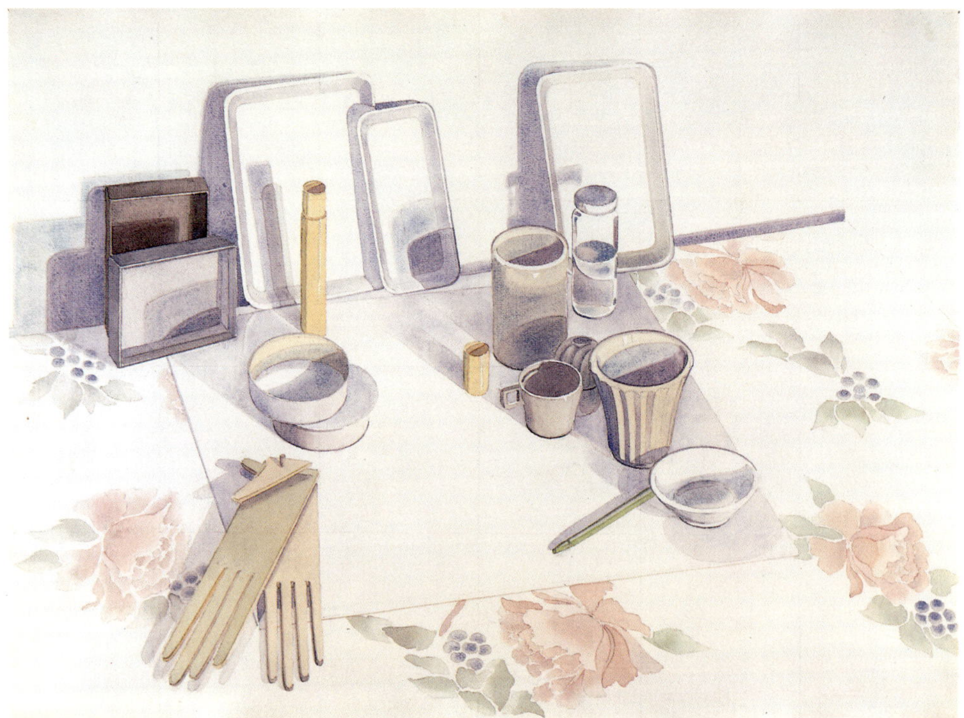

21

MACARTHUR PARK, 1977

Watercolor on paper, 22 × 31 in.
Private collection.

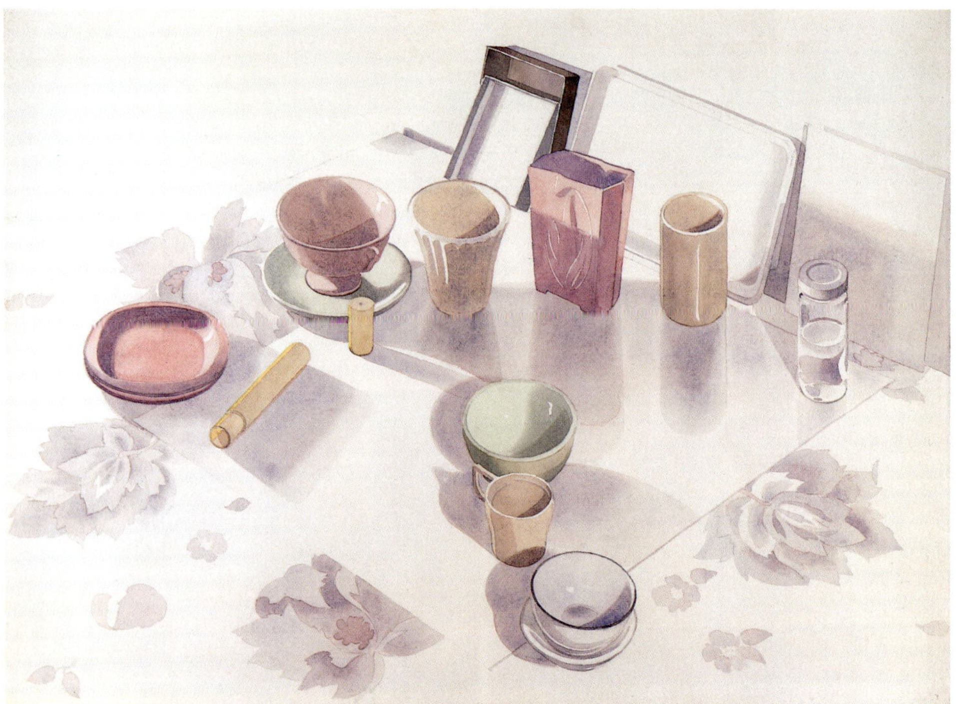

22

THREE L.A. PINKS, 1977

Watercolor on paper, 22 × 31 in.
Private collection.

SEVERAL WATERCOLOR STILL LIFES of 1977 indicate the shift in Moore's work from still life to urban and industrial scenes. Even the titles of these works, *Macarthur Park* (pl. 21) and *Three L.A. Pinks* (pl. 22), indicate his interest in the city. The objects in these works can be read as surrogates for industrial towers and buildings. The layered trays along with the rectangular and oval vases and containers punctuate the wall above the table edge like an architectural vista in the distance from an airplane window. Moore said at the time: "I think of still life in architectural terms and choose specific objects deliberately, like the tall, slim glasses which suggest smokestacks. Industrial architecture has always interested me and shows up in my paintings, seen through a window."[35]

During the summer of 1977 Moore found a place to work on the tenth floor of Conwell Hall at Temple University. The view provided direct access to some of the places he had seen from the train. He set about closing the gap between what he was increasingly interested in and what he could do with brushes and color. *Cityscape* (pl. 23) and *Looking East* (pl. 24) give an idea of his first attempts at the cityscape genre. After the controlled placement of the still-life objects, the amount of detail the city contained overwhelmed him, and he counted on the early morning haze to generalize the forms. Watercolor studies such as these of academic buildings and the neighborhood around Temple assisted him in gathering information for larger oils that he would later complete in his studio.

Moore's first cityscapes show his modernist sensibilities where he first sought forms that unified his canvas. For example in *South* (pl. 25), another view from Temple University's main campus, the shadowed trapezoid of the lower recess directly outside of the window rhymes with the shadows on the first set of academic buildings in the middle distance and with those on the twin red brick structures in the upper section of the outlying city. Two metal rods protruding from the cement in the recess outside the window stand like a pair of isolated De Chirico figures casting long shadows. These forms are then repeated in the middle distance on the green lawn by their human counterparts standing closer together. While not

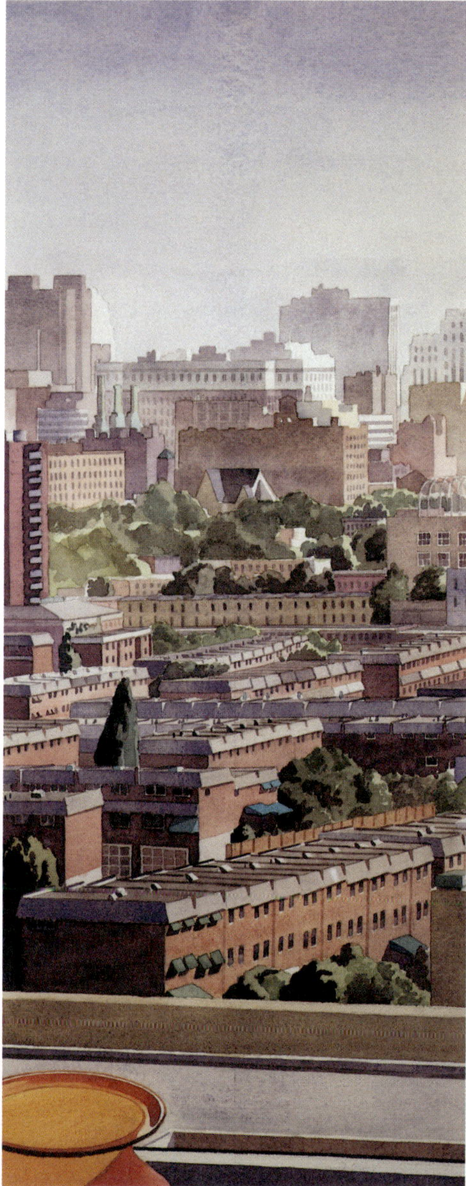

23

CITYSCAPE, 1978

Watercolor on paper, 24 1/2 × 10 in
Private collection.

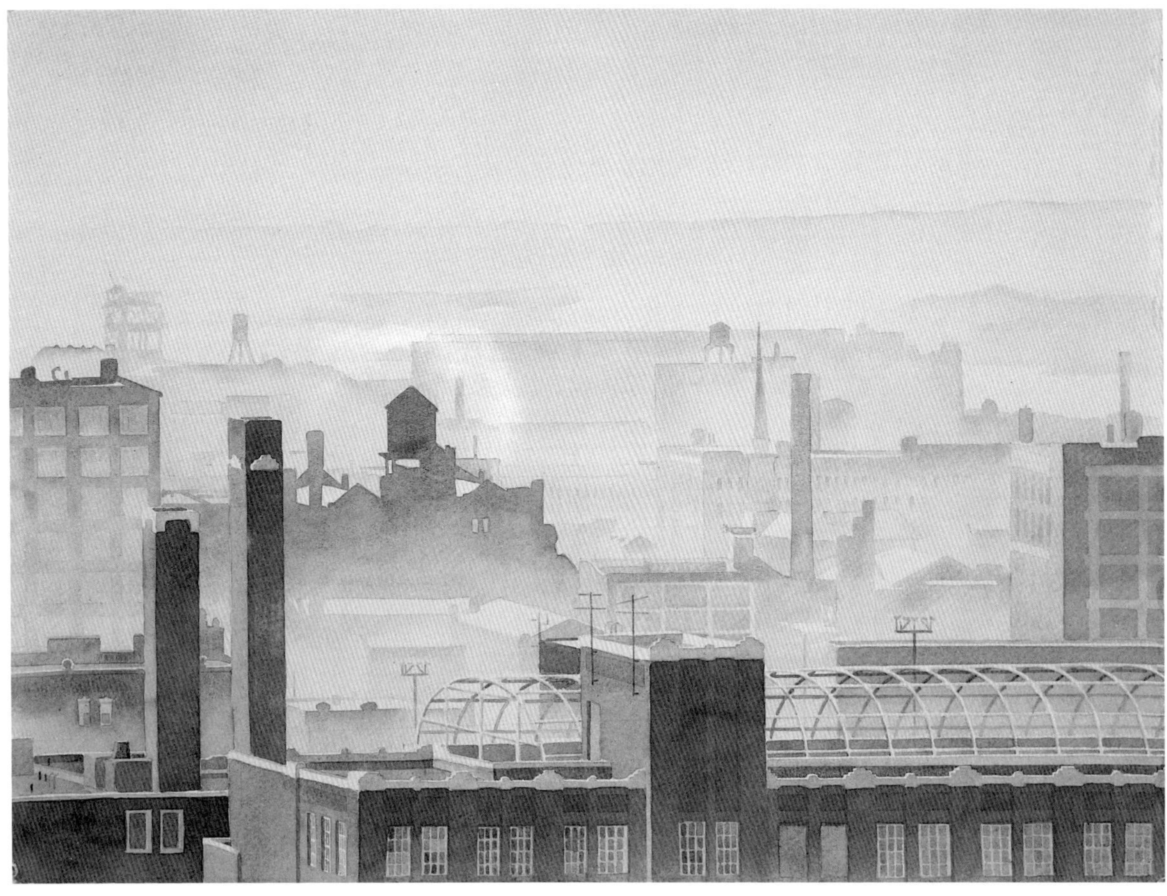

24 LOOKING EAST, 1977

Watercolor on paper, 22½ × 30 in.
Private collection.

denying bulk to the buildings, neither does Moore emphasize it. The stacked perspective and high horizon keep the eye resolutely on the surface of the work.

Moore's choice of view and his structuring of its spaces serve as a realist homage to modernist painting. The city coalesces into an organized unit of almost pure geometry by means of his precise notation of acute angles, straight lines, and clear planes lit by stark patterns of sunlight and shadow. The height and distance of the view minimizes the hustle of the city and quiets its activity, distilling the urban coordinates into disciplined units of form. Moore's cityscape seems idealized, yet remains truthful to a precise time in a specific place. *South* succeeds in taming the kinetic force of the city into a serene and controlled vista. Moore chose the vertical shape of the canvas to accentuate the difference between landscape, which is traditionally horizontal, and cityscape, which forces the eye upward. The experience of seeing the city through the narrow window had the effect of a Chinese scroll for him.

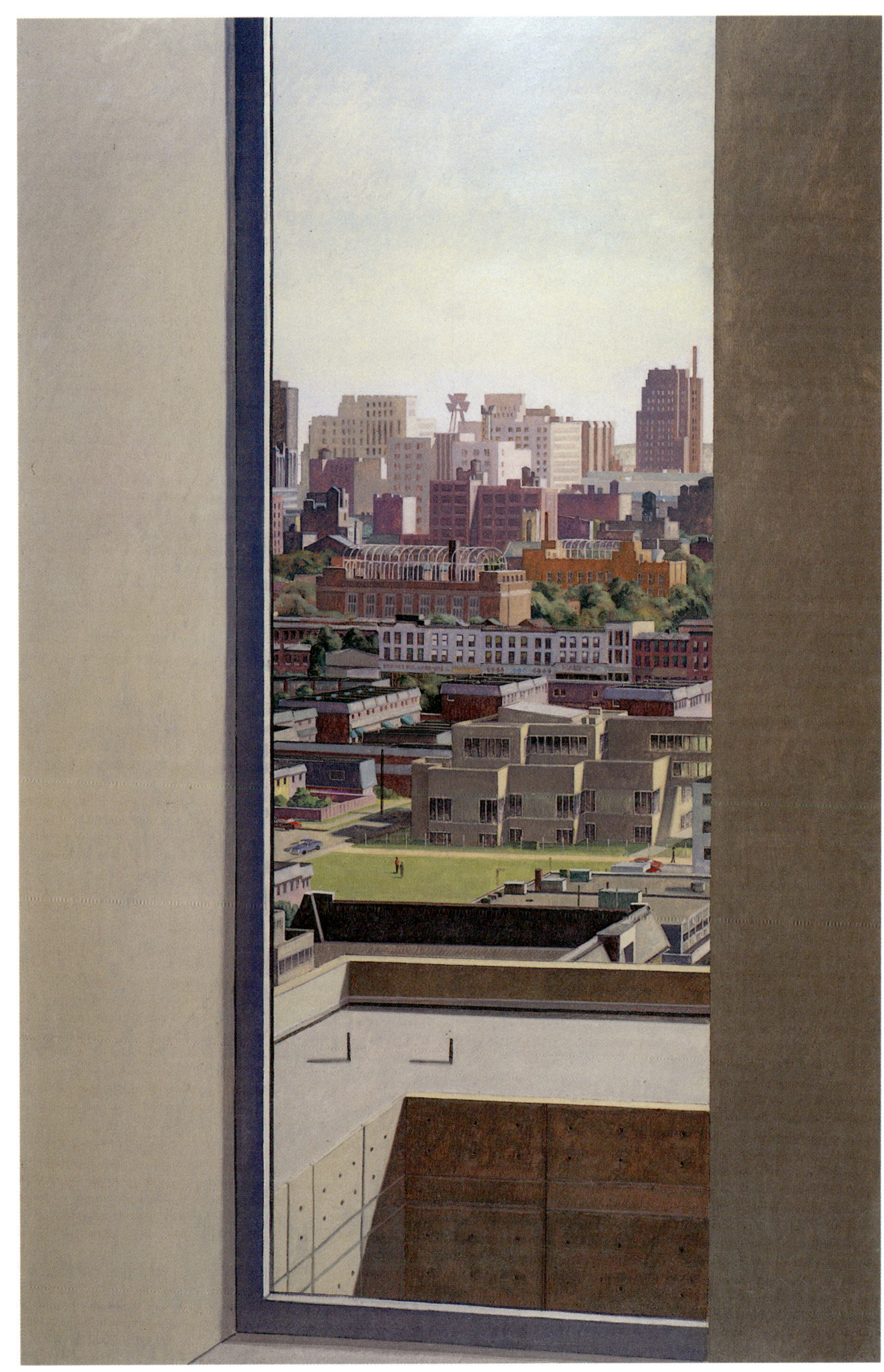

25

SOUTH, 1979

Oil on canvas, 72 × 48 in.
Private collection.

Moore spent a year and a half teaching at the University of California at Berkeley during 1981–82. Always one to avoid the picture-postcard view or any tourist attraction in his art, Moore chose a nondescript but startling site in the large blank facade of a building in his *San Francisco View* (pl. 26). His ongoing interest in the abstract and representational are perfectly wedded in this work. The geometric city forms read alternatively as pattern on the surface and as description in depth. The light brown facade stretching to the top of the canvas prevents any normal vanishing point from receding toward a distant horizon. The cityscape coalesces into a contrapuntal study of squares and rectangles accented by variations on the triangle. Charles Le Clair makes an apt analogy of *San Francisco View* with the push-pull force of Hans Hofmann's work (fig. 8), noting the similarity of large rectangular blocks compositionally tied together by active smaller shapes.[36] Moore thus keeps the language of modernism fresh while remaining faithful to the facts of visual perception in his chosen realist style, finding an underlying order within the architectural world. He discovers a geometry in the city in which facades, windows, rooftops, and steeples shift from illusionistic objects to subtle units of form and color organized across a planar surface. The allover field, flatness, objecthood—hallmarks of late modernist painting—are harnessed to the task of representation. Accuracy in this instance is not sacrificed to abstraction; rather, it is subordinated to achieving clarity through a visual economy of interrelated parts.

Moore allows the shapes and colors of the buildings to organize surface and depth without compromising their individuality as real things in a real world. The unity of the work is both compositional and particularized, investing the act of looking with a deepened sense of modernism's positive heritage, allied with an awareness of Moore's genuine pleasure in describing the world in which he lives. By the competency of the design Moore assures us of his firm grasp on the essentials of his craft while never allowing his skill with detail to overpower the painting to the point where it becomes a fetishistic performance or the sole rationale of the painting. He is committed to the idea of the city as a site that expresses the modern urban condition. His cityscapes tell us that these are places where people work, dwell, and lead their lives. Moore's purpose is not to dilute the power of abstraction but to yoke it to a celebration of the familiar, demonstrating how cropping and composition, along with description of the world, can be analogous to the purity of cubism and minimalism while not neglecting the realities of the physical world.

Figure 8. Hans Hofmann, *The Gate,* 1960, oil on canvas, 74 5/8 × 48 1/4 in. Solomon R. Guggenheim Museum, New York.

Although the title informs us that this is a view of San Francisco, there is no geographical marker such as the Golden Gate Bridge or the TransAmerica building to anchor us in the specificity of a locale. Seeking the specular and not the spectacular, Moore approaches the city as an artistically aware observer, not as a tourist in search of the picturesque view. His city spaces are generic rather than site-specific. Disinterested in the chrome or glitter that fascinated many California photorealists, and avoiding the expressionist drama of Wayne

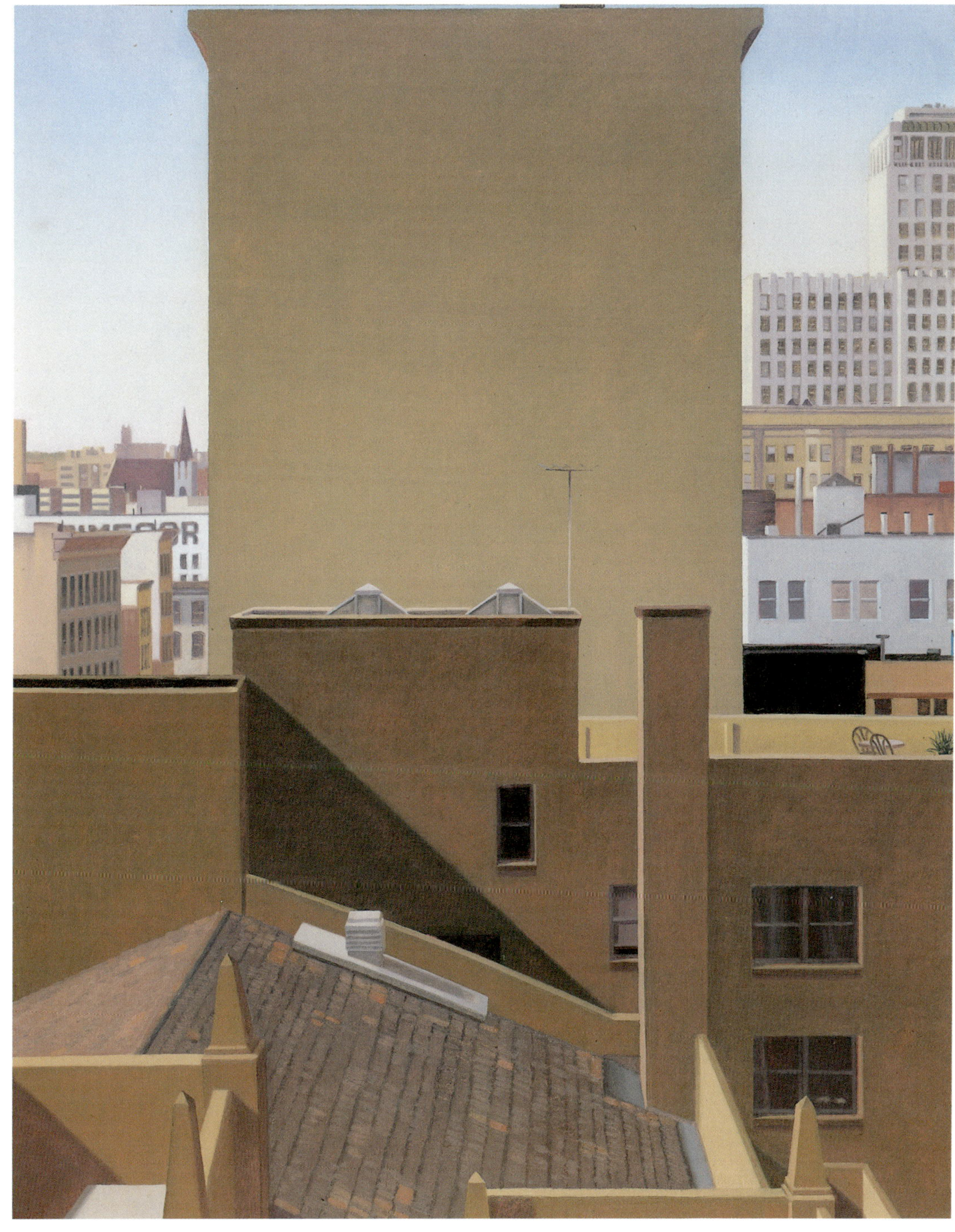

26 SAN FRANCISCO VIEW, 1982

Oil on board, 30 × 24 in.
Boise Art Museum, Idaho, Gift of William Janss.

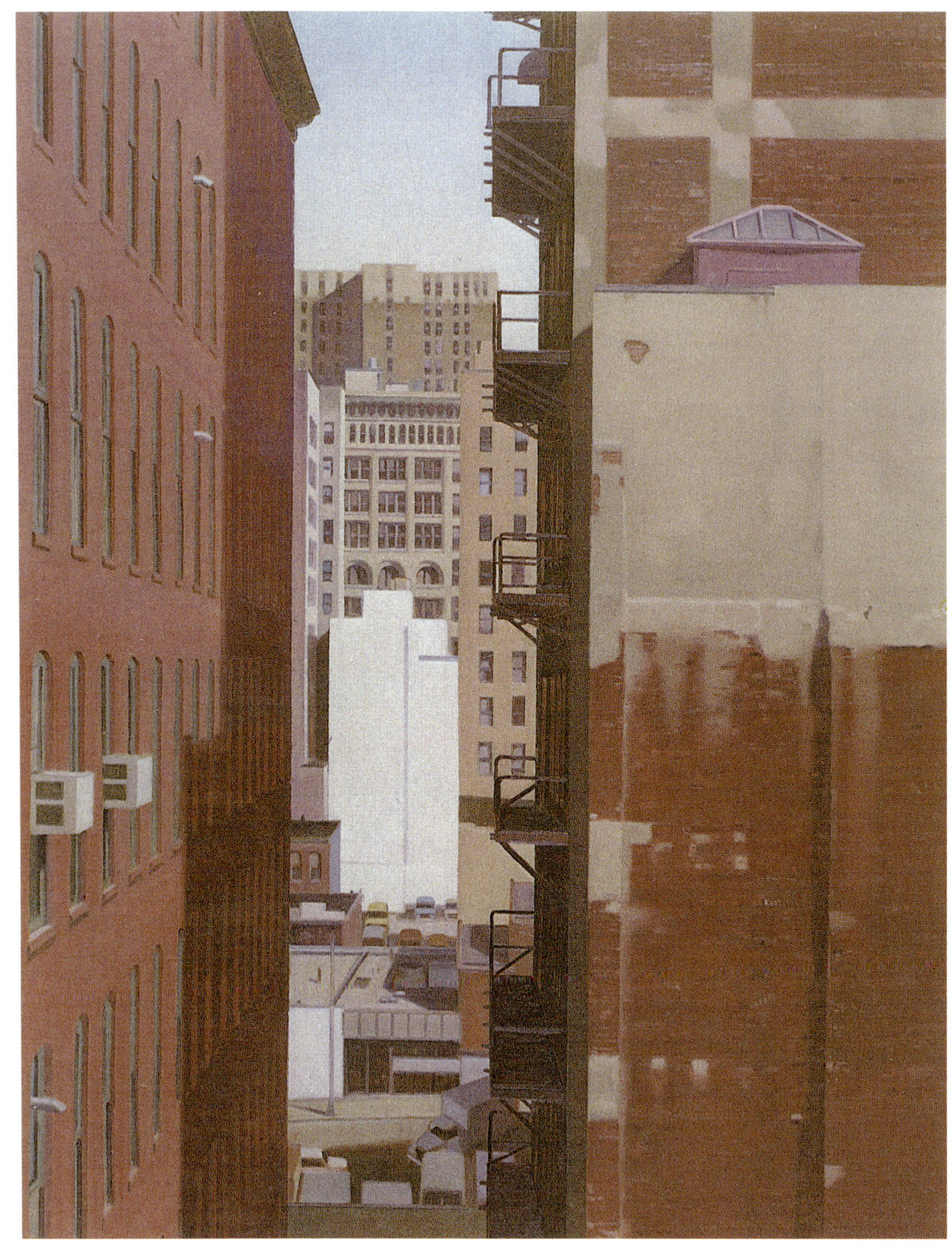

27 TWELFTH STREET, 1982

Oil on board, 30 × 24 in.
Private collection.

Thiebaud's plunging views of San Francisco streets, Moore seems closer to the classic serenity and chromatic sensibility of Richard Diebenkorn in his *Ocean Park* series. As if to humanize the severity of the geometry and to invoke man's presence in the city, Moore includes a small table, two chairs, and a plant on the roof of the chocolate brown building in the middle of the painting, the only circular and organic note in a resolutely angular field, like a gentle aside in a serious soliloquy.

Description in recessed depth of building windows, fire escapes, and trucks alternates with flatness and frontality in *Twelfth Street* (pl. 27). The white facade of the building in the center of the painting merges with the frontal plane of the canvas due to its color value and simple shape, retaining its abstract presence while simultaneously defining a recognizable element in the cityscape. The facade on the right presents patterned brick and faded water stains on cement with a surface as dense and active as a Clyfford Still. Suspended in reciprocal tension, the forms read alternatively as representational objects and abstract entities. By taming the chaos of the city into visually satisfying units of order, Moore provides a positive view of urban life that discovers beauty where others might find decadence and decay. His ability to summarize form directly and intensively assists in the organization of space so that the shape and spatial tension of the buildings serve to enhance the flatness and frontality of the picture plane. No conflict exists between his artistic sense of formal order and his desire to record the look of an American city. By avoiding the bustle of street activity and by his integration of representational detail and structure, Moore allows the painting to function as an object of pure visibility in the modernist sense while not neglecting the truth to social detail that makes the painting legible as a realist account of the contemporary urban world.

Edward Hopper, one of Moore's most important precursors in American urban imagery, is often quoted as saying that all he wanted to do was paint light on the side of a wall. Moore's *Morning Light* (pl. 28) can be seen as a contemporary realist response to Hopper's strong light raking over city facades. While Hopper's works are notably silent and lonely, Moore is interested in arresting a moment that will pass quickly. His aim is to capture a sensation of immediate experience rather than to evoke feelings of nostalgia or reflection. The light passing over the facades animates a scene that is naturally static. Moore's handling of light has become more sophisticated by this stage and brings with it an increase in the amount of information he wants to include along with a greater complexity of design. The additive detail tends to diminish the modernist sense of the canvas as a frontal organization of forms and communicates more of his subjective reactions to what he perceives in the city.

Morning Light depicts the sharply focused edge of bright sunlight cutting across the densely packed city buildings. The deeply hued shadow cast by the foreground building supplies a diagonal foil to the horizontal and vertical elements of the city, enhancing the feeling of light and atmosphere. Moore pays close attention to the subtle chromatic changes of light as it passes from a brilliant white on the east facade of the building in the middle distance to emerge in a softer hue on the south side, thus demonstrating how the same building can seem to be at once crisply new and slightly tattered under different conditions of light. He carefully notes the way incidents of light are reflected off chrome details on the cars, how the shiny metal of a bus is dulled to a matte sheen as it passes through the deeply shadowed street.

The windowed facades of the buildings play a key role in establishing a sense of movement through *Morning Light.* Moore keeps the eye on the surface of the work by moving the viewpoint to the right of the painting, thus cutting off a deep perspective view down the street. The insistent repetition and variation in the shapes of windows—those found in buildings, and on cars, trucks, and buses—create a distinctive urban polyphony that suggests the energy of the city without resorting to traditional narrative devices. Moore's city is not a background for human activity, but provides a multiplicity of building styles, surfaces, ornaments, and color that celebrates the city's diversity. His handling of light is confident, not angst-ridden; his shadows define rather than obscure form. For Moore, the social and visual character of the city are fused in an image that testifies to the idea that there is extraordinary interest in such scenes. Moore's version of the city allows us to contemplate rather than react to the scene presented.

Seen from above, the activity of the city is disciplined into patterned fragments that are abstracted and generalized into an image that is intellectually graspable rather than emotionally overwhelming. In *Cal* (pl. 29), for instance, Moore provides

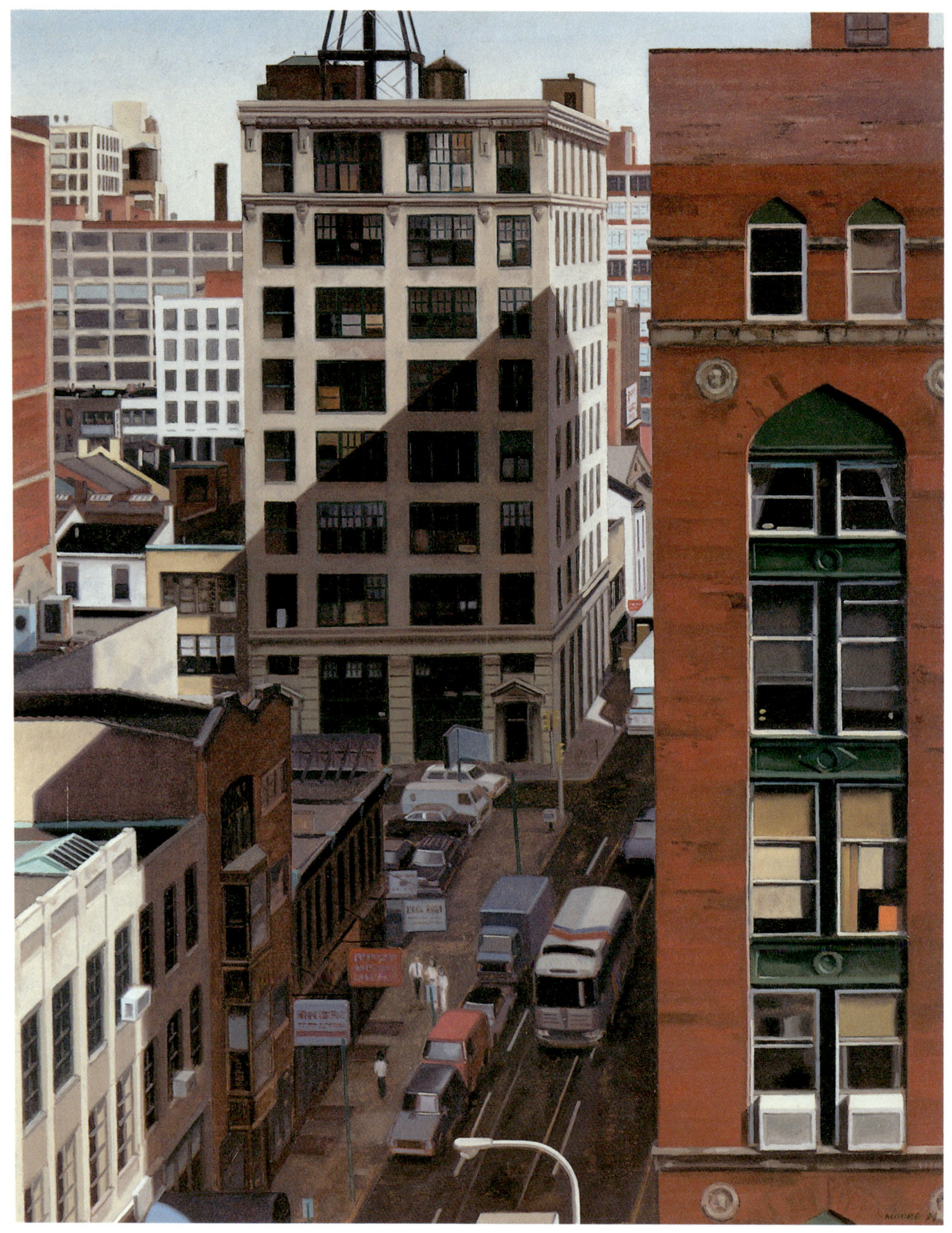

28 MORNING LIGHT, 1984

Oil on board, 30 × 24 in.
Sandra Moore.

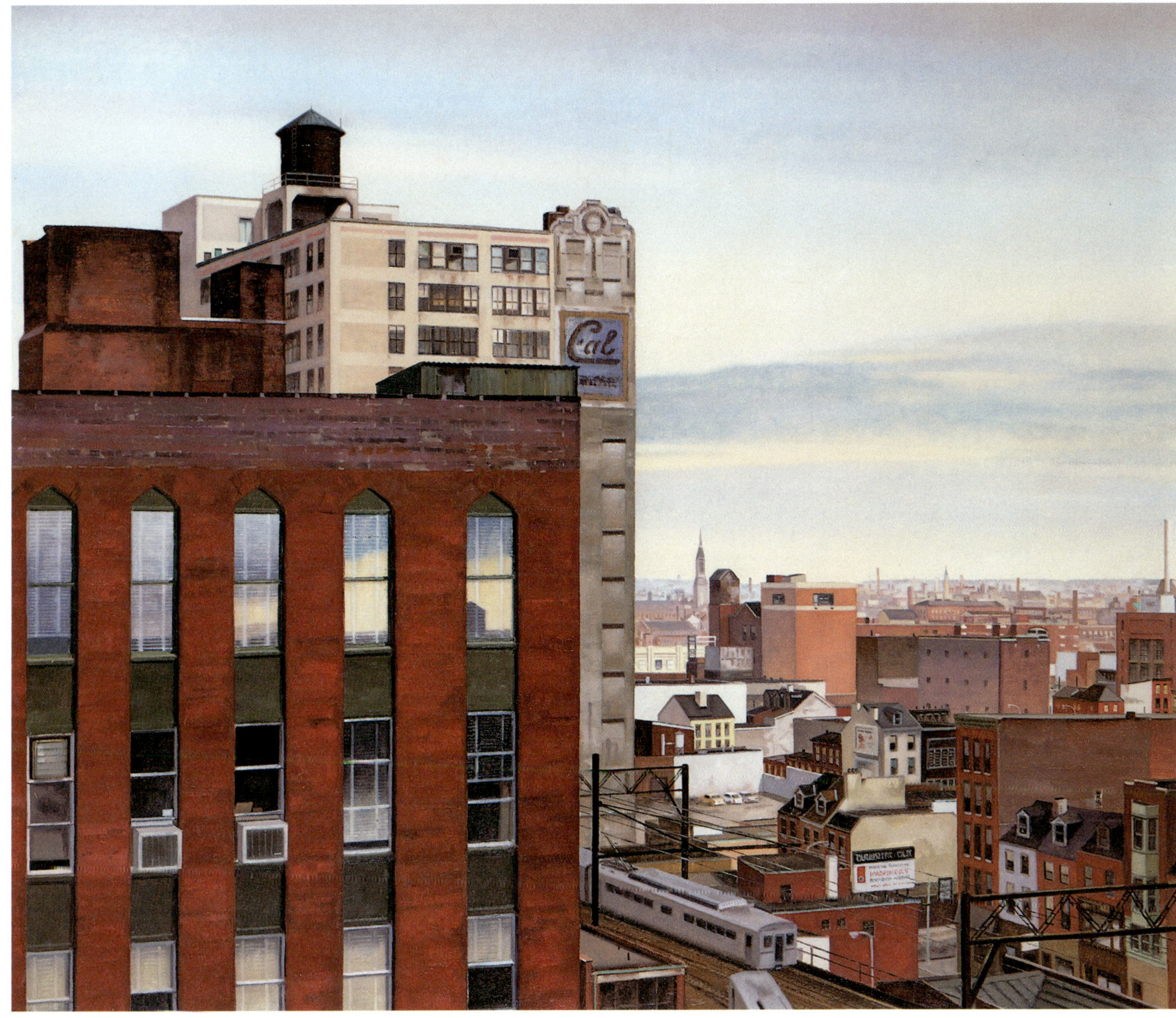

29 CAL, 1984

Oil on canvas, 41 × 49 in.
Private collection.

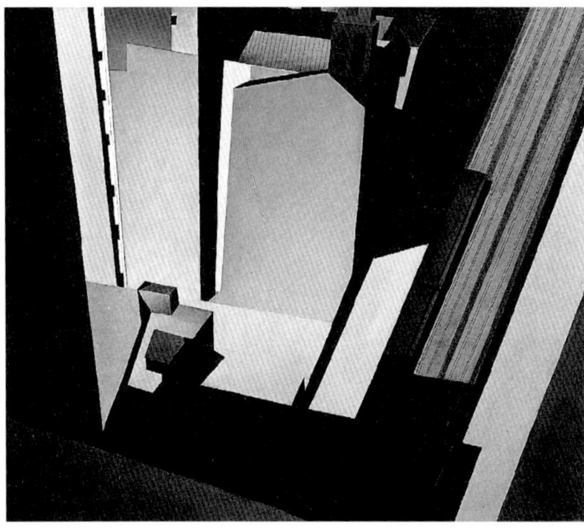

Figure 9. Charles Sheeler, *Church Street El*, 1920, oil on canvas, 15½ × 18½ in. Cleveland Museum of Art, Mr. and Mrs. William H. Marlatt Fund.

fragments of buildings that ultimately coalesce into a pictorial unity beneath a cloudy late-afternoon sky whose fading light is reflected in the windows of the brick building in the left foreground. He considers the city a landscape filled with different textures whose details are described in a muted but convincing manner. How the buildings create a locale that has its own regional and class individuality, how they interact with the buildings surrounding them, and how together they form a complex that is ultimately more interesting than their individual parts, forms the substance of Moore's work.

The title *Cal* calls attention to the blue sign on the side of the tall building in the middle distance whose Art Deco facade abuts a more modernist building and serves as a perfect metaphor for the grafting of old and new styles that is an important part of Moore's own art. The calligraphy on the sign supplies a well-known detail of urban popular culture and provides, along with the sky whose colors it combines in its weathered face, a lyric counterpoint to the cubic facades and several upright towers and smokestacks fretting the horizon.

Cal bears comparison with Charles Sheeler's 1920 *Church Street El* (fig. 9) as both paintings focus the gaze on an urban view of buildings and look down on a train. Sheeler strips his buildings of detail, depersonalizing their forms into slanting cubic shapes whose shorn surfaces evoke urban anonymity. The weathered surfaces of the buildings Moore paints are rubbed with a patina that speaks of age and experience, suggesting the residue of human activity and use. Sheeler brings the newness and speed of the modern city to the foreground in his sharpened view. With *Cal,* Moore has slowed an urban moment into a visual celebration of the familiar. His focus is on a working-class neighborhood where older factories and tenements congregate with newer facades in a stylistic mix that suggests the diversity of the lives of the workers and residents who inhabit these spaces.

Moore attends to the drama inherent in light and shadow as they paint buildings and windows in differing shades in *Tenth Street* (pl. 30), a neighborhood scene on the edge of the commercial district of center city Philadelphia. He converts the nearly blank facade of the tall building rising on the horizon into a tactile mauve field whose chromatic nuances on its flat surface haloed by light are as painterly as a Mark Rothko. The setting sun converts windows on the factory in the middle right distance into gilded tesserae worthy of an apse in Ravenna. Even the tenements partake in a jeweled brilliance that modifies their dullness into a temporary regal splendor of purples, reds, and gold. By a skillful juxtaposition of positive and negative shapes, Moore adds movement in depth and tension across the surface in an otherwise static composition. Contrasts of light and shadow endow the buildings with a crispness of edge and a vivacity of color suggesting that the buildings are freshly painted and refurbished, even though we know that in this case the urban renewal is the result of ambient light rather than economic infusion.

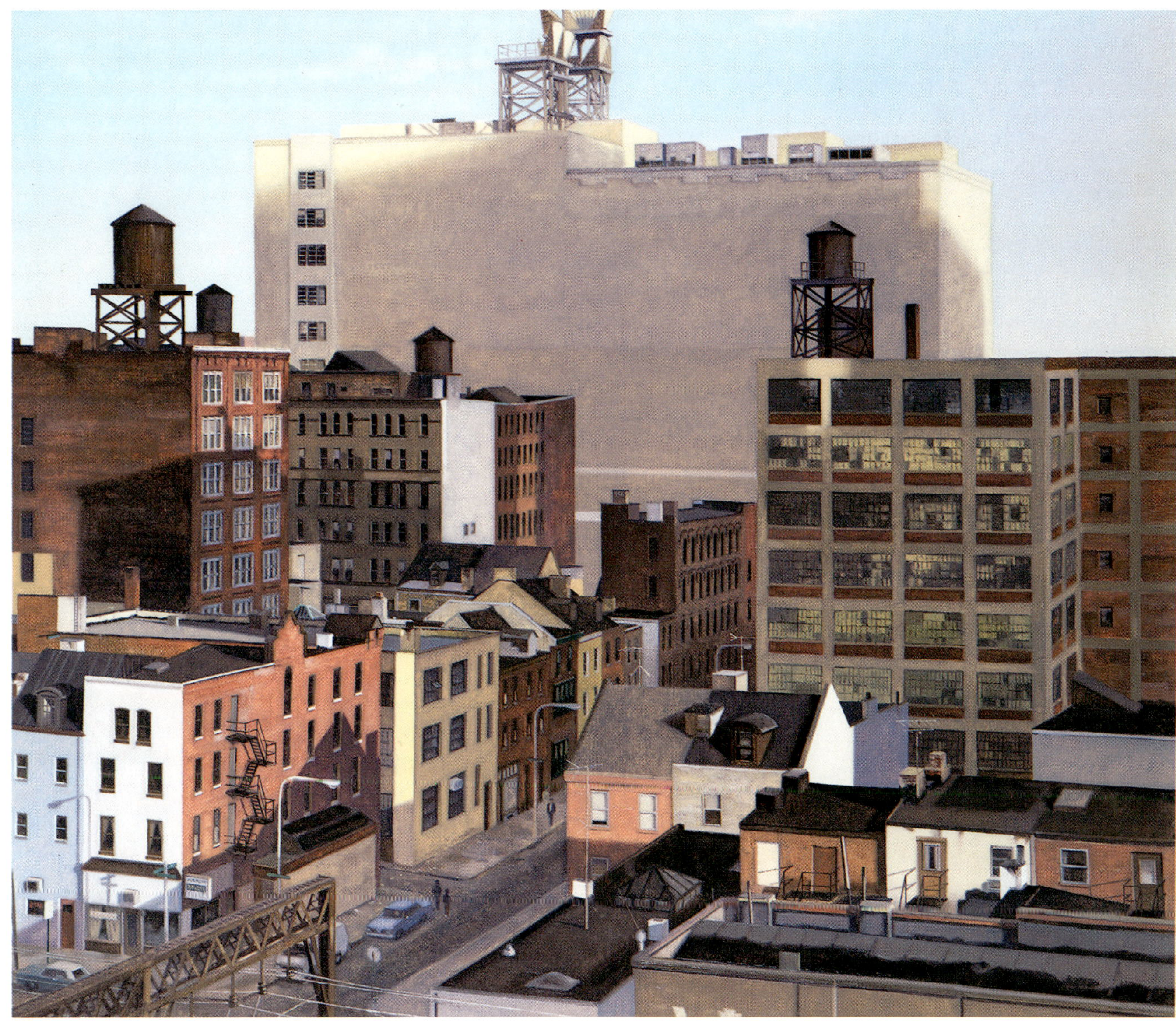

30 TENTH STREET, 1985

Oil on canvas, 41 × 49 in.
Private collection.

By portraying his subjects faithfully with much of their lower-class detail, Moore manages to make an area of the city deemed uninteresting by a more cosmopolitan taste hold its own as a visual field of complexity and delight. He discovers the potential of an image to reveal pictorial passages that resonate a modernist involvement with the compositional rhythms of geometry and a fascination with abstract color fields, while never neglecting the class associations of the site. This fusion of the aesthetic with the culturally aware is Moore's way of relating humanistic concerns.

Moore's keen observation of the pictorial incidents that make up a city are intended to assist the viewer in achieving an intensity of vision that has been blunted by routine and numbed by the nagging details of daily existence. His carefully rendered view of an industrial neighborhood at a certain time of day records a way of life in urban America. Painters such as John Marin and Joseph Stella celebrated the city's vitality with kinetic images of famous skyscrapers and bridges. Moore opts for the areas of a city as often neglected in art as they are in city funding, and if he lavishes his skill on water towers rather than scenic buildings, on fire escapes instead of beaux-arts decoration, it is because of his conviction that the picturesque is an evolving concept.

A commission in 1985 from the John Hancock Mutual Life Insurance Company took Moore to Boston, where he conceived his ideas for *Boston Common View* and *Winthrop Square. Boston Common View* (pl. 31) presents a street-level view of offices, shops, and apartments around Beacon Hill. Moore's intention, however, is not to document a site with topographical exactitude: although several of the buildings are in this location, their configuration is altered by his individual compositional requirements. He locates the truth of the painting in the urban mix of the commercial and the residential, highlighting the stylistic blend of the distinctive modern regularity of the glass-and-steel bank headquarters behind the eclectic older red brick buildings with their balustrades and porticoed Palladian-style entrances above a boxy luncheonette. Vignettes of people standing in windows and working in fluorescent-lit offices pay tribute to Hopper's paintings of similar subjects. Even the figures seated at the counter of the darkened luncheonette might serve as Moore's Boston variation on the *Nighthawks,* but here miniaturized and viewed from a distance, as if seen through inverted opera glasses.

Moore's choice of dusk for the painting assists him in his creation of a fictive reality. The ebbing light mutes the details of the scene to a slight vagueness that enhances the various narrative uncertainties contained in the picture. A man and a woman in the left foreground suggest a variety of possible encounters familiar to the city. Are they solitary pedestrians or are they together as a couple? Is he gazing at her or has he halted for a moment of introspection? Will he turn to ascend the steps to his left or follow her through the park? This ambiguity is continued in details such as the patches of paint around the refuse container anchoring the lower right corner. Are they leaves or garbage, or a mixture of both? Is the vapor at the back of the red car parked in the street exhaust from the tailpipe or steam from a street vent? Is the figure in the lit window above the door waving to an outsider or scratching her head? Moore nourishes our imagination with these few visual clues and indicates that, for him, these figures serve as more than mere staffage. Incertitude plays deftly against the graphic accuracy of style as Moore fastens on details of architecture and elements of atmosphere with a precision that secures a lived sense of time and place.

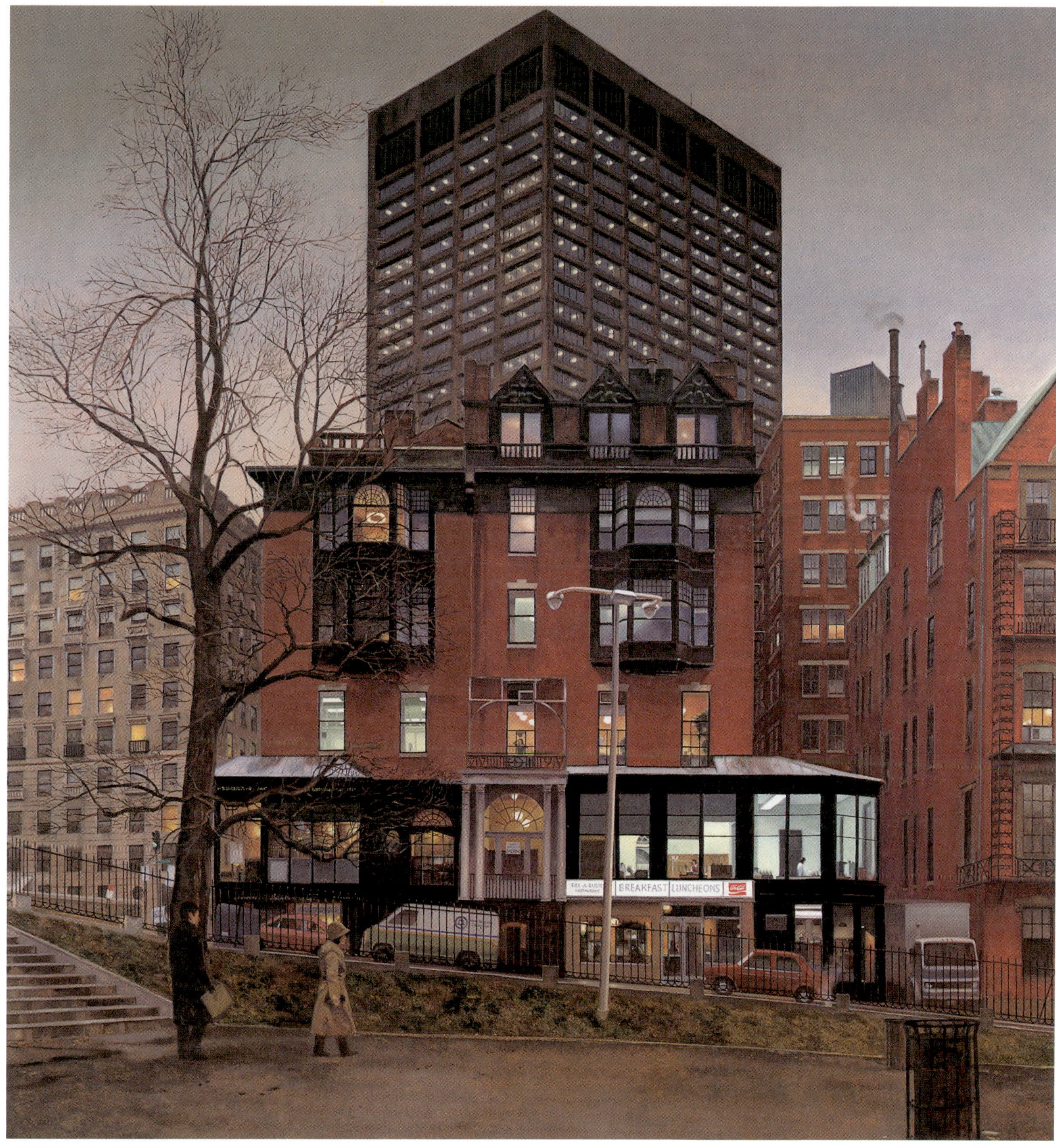

31 BOSTON COMMON VIEW, 1985

Oil on canvas, 75 × 72 in.
John Hancock Mutual Life Insurance,
Boston.

Moore concentrates on familiar rather than unique moments in the city. A New England Telephone Company truck parked in front of a restaurant named Fill-a-Buster communicates the prosaic quality of city neighborhood sites that register in the mind as typically American. The multiple window styles with their lights ranging from cold white fluorescent to warm golden incandescent possess an almost psychological individuality that connotes the various living styles possible in urban culture.

Moore employs the architecture of the city as both subject and locale. He provides a convincing illusion of buildings from different periods of the nineteenth and twentieth centuries that fix regional characteristics and allow contemplation of the social values reflected in the ways our cities are built. "The look of American cities—Philadelphia or Boston or New York—says something particular about the American character, American economy, American values," Moore observed. "An Italian village with its stucco houses and a church in the center of town shows something about the role of religion. When you go to American cities, banks and insurance companies are the biggest buildings."[37] Corporate verticality towers over domestic horizontality, visually capturing the power of capital that dominates the life of the populace. Moore's title *Boston Common View* plays with the idea of a well-known esplanade that serves as a major city landmark, but the title refers less to geography than to the daily familiarity that characterizes life in a major American metropolis.

Winthrop Square (pl. 32) provides a further instance of Moore's preoccupation with the city at a moment of sharp white sunlight and deep blue shadow. A woman about to cross the street halts to look back at two policemen standing by their wagon parked in a narrow alley between blocks of city buildings. A man and a woman at the far end of the alley have stopped to stare in typical urban curiosity at the scene. In the left foreground a man in a business suit only slightly darker than the shadow that surrounds him is about to emerge into the light and cross the street. A shopkeeper quietly gazes out of the window on the lower right, perhaps hoping that these strollers will be attracted by his storefront mannequin, whose rigid stillness along with its blue-and-white outfit almost parody by their reversals the woman in the center of the picture. Moore casts these familiar incidents of urban existence against the gridded stability of the architecture and streets. A network of glances, gestures, and directional lines creates a rich visual and social intricacy.

Winthrop Square focuses on a perceptual moment in the transient life of the city. And if no significant drama can be witnessed by the policemen and the pedestrians, or by us, further anonymous viewers of the work, Moore provides his own by the theatricality of the chiaroscuro that illuminates the facades in a brilliant morning sun and casts parts of the streets, alley, and windows into a richly textured shadow. The commonplace is awarded a moment of clarity and abundance. Moore has stilled a moment of flux in urban living and commemorated it with meticulous fidelity in a stately composition. The primary colors of red, white, and blue dominate the painting in various hues, effecting a witty conceptual play on the patriotism of John Winthrop, the first governor of Massachusetts and head of an illustrious Boston family, for whom the square is named.

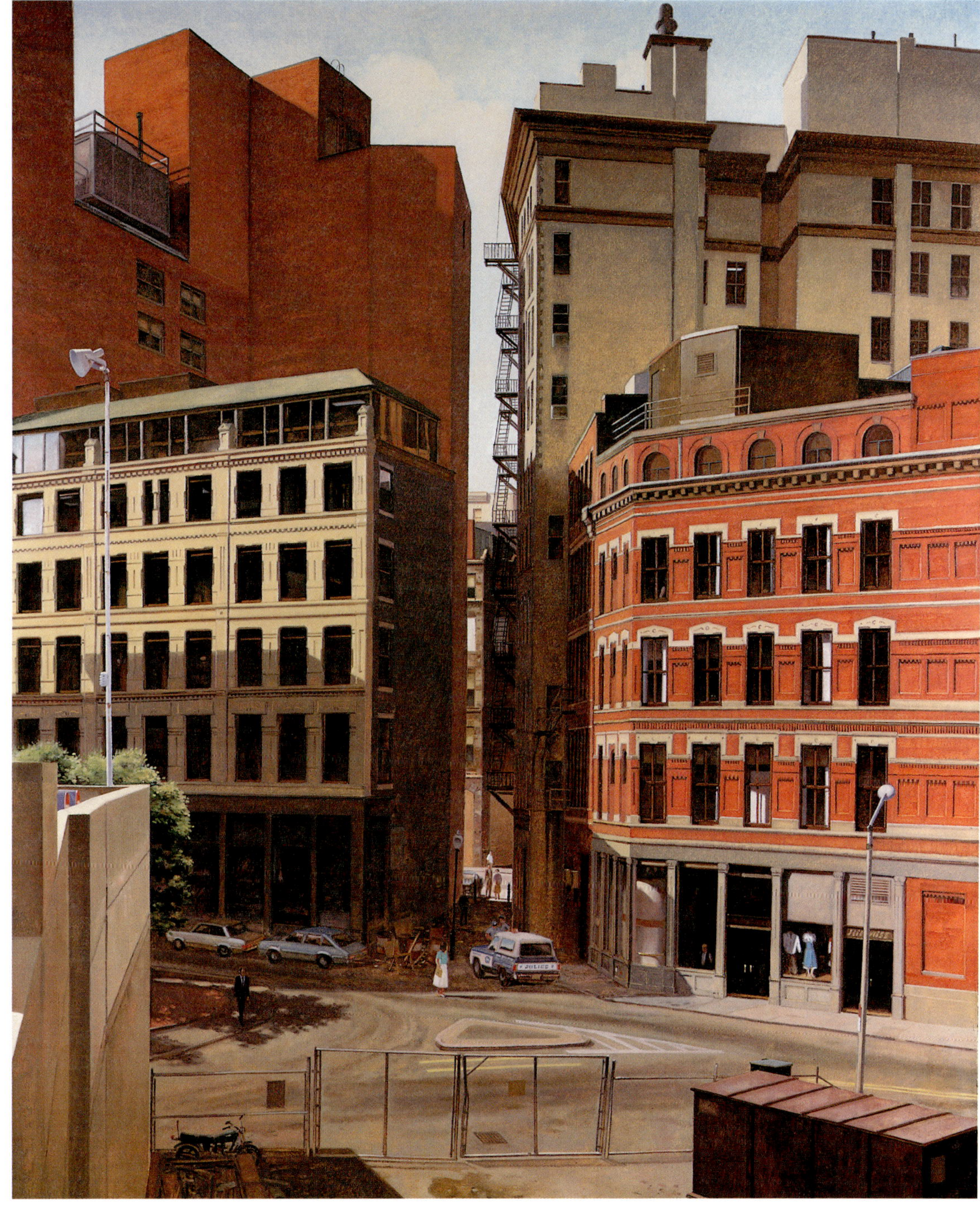

32 WINTHROP SQUARE, 1985

Oil on canvas, 84 × 70.
Private collection.

Moore's interest in what he calls "celebrating the margins of the megalopolis, the moments that occur in the supporting shadows of the city," can be seen in *Weehawken, Tunnel View,* and *Turbo Dogs. Weehawken* (pl. 33) provides a view of a rectangular brick building backed by a baseball field that one sees from the highway off the New Jersey turnpike leading to the tollbooths of the Lincoln Tunnel to Manhattan. Moore's picture suspends a moment of urban life seen daily and probably experienced subliminally by thousands of commuters as they pass out of New Jersey and into Manhattan. What Moore has done is to fix the inherent irony of the site, with its juxtaposition of the bucolic pleasures suggested by the playing field and the edge of a swimming pool set above the congested lanes of traffic. Weehawken, a town that resonates with the memory of scenes painted by John Marin and Edward Hopper, is literally sub-urban; the view directly to the left of the site is the dramatic Manhattan skyline whose buildings have dominated the subject matter of cityscapes in the twentieth century. By cropping out this most familiar of views, Moore privileges the mundane, where beauty is not as evident as it is in the spectacular skyline but must be sought out and contemplated from a standpoint that is both physically and aesthetically distinct.

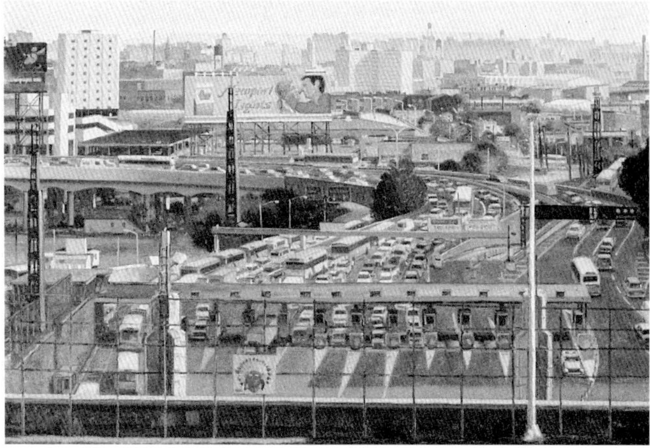

Figure 10. John Moore, *Weehawken,* detail.

Moore plays on the dichotomy between the chaotic tug of urban activity in the distance, which he details with great specificity (fig. 10), and the order and regularity of the foreground, with its geometric shapes muted under a deep shadow. He thus combines in one image the kinetic visual and social energy of the metropolis with a sense of the detachment and anonymity that the city engenders. If the need for observation is as powerful as the demand for creation in Moore's realist canvases, it is because of his belief that life and art contain a world of values that can be articulated in a style of art that gives the "act of painting something to do," to quote his colleague Rackstraw Downes.[38] One could say about Moore's image what Hopper wrote about Charles Burchfield: "His work is most decidedly founded, not on art, but on life, and the life that he knows and loves best. From what is to the mediocre artist and unseeing layman the boredom of everyday existence in a provincial community, he has extracted a quality we may call poetic, romantic, lyric, or what you will. By sympathy with the particular he has made it epic and universal. No mood has been so mean as to seem unworthy of interpretation."[39]

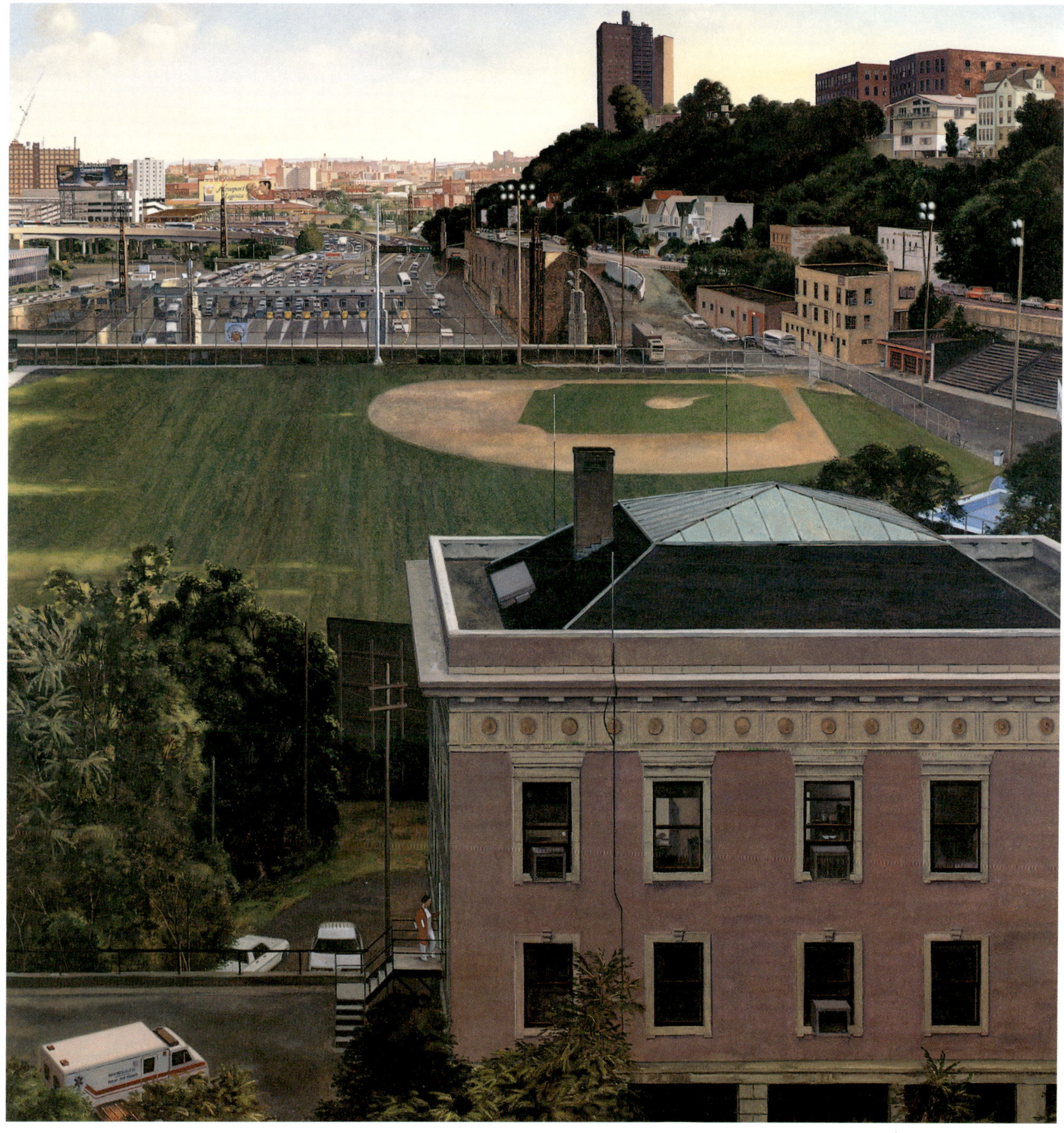

33 WEEHAWKEN, 1987–89

Oil on canvas, 75 × 72 in.
Private collection.

Tunnel View (pl. 34) proceeds from a deeply shadowed foreground, as if an invisible colossus towered over the site near Holland Tunnel in New York, to a horizontal perspective of bridges, tunnels, buildings, and factories under a serene wintry sky. Moore possesses a canny eye for freezing details that are registered mostly in a blur, if at all, as we pass by scenes such as these. He challenges the viewer to work through the random detritus of rocks and rubble in the lower foreground, to register the rhythmic succession of arches on the tunnels at left and the staccato sequence of corrugated metal on the bridge to the right, and to note the syncopation of building profiles that stipple the horizon in the distance. This sense of movement, rare in Moore's work up to this point, is especially apt in an image depicting tunnels and bridges that daily transport masses of people in and out of the city.

Moore multiplies the options for the eye to try to register the vast amount of information the city contains with its mix of traffic and buildings. Most of what we see in the scene is fragmented: the highway disappearing around an implied curve in the center of the painting, the bridges continuing beyond the right edge of the canvas, the buildings interrupted by water towers and light fixtures, their facades overlapped by billboard advertisements in an urban collage of color and shape. The visual density and physical energy implied by the subject of the painting allegorize the many sensations available in the experience of a city.

For the most part the American city has come into existence in a piecemeal manner, with the diversity of styles and shapes of buildings expressing the public and private function of their use. Moore is fascinated with the interactive values present in the city, with the physical heterogeneity supplying a visual analogy for the cultural. Thus he particularizes rather than idealizes the urban environment. Moore offers a vision of the city that is totally independent of stylization and fetish, but never devoid of the cultural and economic blend that constitutes its reality. *Tunnel View* reverses the traditional concept of tunnel vision, for Moore opens up rather than closes in upon a wide variety of visual foci that allow the mind to follow the eye by engaging in the elisions and idiosyncracies that appertain to the experience of the city.

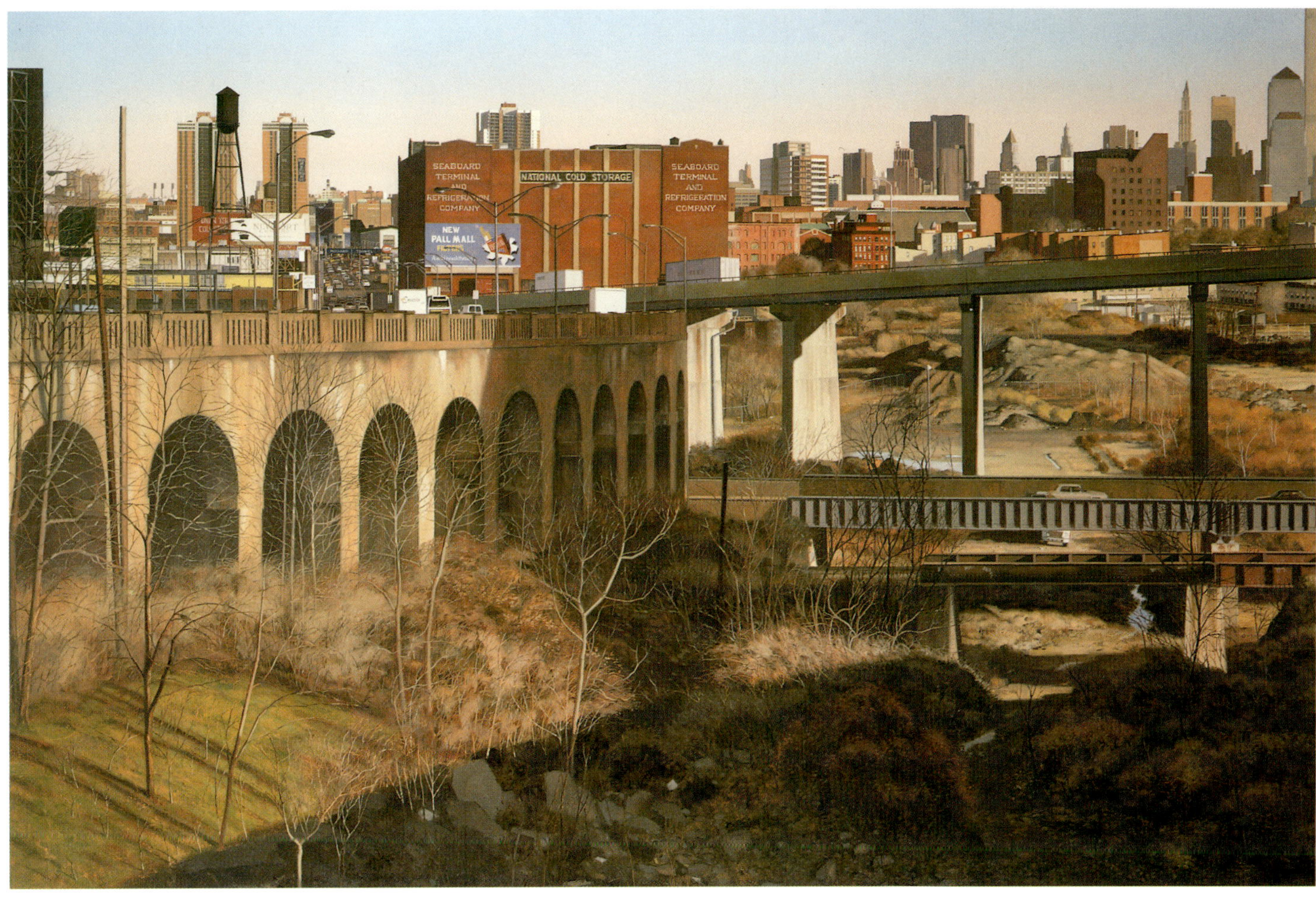

34 TUNNEL VIEW, 1988–89

Oil on canvas, 60 × 90 in.
Private collection.

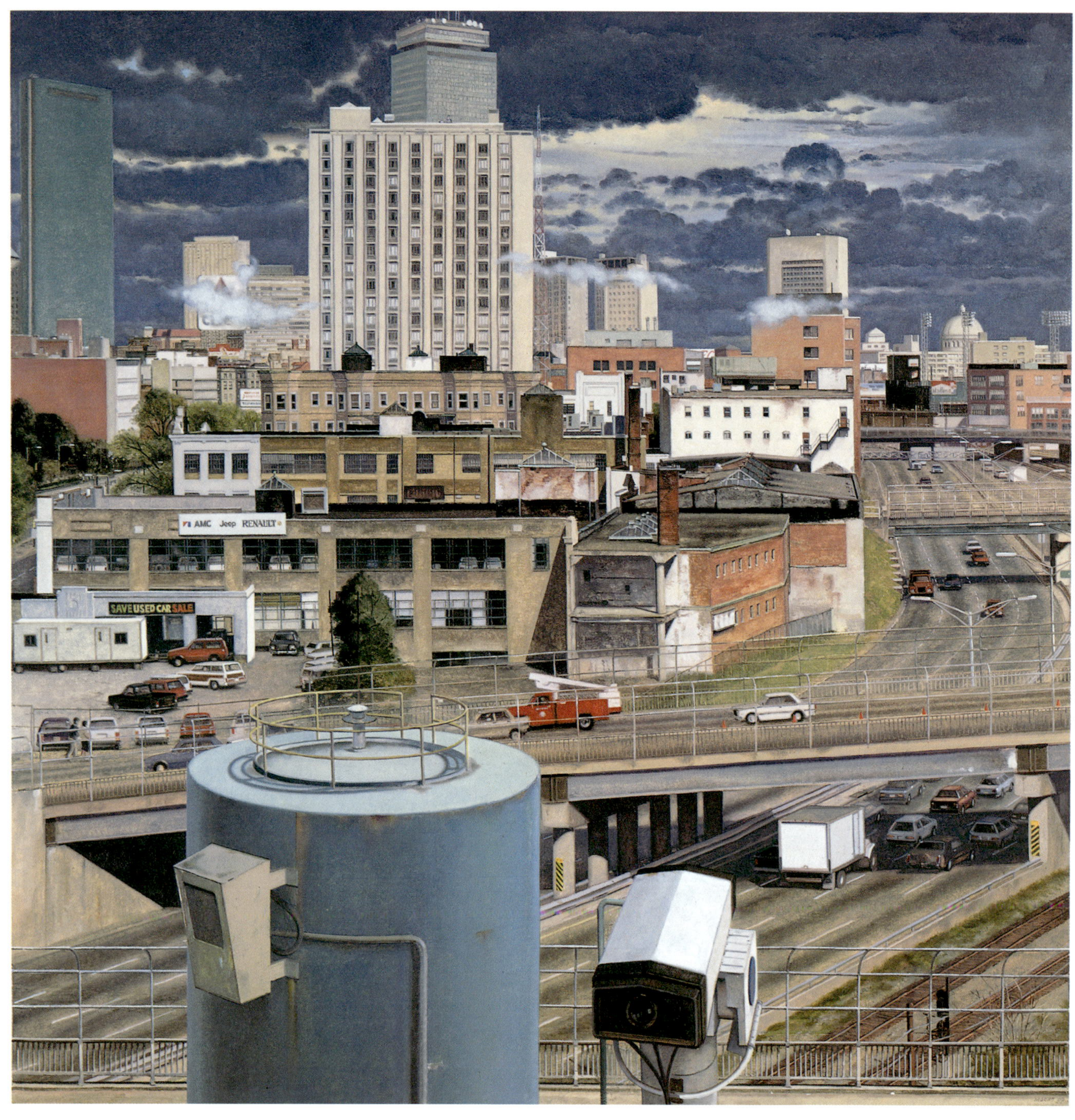

35 TURBO DOGS, 1989

Oil on canvas, 60 × 60 in.
Courtesy Hirschl & Adler Modern.

Turbo Dogs (pl. 35) looks across a section of highway in Boston to overlapping planes of buildings depicting car lots, older industrial buildings cheek to jowl with newer commercial skyscrapers, and high-rise apartments against a dramatic cloudy sky. In the foreground Moore positions an industrial tank and a traffic scanner on a bridge, surrogate sentinels watching the daily life of the city. He contrasts active curving highway and the notion of transit with cubic architecture and the idea of stability. The highway ramp cutting across the lower middle section of the painting leads the eye out of the sides of the work, while the road beneath it acts as a force that draws the eye into a deep perspective in the right side of the painting. These contrasting vectors have the sweep and energy of a Franz Kline painting, but Moore's painting is held back from the raw edge of expressionism by the precision of his detail and the geometric solidity of the buildings.

Turbo Dogs describes a scene so familiar to the city commuter that it is eminently forgettable and thus somewhat surprising as the subject of a work of art. Moore takes the commonplace and makes it seem fresh and worthy of viewing. Time is implied by the passage of cars, while the different focal points of the painting, which insist on being read at separate intervals, slow one's progress through the work. The painting offers a wide variety of visual events of no great narrative significance—not even a traffic jam for the scanner on the bridge to record. It provides a characteristic urban experience seen through an eye attuned to the particulars of daily life, and it serves to remind us that a subject we think we know all too well can always reveal something new.

Moore chooses an area of the city that most would describe as a place to get through in order to go somewhere else. He then challenges this notion with a palette that reveals great visual interest in different shades and textures of brick and concrete, asphalt and chrome, the shapes and colors of commercial logos, the energy and intensity of the urban setting. Moore shows in this image how human economic needs have shaped the land, converting brown earthen furrows into gray asphalt highways plied by traffic rather than plowed by hand. The cyclical has yielded to the linear, glass and steel structures have replaced organic growth on the slope to the left of the highway, and the land that was once natural is now social. Commercial and political concerns have so dominated the site that the sole witnesses to the pastoral are a few surviving trees and a narrow strip of grass bordering a railroad track in the lower-right corner of the painting. Moore's view of the city is neither sentimental nor cynical. He applies his paint in a straightforward manner that values firmness over flash. He educates us in the process of vision, taking something we feel we know in an instant and then proving that recognition and contemplation are separate definable acts.

Moore's choice of subjects often evokes Hopper, paraphrasing select compositional devices. *Southside Light Clue* (pl. 36) isolates a building across a horizontal road in a manner similar to Hopper's *House by the Railroad* but substitutes clear light and crisp detail for Hopper's angst-inducing chiaroscuro. *Village View* (pl. 37) recalls Hopper's *City* in its elevated view of urban architecture and the use of strongly angled sunlight cutting across facades. Representation and abstraction are balanced across these works to ensure the vision of the city as a source of formal order and a source of pictorial ideas.

The soaring verticality of the isolated building on the left in *Southside Light Clue* can be interpreted as a postmodern response to the many paintings of skyscrapers that towered in the paintings of early American modernists such as John Marin and the Ash Can school. Whereas these painters invested their work with a sense of energy and optimism, Moore cultivates the image from the other side of the century of progress and notes the dwellings of people displaced to the farther edges of tourist centers and expensive hotels. These are buildings that most likely overlook vacant lots rather than scenic parks, where necessity rather than indulgence dictates the minutiae of daily life. Moore wants an image that relates his experience of urban life in terms of the mind as well as the eye, that authenticates through composition and detail what he feels about the city.

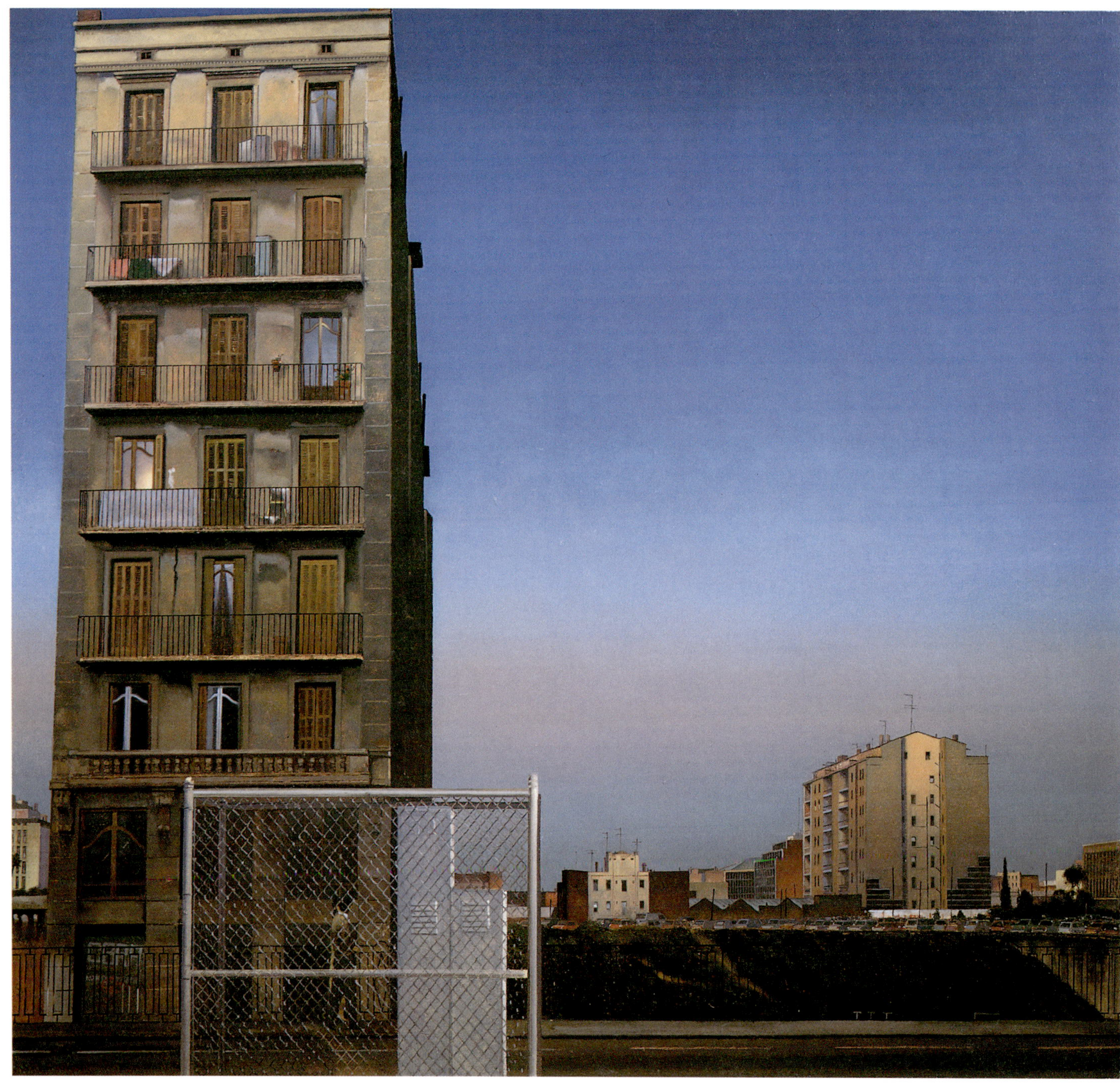

36 SOUTHSIDE LIGHT CLUE, 1991

Oil on canvas, 50 × 54 in.
Sandra Moore.

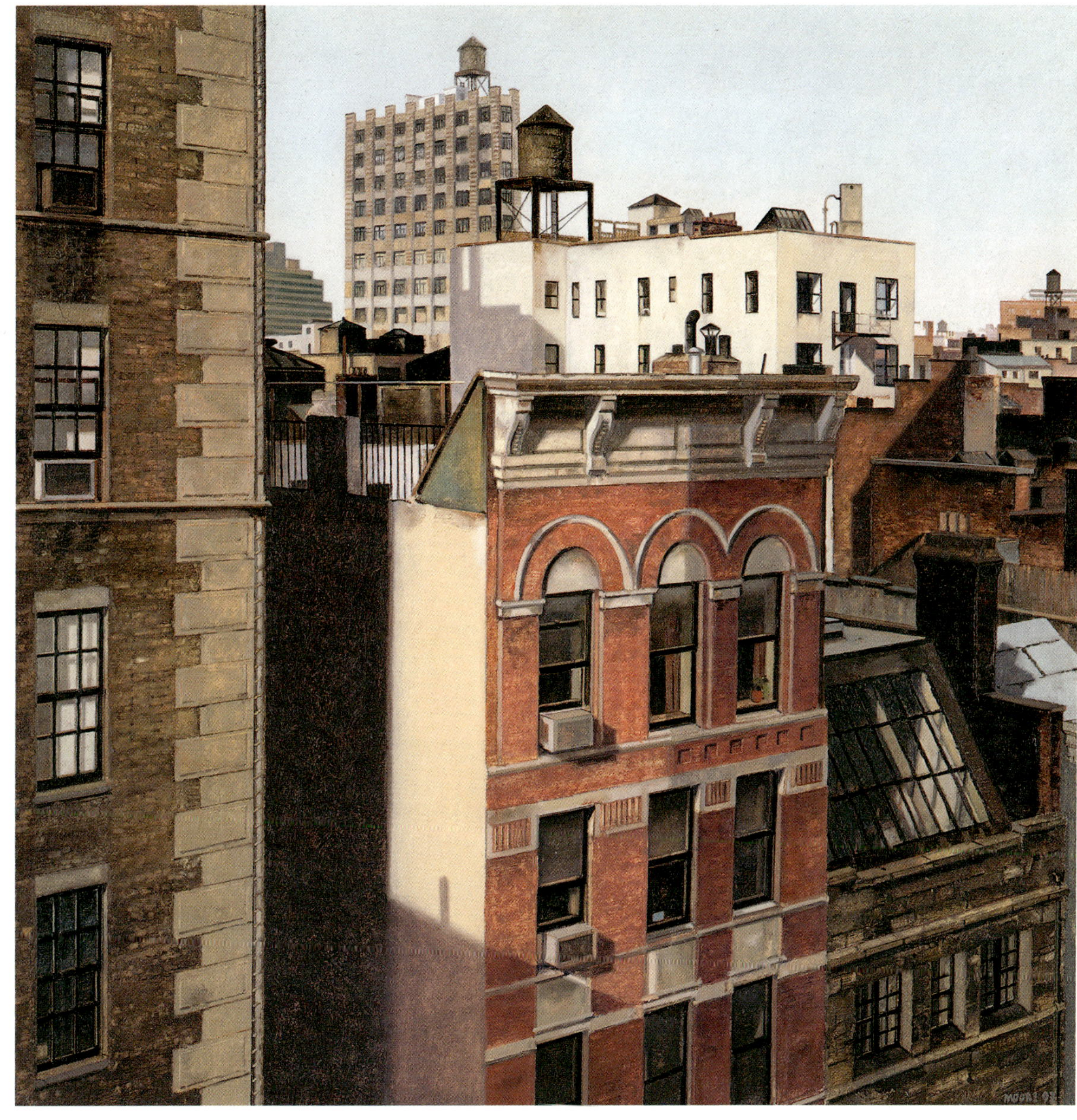

37 VILLAGE VIEW, 1992

Oil on canvas, 24 × 24 in.
Courtesy Hirschl & Adler Modern.

Although most of Moore's cityscapes are unpopulated—in this instance he obscures pedestrians behind a chain-link fence—they are not without humanity. He carefully notes things such as curtains pulled against a window and laundry drying on balconies, small synecdoches of the lives that are conducted behind the facades. Moore remains uninterested in the city as an arena for human activity, trading the bustle of movement for the stability of buildings that are as revealing of class by their ornamentation or lack of it as are costumed characters in a play. Perhaps for this reason Moore's work has so often focused on windows and doors that punctuate urban facades, dealing with the interplay between outside and inside, the public and the private that are part of the complex mythology of urban existence.

Like Hopper, Moore is an architectural realist whose attention to light aids in organizing the composition. In *Village View* Moore paints the area of Washington Square where Hopper lived and worked, angling his buildings into the picture's depth with a wedge of light that serves as a compositional homage to his predecessor in American city painting. Moore surveys the city, finding the facades as fascinating and full of individual personality as a Dutch portrait painter before an animated group of sitters. With careful attention to texture and a keen eye for the individuality of each edifice, he records the iconic geometry of the city. The overlap of outlines combined with the compressed space creates a rich visual field that blends grandeur and intimacy. A strong wedge of sun, a familiar device from Hopper's paintings, throws a dramatic spotlight on the ornamentation of the older brick building in the center, whose richness is contrasted with the severe plainness of the starkly lit white building behind and slightly above it in the middle distance. A moment that will pass quickly is suspended in time so that the familiar can seem new again. Thus Moore allies the evanescence of time with the endurance of monolithic structure, drawing out of a city view a wide range of emotions. He controls the extraordinary amount of detail in the site so that it never detracts from the unity of the painting. The terse masonry of the brownstone building on the left in *Village View* closely abuts a more loquacious red brick facade that speaks of other eras and different tastes. His careful notation of textures imparts a sensuality to the facades that distinguishes them from the austere surfaces of Hopper's paintings.

The notion of America as a melting pot is clearly evident in the face of most of our cities, and for this reason Moore stays away from familiar landmarks that serve as signatures for individual city skylines, preferring a more generic view of buildings that analogizes the ethnic mix of the urban milieu. Different styles of architecture serve as tangible reminders of the interchanges between tradition and innovation, visible manifestations of man's nature and diversity expressed in an American vernacular.

The homage to Hopper in site and motif acknowledges Moore's awareness of the cityscape tradition. Moore invites a reading of his painting across and through Hopper, authenticating his own voice by contributing to the metropolitan image, conscious with every stroke of other works that have nourished him. Moore often defines his realist style against the legacy of earlier artistic practices, giving form and identity to his subjects through a dialogue with sources that have prompted him to articulate his individuality.

Moore spent some time in Barcelona, Spain, following an exhibition of his work in the spring of 1990. "I began to work from locations in that city that seemed to resonate with layers of time and change and experience; industrial edged urban neighborhoods, urban vistas, city parks and streetscapes, places that suggested the uneasy accommodations of the past and present that give weathered weight and meaning to basic experiences of city life. I have continued to use material from Barcelona and combined it with other places I have worked and lived, although the intent is not to describe the solely literal but to juxtapose, alter or collage aspects of places into a seamless image that honors the rich tapestry of everyday life."[40] One such painting is *Mediterranean Hotel* (pl. 38), where Moore paints an area of the city that most would describe as an eyesore. He tells the truth about mud and grime, drabness and urban blight. This is at a far remove from the romantic trope of the picturesque ruin, where decay was prized by figures lost in reverie about the classical sublime. Moore informs us that there are several views of urban life that are characteristic, and his painting enables us to understand how we see the world at different times under different living conditions. His paintings give the eye a lot to do. In *Mediterranean Hotel* there is the familiar confluence of roads, residences, and commercial buildings embodying a part of the urban experience that rarely finds its way into painting.

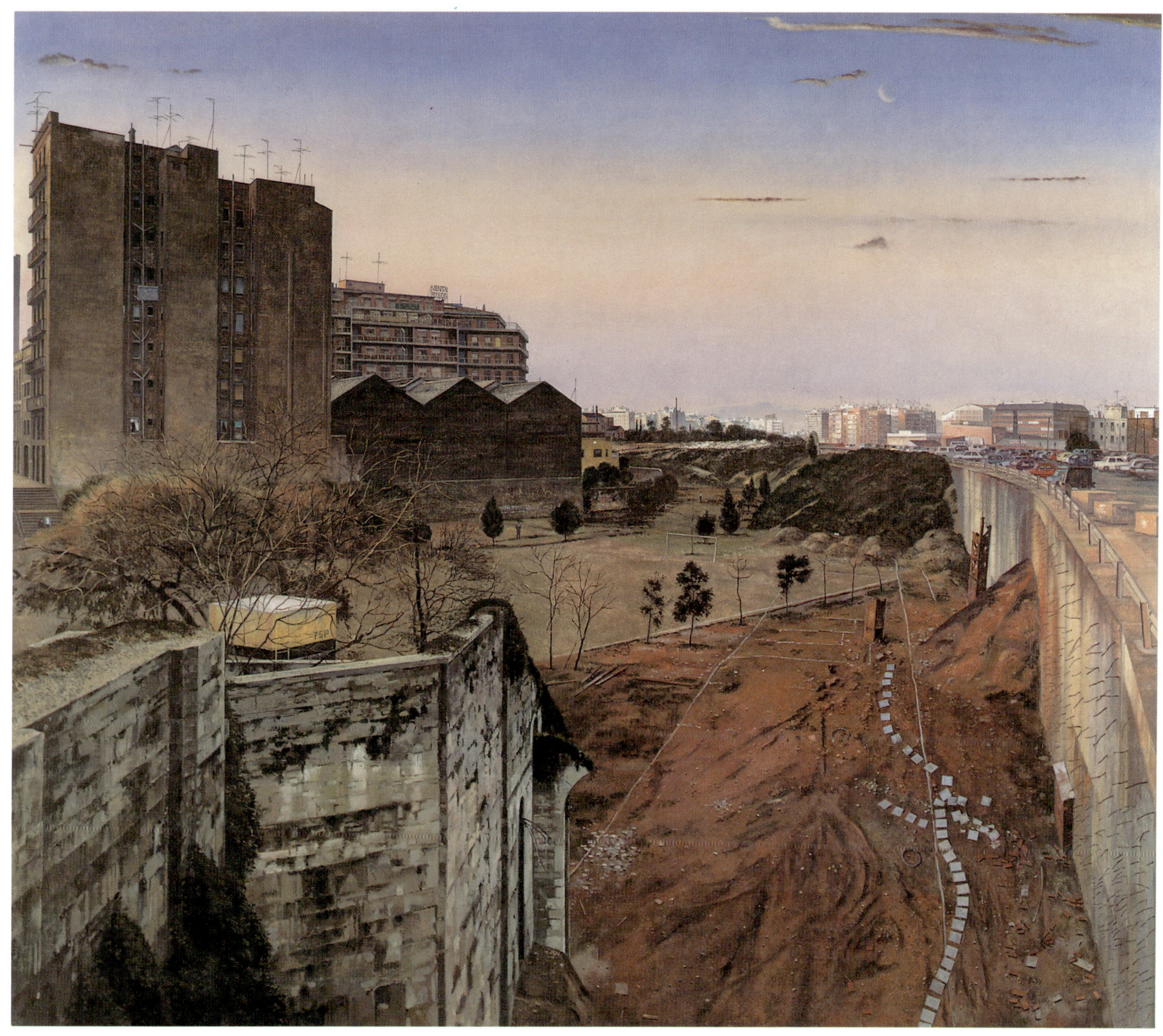

38 MEDITERRANEAN HOTEL, 1991–93

Oil on canvas, 72 × 84 in.
Aaron Moore.

On the far right an aborted expressway, sprouting wires on its side like unshaven stubble, leads the eye into the far distance of the painting. The center foreground is a muddy field laid with paving stones in a plotted path, its snaky contour a reminder that where nature once ruled, culture will prevail. A yellow construction vehicle provides an oddly cheerful note amid the dank browns and sullen grays, like a canary alighted in a bog. The angulated lines of a stone wall dipping into an irregularly shaped brown field whose swirls of mud mimic a free gestural paint handling, the crenellated tops of the apartments on the left, and the sweep of the abandoned road on the right into the disappearing center of the painting, give the work an abstract visual energy.

Moore loves the stony path for the evidence it gives of a desire to shape one's world and somehow domesticate a site that is hostile to this effort. "This is futile," he observed, "but it is a beautiful gesture."[41] He is interested in how the playing field in the middle distance—its neatly tended grass an ironic contrast to the bewildering chaos surrounding it—humanizes an inhospitable environment. He shows us the material world being shaped by its distance from capital in both its economic and geographic sense. He presents a locale and preserves the idea of place by focusing on the lesser dramatic entanglements of urban existence. His apparently mundane objectivity in selecting such a view belies a profound commitment to imposing unity and stability on the immediacy of experience and for capturing the site in terms of human sensibility. Like Walker Evans's photographs of the weathered utensils of sharecroppers, Moore's surfaces speak of use and abuse. *Mediterranean Hotel* combines details of sites in Barcelona and in Charleston, Massachusetts. Moore often joins elements of buildings and landscape from many sources in order to achieve an image that resonates with a sense of the uneasy accommodation of the old and the new, of all the things in a site that communicate something about the condition and character of the city.

Moore travels several times a year from his home in Boston to New York. Although he brings reading material to pass the time, he finds he often spends more time looking out the window, where he will occasionally find new subject matter. One such view from the train is *Dutch Pink and Italian Blue* (pl. 39), which depicts the colorful towers of a Greek Orthodox church overlooking Astoria, New York. Moore was attracted to the church, which he saw as a measure of the place, signaling its immigrant base. His interest focused on detailing the postwar rowhouses and factories, portraying how each block was adapted to the site, with Tudor style chosen in one instance for a section of homes on the left. For him, this gives evidence of the dreams people have of making one area look like something else, of trying to put a mark on a place and have it feel like the home from which they migrated or the fantasy to which they aspire. The factories in these working-class neighborhoods are down to about thirty percent capacity. These, along with the monuments to money on the distant horizon, are all recorded in one painting.

Moore draws the eye by means of deep perspective to the New York skyline where exhaust from factory chimneys merges with the dark gray storm clouds above, suggesting a tornado funnel about to descend on the scene. Drama and color are brought to a plain scene that is rendered accurately and with an almost overwhelming attention to detail. Moore keeps the eye from progressing too quickly through the vast center of the painting by placing a tree in the middle distance to break the line of rooftops and by inserting a long yellow factory in the far distance to force the sight to extend laterally before it reaches the horizon. To represent the city as a perceptual blur would mean for Moore to lose focus on the social differences and divisions that establish identity. He seeks out regular patterns in the urban landscape, discovering elements of repetition that naturally unify the scene without dampening the variety of pictorial incident the painting contains, thus maintaining the tension between deep space and surface in the design.

This six-foot-square canvas testifies to Moore's love of making images that require a slow investigation of scenes whose familiarity tends to breed if not contempt, at least a complacency that dulls the awareness of the abundance of visual riches available in such locales. The time required by careful sight can provide compensatory insight into the city's multitudinous contents. High above the streets, the intractable city can be monitored by the eye, allowing a mastery of the chaotic elements that threaten coherence at close range. Despite the mythic implication of such elevated views, Moore does not offer the promise of paradise regained. Elevation in this case does not bring the elation that was an integral part of nineteenth-century American panoramas. Moore's high viewpoint produces social rather than sublime vistas.

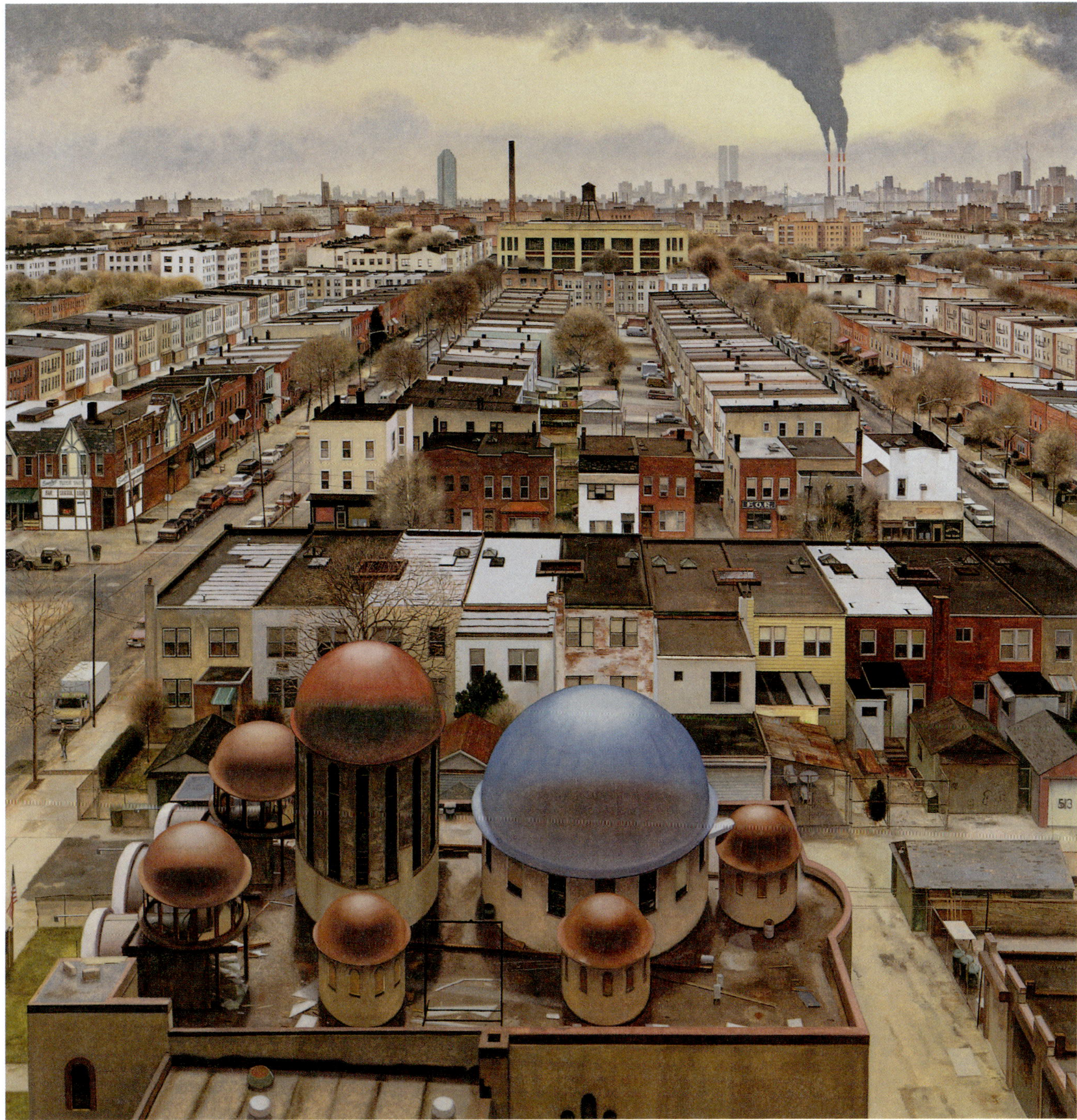

39 DUTCH PINK AND ITALIAN BLUE, 1992–93

Oil on canvas, 72 × 72 in.
Private collection.

Images of the city by earlier American modernists often stressed the verticality of buildings seen from below, with the soaring upsweep suggesting the hope of progress. Moore's view from on high causes the lines of force to converge on the city in a perspective that sucks the visual energy of the painting toward the horizon, where skyscrapers preside in gray sentinel over the working-class site to which the scene is visually and economically tied. Moore's vision of the city pries it apart from the modernist optimism that often marked the American cityscape at the beginning of the twentieth century. He provides an illusion of the city that is more intense than normal vision, and by isolating it allows his subject a distinction and an amplitude that reveal the visual power it contains. He seems to imply that there is much in life around us that we fail to note in our routine progression through it. He proves Hamlin Garland's point that the tourist cannot write the local novel.[42] Only an eye trained on the everyday nature of such American sites could understand its habits and discover such scenes to be paintable.

Moore's canvases work against the tendency to locate the meaning of the art in an intellectually fashionable statement that the painting ends up illustrating. The details act as guides to an overall sense of place and time in contemporary American life. Moore wants the physical character of the urban landscape to function as both aesthetic exemplar and social document in a reciprocity that keeps the fictive realities of paint sustained by the actual sites that inspired them.

Moore's move to the Boston area in 1988 brought a renewed interest in nocturnal scenes as a subject and a notable increase in the amount of information he wanted to record. Most of his night paintings are quiet in mood with a minimum of human activity. He combines a concern for rendering detail with the challenge of making it hold its own weight under obscured light and dusky shadows. Robert Henri wrote that low art "is just telling things, as, there is night. High art gives the feel of night. The latter is nearer reality although the former is a copy."[43] The "feel of night" is the most compelling feature of these paintings. By reducing the color range, Moore found he could heighten the moods connoted by evening. With probing scrutiny, he investigates the evocative aspects of darkness and shadow, invoking but never cheaply exploiting the mystical elements present in the varying degrees of night's luminescence. Light, as much as architecture, has been Moore's enduring interest. Despite all his precision and attention to detail, Moore's light is never photographic or purely about recording information. The variety of light effects he pursues allows him to suggest his subjective reactions to the scenes he creates, permeating his surfaces with a concern for communicating the transitory rather than fixing the permanent. His light enables him to achieve a sense of temporality, illuminating the multiple narratives occurring at separate intervals yet united on the surface of the canvas in a way that provides the viewer with a variety of visual opportunities to explore and contemplate.

In 1989 Moore painted an area of Boston viewed from on high at sunset in *Area D* (pl. 40). Seen from above and at a distance, the activity of the city in this work is stilled into a contemplative panorama, while the fading light softens the harshness of the angular buildings and dims the grime to a tonal density. He overlays the prose of the city with the poetry of the sunset, as if Thomas Cole had been called on to complete a John Sloan cityscape. Moore's love of dusk allows a conceptual play with the idea of realism and its alleged truth to the visual model.

The lower central foreground of the painting depicts an empty construction site. A blue sign on the fence, illegible under the waning light, announces a forthcoming project. A pile of debris next to a construction trailer indicates that work is about to begin. The vacant lot, surely a brown field of mud and muck during the day, seems transformed at this time of night into a rich velvety field of fertile loam ready for planting. In the lower left corner of the painting, a figure—it is unclear whether it is male or female—approaches a subway entrance, where a form that could be either debris in a white bag from the construction site or a recumbent piece of public statuary rests on the platform outside. Moore plays this visual ambiguity in the foreground off of the fascinating precision of such details as architectural moldings and cornices clearly visible in the distance. He provides Hopperesque vignettes through office windows on the right, where file cabinets and manila folders on shelves are as legible a piece of Americana as the Marlboro man who strikes his cigarette next to a Windsor liquor billboard.

Moore achieves the accuracy of the inaccurate, true to a time of day when lavender shadows veil the rawness and vastness of the urban environment into a crepuscular field of blunted forms and softened shapes. His sensitivity to the many

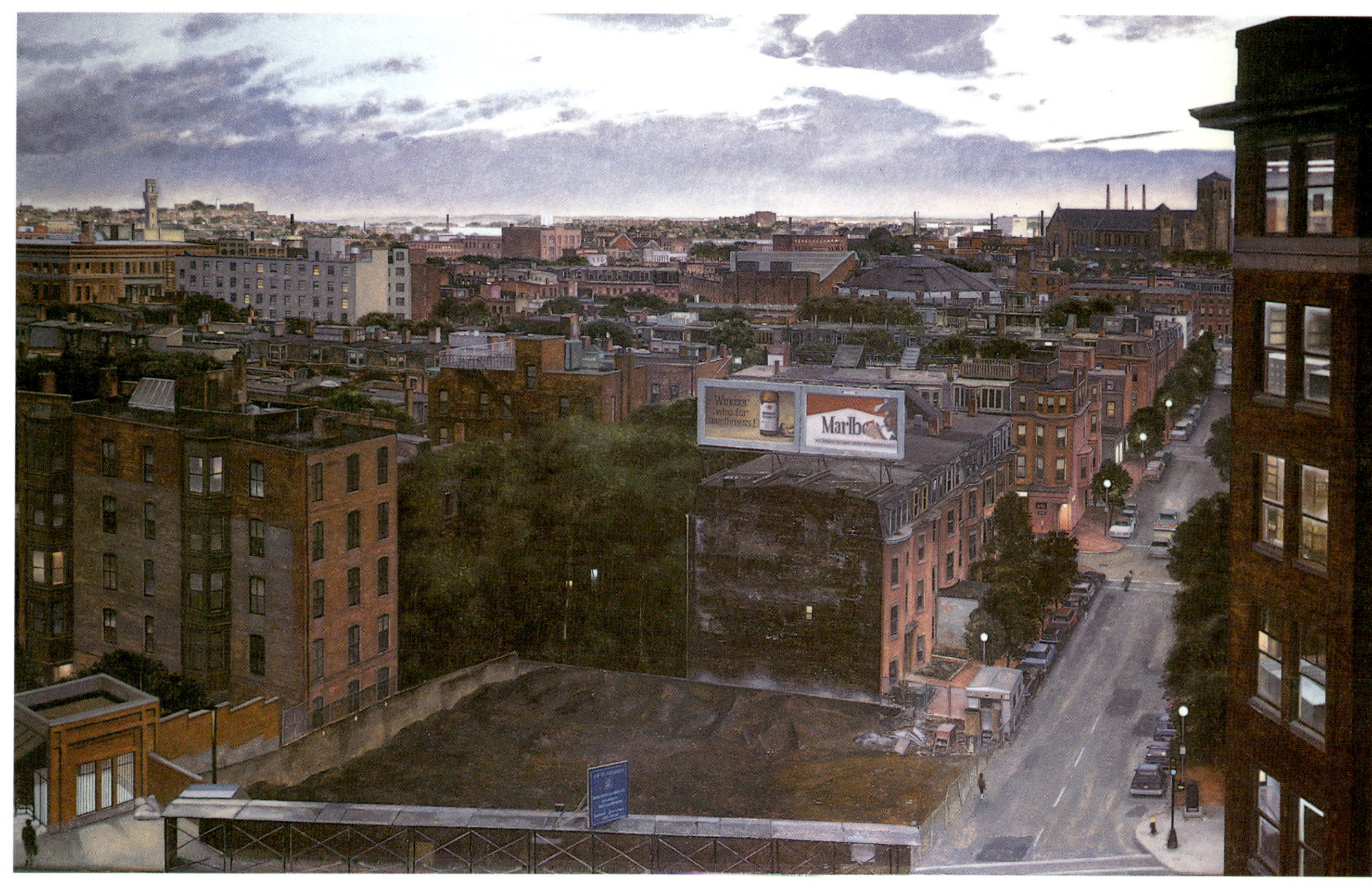

40 AREA D, 1989

Oil on canvas, 54 × 90 in.
Commerce Bancshares, Inc., Kansas City, Missouri.

different kinds of illumination available at dusk endows the picture with an edge of familiarity as the viewer distinguishes the artificial sources of street light, office light, and car light from the elegiac natural light of the setting sun.

Like Nathaniel Hawthorne's watchman, Moore surveys *Area D* from a position that is "all-heeding and unheeded."[44] The choice of a high viewpoint enhances the quiet time of day, thereby eliminating the sense of flux and restlessness characteristic of urban life. By keeping stillness and movement, distance and intimacy, darkness and light in a carefully calibrated balance, Moore orchestrates rather than dictates the mood of the painting, thus allowing the viewer's sensibility the scope to develop in time and engage the work in a private manner. The varied incidences of this panorama can be taken up at any point in the painting, giving the viewer the freedom to move between characteristic details that parallel life in the urban milieu.

The painting of the city skyline from an elevated point recalls the American landscape tradition of the panorama, favored by artists wishing to call attention to aspects of the wilderness and the frontier as visual challenges reflecting a moral imperative. Thomas Cole's mountains and Frederic Church's gorges have been transformed by Moore into an account of man-made structures of concrete and glass with canyonlike streets that address the twentieth century's use of space. The nineteenth-century depiction of mountains, valleys, and oceans, with their attendant values of awe and wonder, pride and optimism, yields in Moore's art to buildings and streets where commerce, progress, and business address the transformation brought about by an urban culture. The older tradition is read through the new, yoking them in ways that enrich both by their continuities and differences.

Waiting at St. Cecilia's (pl. 41) represents the back of a large Romanesque-style brick church seen from across a fenced-in park where a woman clutches a chain-link fence and seems to stare at the viewer. Moore chose to paint a view of the church that is uncharacteristic, focusing on the blunt architecture at the rear of the church rather than on the more decorative or ceremonial front entrance. While he was sketching on site during several evenings in the summer of 1991, he noticed a woman who would stroll behind the back of the church, meet with men, and then disappear into the bushes at the left. He eventually realized that she was a prostitute and that the park behind the church was her place of assignation. Her inclusion in the painting not only provided the title but supplied a narrative dimension to the work.

Moore pays close attention to the effects of light and atmosphere created by the ebbing sun and the electric illumination that throws portions of the church facade into dramatic relief. As a realist, Moore is attracted to the character of a setting, seeking out its individual traits along with its oddities and building his art on them. He investigates the nature of the different lights in the work, their direction and hidden sources, from the spiritually affecting light of the stained-glass window in the church to the harsher glare of the incandescent street-lamps, to the electric and fluorescent light emanating from the interiors of nearby apartments and stores. The interplay of lights and darks used throughout the work evokes the sacred and profane.

Moore takes the common visual currency of the urban landscape and, by means of a process of slow testing and exacting observation, translates it into an image that opens a perspective on the complex psychology of the city without narrowly dictating its direction. His sense of the local and the specific is conveyed by details that are never allowed to become incidental or fragmentary, but are selectively rendered to enhance the ambience. The intense specificity of the way Moore has organized his visual information provides access to pictorial as well as social energy in the painting. What results is not traditional narrative but an urban mythology that suggests a sense of the metaphorical struggle connoted by the contrast of natural and artificial light. Whereas Hopper often imposed a feeling of melancholy and loneliness on his city scenes, Moore's paintings create moods that arise from subtle permutations of light, density, shadow, and scale skillfully adjusted to present the materials of a human situation in a way that is less narrowly circumscribed, more nuanced with mystery and doubt. The painting invites a reading according to the conventions of narrative realism, then undermines it by refusing to provide adequate certainties to secure a fixed meaning. This effect is not intended as a sly irony or a facile dramatic ploy, but offered as a means to reconsider the conventions of realist portrayal.

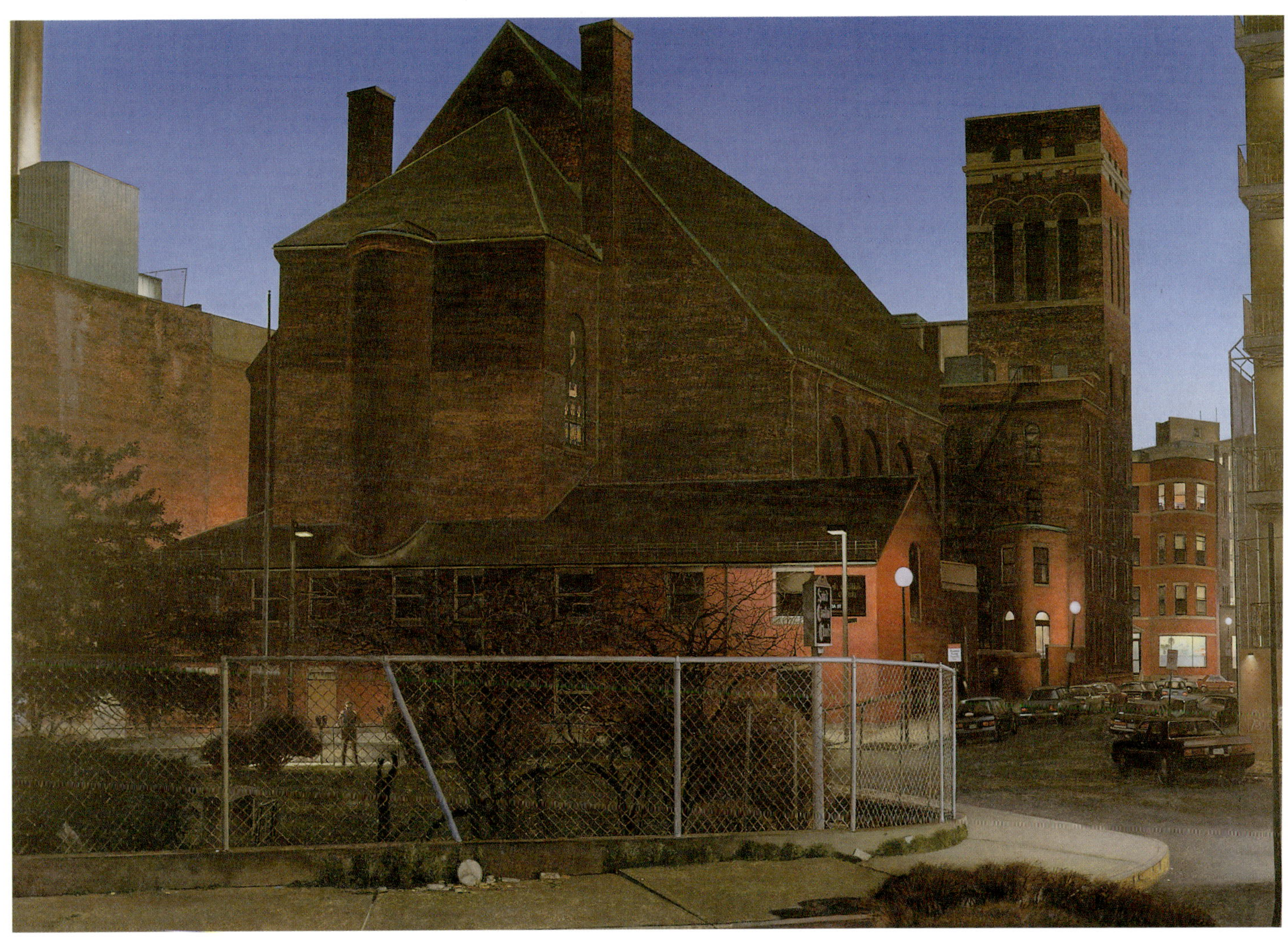

41 WAITING AT ST. CECILIA'S, 1991–92

Oil on canvas, 75 x 108 in.
Courtesy Hirschl & Adler Modern.

Childe Hassam once remarked that the portrait of a city resembled that of an individual: "The difficulty is to catch not only the superficial resemblance but the inner self. The spirit, that's what counts, and one should strive to portray the soul of the city with the same care as the soul of a sitter."[45] Moore uses a particularized instance of urban life to give visual witness to the idea of the city as a subjective experience. The configuration of encounters possible in the city, the meanings associated with specific buildings—be they commercial, domestic, or in this case ecclesiastical—the types of natural and artificial light with their different emotional registers, and the interaction of the private self in the public domain, are important for him to register to satisfy his sense of what makes a painting.

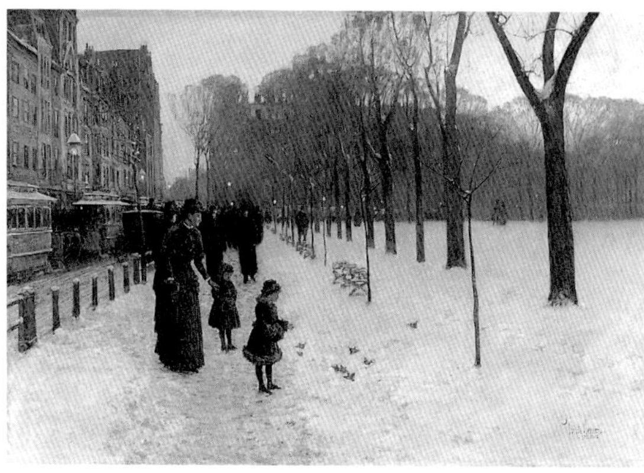

Figure 11. Childe Hassam, *Boston Common at Twilight,* oil on canvas, 42 × 60 in. Museum of Fine Arts, Boston, Gift of Miss Maud E. Appleton.

Outbound (pl. 42) provides a response to Childe Hassam's *Boston Common at Twilight* (fig. 11), substituting the grittier truths of contemporary urban life for the genteel order of nineteenth-century leisure activity. Well-dressed children on Hassam's snow-covered sidewalk feed birds under the watchful gaze of an indulgent mother or nursemaid; Moore's pedestrians, in contrast, are dissociated commuters who confront a debris-strewn subway exit. Buildings, trees, and trolley cars recede with perspectival regularity in Hassam's work, marking the space in a lucid progression that visually secures the coherence of the scene. In this instance, Moore's avoidance of one-point perspective duplicates present-day urban complexity and dislocation as light fixtures, railings, bridge supports, and underpasses careen toward multiple vanishing points. Moore calls attention to corporate power in the urban world by drawing the eye to the office building silhouetted against the evening sky, its sleek and chilly modernity at a far remove pictorially from the ready charm of Hassam's upper-class neighborhood facades. The pearly winter twilight that unifies Hassam's Boston Common gives way in Moore's work to a contemporary lexicon of lights—incandescent street light, car headlight, fluorescent office light—all of which compete with the natural evening light.

Moore offers neither suggestions nor reprimands in his art. *Outbound* is not painted as a polemic, but by encoding the new against a reading of the old, he documents the powers of attraction and repulsion, the diversity of emotional resonance that separates his scene from the genrelike simplicity and visual coherence of Hassam's. Viewed from the top of subway steps, Moore's painting is not intimate, but neither is it indifferent. The insistent directional pathways carry the eye and subsequently the mind out of the painting, suggesting that the scene is linked to a larger world that lacks the secure intimacy and closure of Hassam's. *Outbound* lacks a fixed center and thus resists a totalizing gaze. The inability to grasp the scene in a unifying glance, the discontinuity created by the divergent vectors mapped across the picture plane, charge the work with a visual tension that is psychic as well as physical.

Moore's work takes its place in the lineage of American cityscape painting, contributing to its cumulative heritage by discovering increased pictorial challenges to further its expressive range. If Hassam's is the age of innocence in the city, Moore portrays the age of experience. Leery of too easy a beauty or the merely scenic in a sunset scene, Moore seeks the intensity of a fleeting moment in which the drama of the sky serves as a backdrop for the commonplaces of urban life. The random mobility of the clouds brings into sharper relief the rigid artifacts of the metropolis.

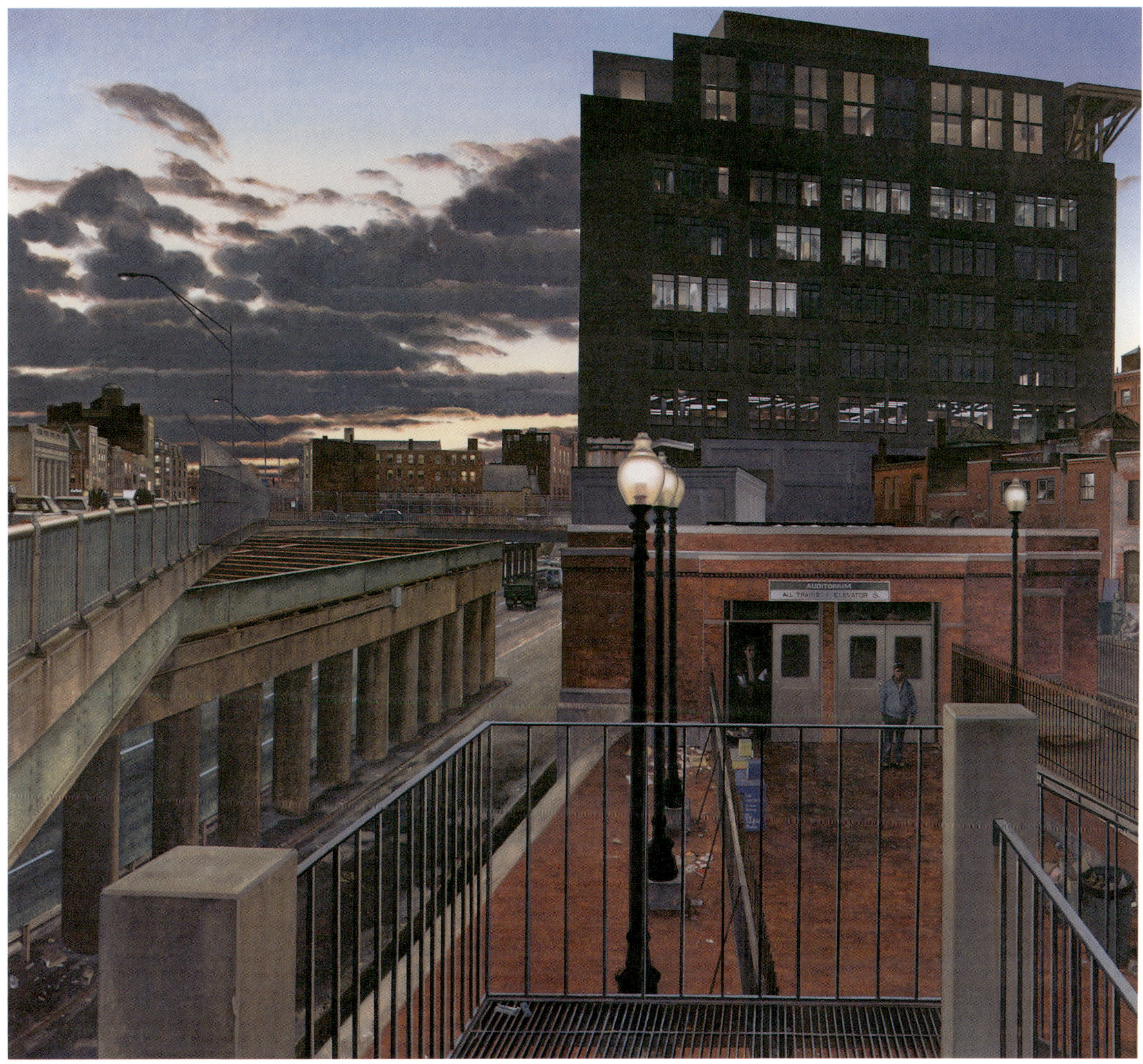

42 OUTBOUND, 1991–92

Oil on canvas, 72 × 80 in.
Private collection.

Weekend Conversation (pl. 43) looks down past commercial heating vents to an illuminated street corner and out past a brick building to the night skyline of city buildings on the horizon. Moore positions the viewer of the painting as a voyeur in a window whose edge is unobtrusively visible on the right. Like Hopper in his etching *Night Shadows* (fig. 12), Moore angles the view sharply from above, but also draws the eye to the horizon beyond. He establishes an emotional relationship with the entire scene rather than solely with the anecdotal event that titles the painting.

Moore frequently poses the viewer of his paintings on the threshold between the private and the public spaces of the city. His early city paintings such as *South* included window frames that defined the spectator's position in space. The window imposed an order on the cityscape, arranging its fragments into cubic regularity and converting the random into the permanent. *Weekend Conversation* dispenses with all but a fragment of the physical frame of the window, indicated by a dark angle on the right, but tends to imply it as a critical factor by the point in space from which the scene is viewed. The repetition of other windows as organizing elements in the painting is allied with the shape of the canvas itself and functions as an analogy for seeing and being seen. The window, whether implied or actual, provides the physical and moral vantage point from which to observe and read the city. The variety of windows present in Moore's cityscapes serves as a reminder that looking at and looking through are means of connecting the internalized imagination with the exterior forms of reality. This skillful interplay between inside and outside, the almost constant use of a distancing device between the viewer and the subject, also approximates the physical, social, and psychic barriers intrinsic to urban living.

No single building is addressed here, only fragments of facades noted like snatches of conversation. Moore keeps the painting from the high drama of street interaction by the distancing position from above, yet he relieves the scene of any banality through stimulating detail and complex spatial organization. The multiple light sources, some hidden and some revealed, break up the scene in a modified cubist manner

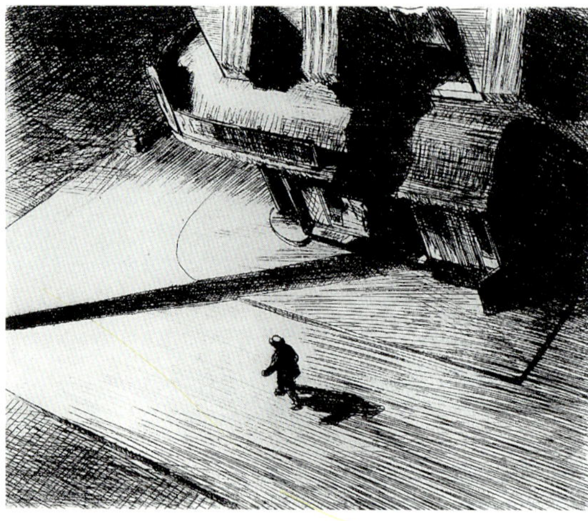

Figure 12. Edward Hopper, *Night Shadows*, 1921, etching, 6⅞ × 8¼ in. Whitney Museum of American Art, New York, Josephine N. Hopper Bequest.

by illuminating surfaces from many different angles. Moore's natural attraction to pattern and repetition in the urban landscape is brought into focus by the gentle puffs of steam floating in the front plane of the canvas. Their amorphous shapes about to disappear serve as reminders of the tug between the randomness of visual information available in a cityscape and the need to order it into formal coherence to make the scene visually engaging and intellectually satisfying.

Instead of capturing a fleeting impression of a busy boulevard, as did Claude Monet or Camille Pissarro, Moore sacrifices instantaneity for a unified visual realm where geometric hierarchies and spatial organization are heightened beyond what the eye normally perceives. His is a human vision that allows the cityscape to be both spacious and intimate, impressing us with its amplitude while including an anecdotal occurrence on a city corner that reminds us of all the minor moments and small events that are integral components of urban life.

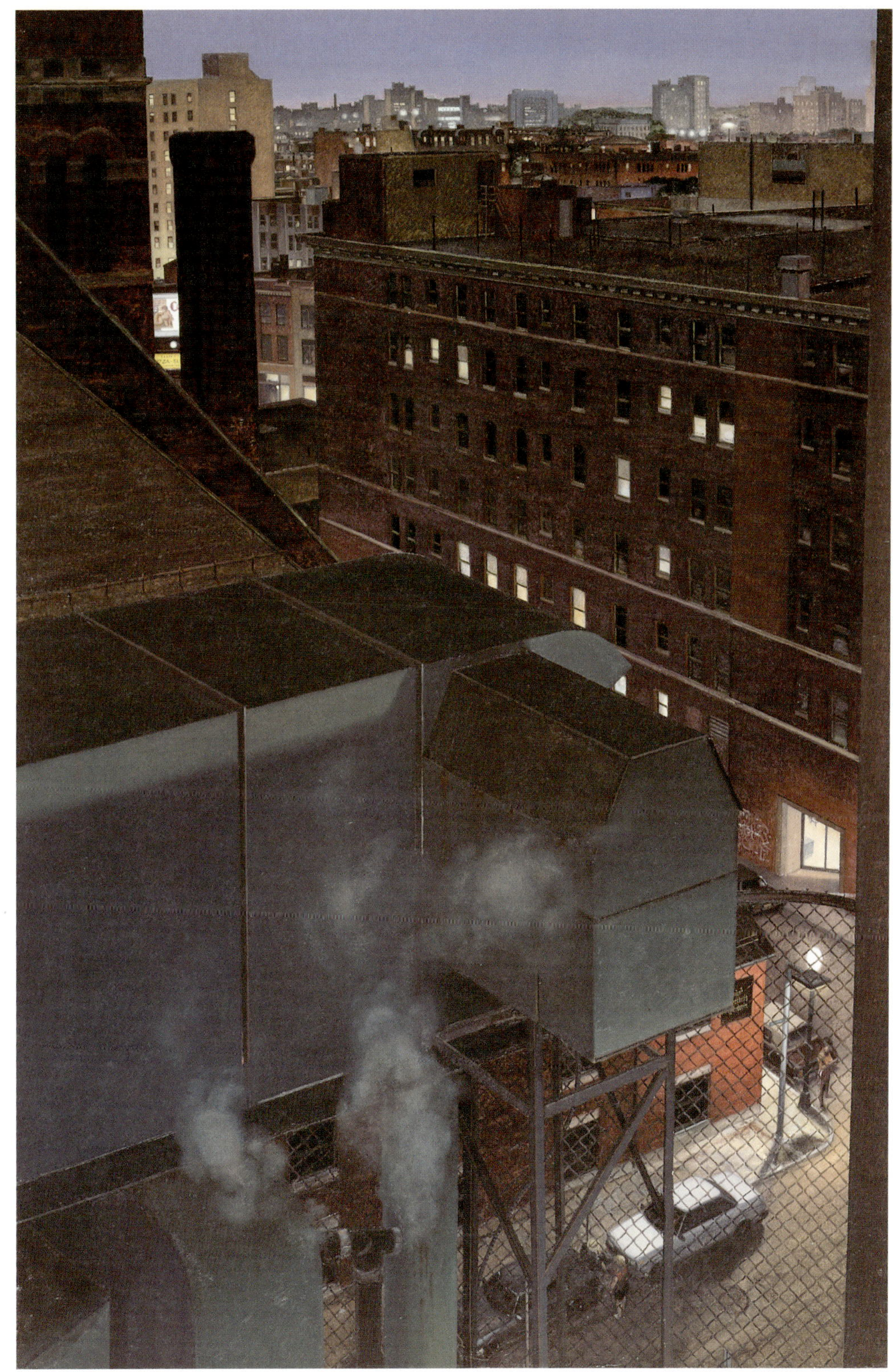

43

WEEKEND CONVERSATION, 1992

Oil on canvas, 54 × 36 in.
Aaron Moore.

Moore wittily reverses the idea of the detail fading in perspective depth by placing the dark green heating vents in the frontal center of the painting, their blocky green shapes as unadorned as a Donald Judd wall sculpture. On the horizon the buildings become an activated field of scattered lights and spirited profiles, drawing the eye to investigate their detail and delight in their sprightly progression across the night sky. The presence of the purified modern forms of the vents in front of a fragment of a Romanesque brick tower and buildings from all decades of the twentieth century serves as a cognate of Moore's postmodern realism, with its visual roots in modernism, tradition, and contemporary style.

The many visual events in the painting act as metaphors for temporality. Although one can grasp the whole canvas in a visual embrace, it is impossible to experience all of its events at once. The gaze is drawn from steam in front to people below, to buildings between, to lights beyond. Each section of the painting has its own individualized rhythms. This suggests ways of seeing and being in the city that work against universalizing truths. Like the city itself, the painting is a series of discrete visual events that overlap one another in time and space.

Two Boots (pl. 44) takes its name from an East Village, Manhattan, restaurant that Moore has tucked away in the upper middle of the painting. Moore and his wife, Sandy, had celebrated the sixtieth birthday of a friend at the restaurant, and Moore fell in love with the name. As is typical of Moore at this period, the site combines buildings from various cities, in this instance New York, Washington, and Boston.

Twilight descends on the city as office workers finish their day's work in the upper floor of the building in the right foreground, while others in a rug emporium on the first floor read the newspaper or wait for customers. The many directions lives can take in the city are suggested by the multiple entrances and exits of doorways and subways, streets, and bus depots mapped onto the active but controlled surface of the canvas. The visual impossibility of grasping this scene as a whole is conveyed by the way the eye is teased through windows, drawn down a flight of steps, or shifted around the generous curve of a street. Moore is like the *deus absconditus* of the Old Testament, seeing all, knowing all, controlling from afar, caring about the larger issues but always attentive to the small details. While Moore's cities are urban, they are never cosmopolitan in the sophisticated or blasé sense of the word. Georg Simmel in "The Metropolis and Mental Life" defined the blasé attitude as "the indifference towards the distinctions between things. Not in the sense that they are not perceived, as in the case of mental dullness, but rather that the meaning and the value of the distinctions between things, and therewith the things themselves are experienced as meaningless."[46] Nothing could be further from Moore's city scenes. His willingness, indeed his need, to detail the quotidian incidents of an invented urban milieu, such as the visual wit of the graffiti on the subway wall in the lower right of the painting—the disembodied head a metonymic pun on the passengers who traverse that space—testifies to his commitment to tell his own truth about the city in its prolixity. "Compose by shadow and chrome," wrote Moore's friend and colleague, the poet Rosanna Warren, in "Music for Railroad, Telephone Wire, and Easter."[47] Moore has done just that in *Two Boots,* portraying with exquisite care and craft the multiple textures that make up the urban vistas he has chosen to create.

Moore moves to the suburbs for *Downhill Street, Feather Light* and *Pause.* Both scenes are portrayed at the transitional moment of dusk, when detail and color tend to change from articulate clarity to tonal nuance and obscurity. Moore's combination of muted color and precise observation in *Downhill Street, Feather Light* (pl. 45) describes a neighborhood dominated in the foreground by a building whose smokestacks stretch across the canvas like a pipe organ ready to play to the town below. The bird's-eye perspective of the area is literalized by the pigeon who has departed from the group perched on the building that anchors the lower center of the canvas. The bird's flight out of the canvas creates an interesting visual tension that counteracts the deep pull of the distant perspective.

A combination of houses in Springfield, Ohio, with a hill located in Coatesville, Pennsylvania, and the view from Moore's Boston studio, *Downhill Street, Feather Light* is a composite neighborhood scene where a sense of middle America is depicted. Ambience and mood rather than topographical accuracy are his primary concerns. Moore would like his paintings to possess the direct honesty and innate

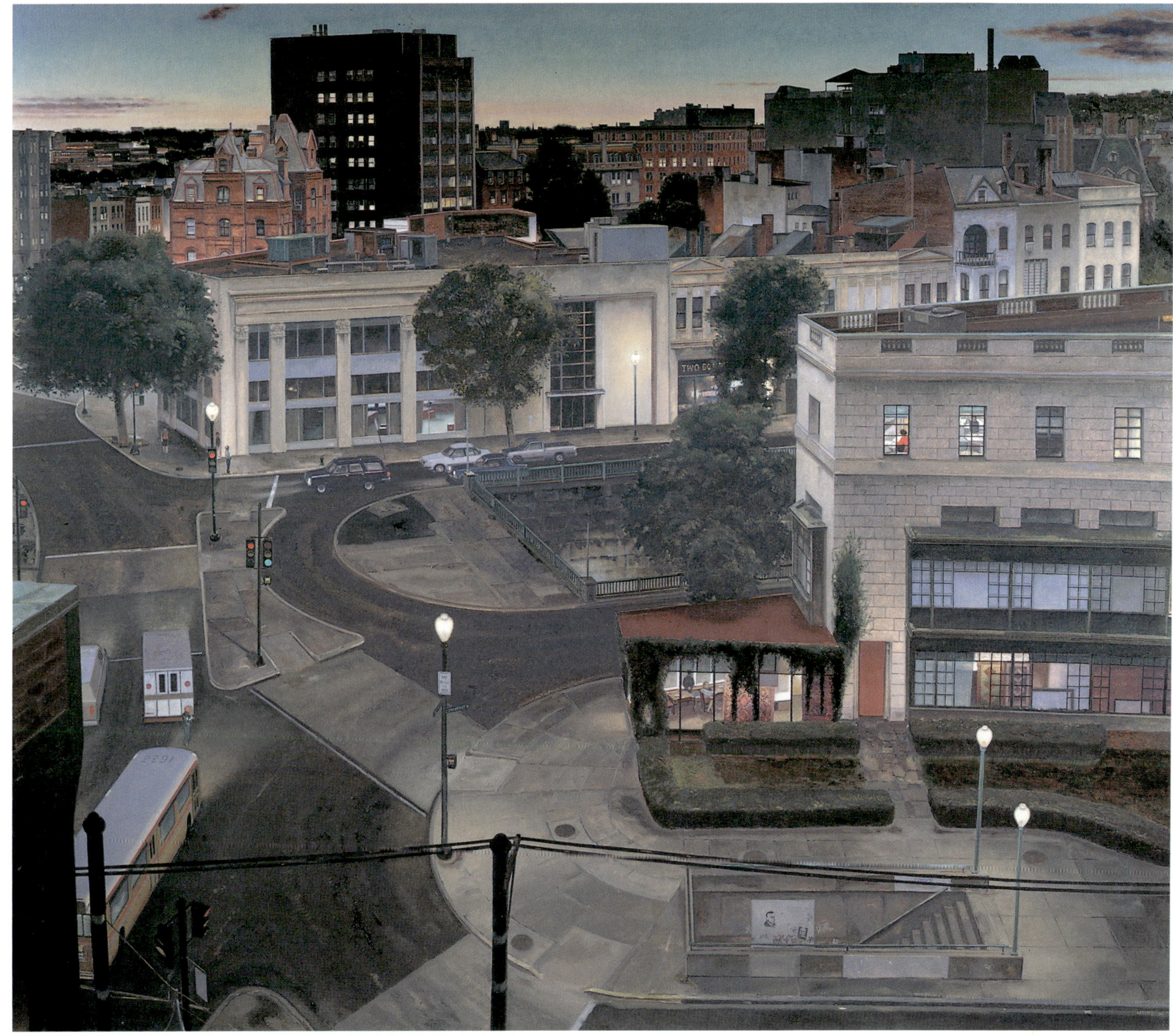

44 TWO BOOTS, 1994

Oil on canvas, 62 × 72 in.
Courtesy Hirschl & Adler Modern.

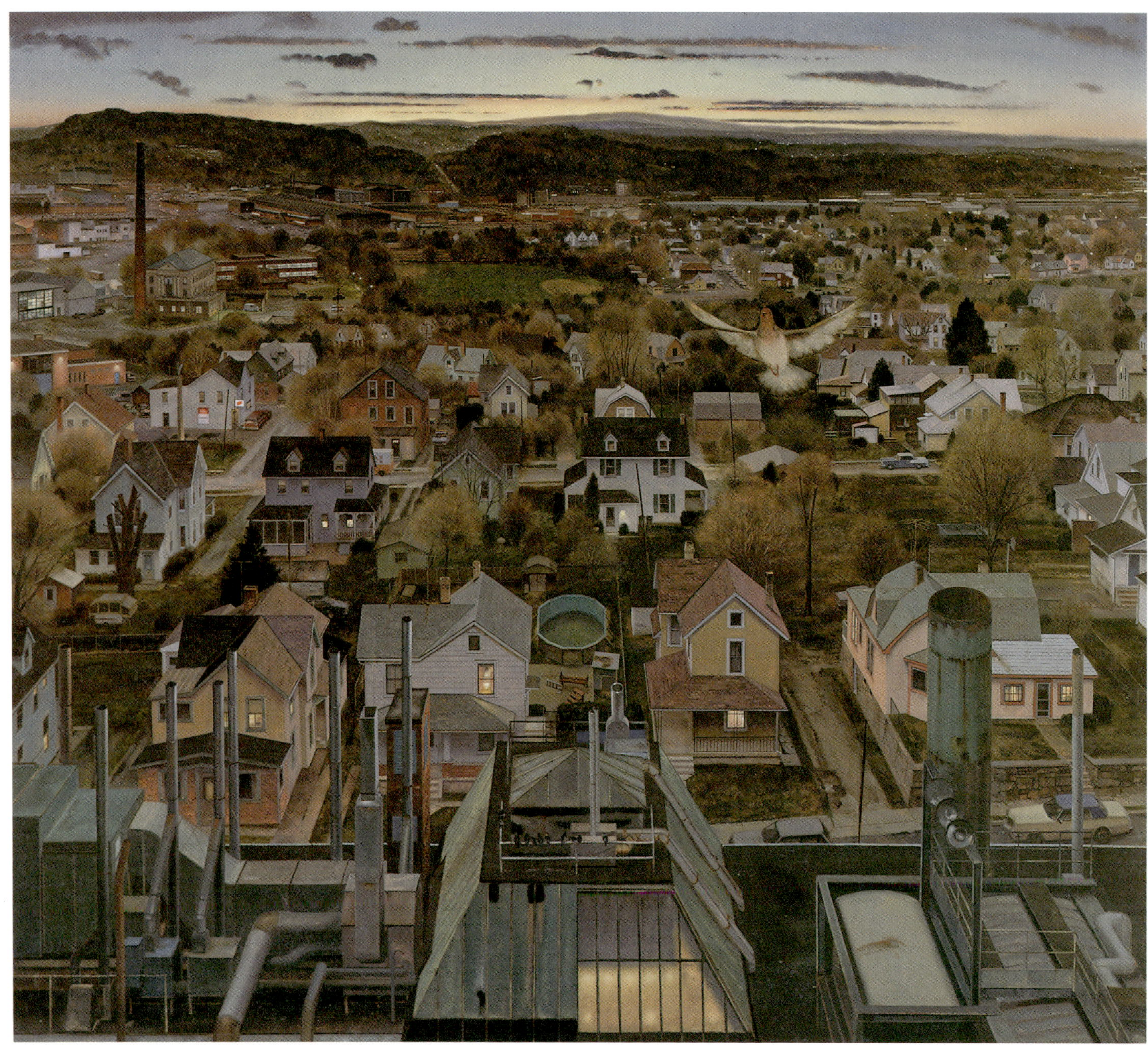

45 DOWNHILL STREET, FEATHER LIGHT, 1992–93

Oil on canvas, 72 × 82 in.
Private collection.

mix of the formal and the specific that the Scottish immigrant painter John Kane recorded in his views of Pittsburgh. Kane paved the streets and toiled in the factories that he then painted in views that fully brim with his knowing and feeling and loving a site. Moore works for a similar sensibility in his scene of a working-class neighborhood, allowing his deeply felt accuracy about light and space to shape the landscape and suggest the character of a place and his affection for it.

Moore takes undistinguished sections of suburban life and discovers details that transmit the cultural life of the area. He is fascinated by the way American neighborhoods have come into existence piecemeal, with homeowners asserting individuality by additions of porches, shutters, garages, and personal color choices in houses that were originally identical. Views through windows, porch lights turned on, cars making their way down quiet streets manage to convey human presence without depicting it directly. Moore chronicles the visual nuances of multiple light sources, modulating the landscape into a patterned quilt of forms that shifts from an embracing abstract field of shapes to a detailed inventory of American domestic architecture. No single object holds the attention long enough to dominate the scene. This presentation of an unprejudiced field of vision, where everything is seen democratically, connects to the larger context of individuality in community. The many ways the eye is invited to scan the scene and fasten on the diversity of details gives the impression of an observer's active presence, even though there is no physical foothold in the work.

Moore's infatuation with the particularity of the ordinary conveys an image of America where formal intricacy duplicates social complexity. The legibility of the community is ever present in his details that reference everything people living in a geographic region do, the symbols and values they establish through the material evidence they surround themselves with, from the backyard pool to the local convenience store and the community baseball field. Moore documents the human ecology of the community by calling attention to the objects of the social landscape rather than the activity of human interchange. *Downhill Street, Feather Light* provides a visual exemplar of Wallace Stevens's words: ". . . no sign of life but life,/Itself, the presence of the intelligible/In that which is created as its symbol./It is a new account of everything old."[48]

In *Pause* (pl. 46) Moore moves onto the street to imagine what happens in such suburban neighborhoods. Two children stop playing for a moment to focus on the scene through the windows of the house next door (fig. 13). On the right a man sits in a plain wooden rocking chair dejectedly watching a small television in a room as bleak as his mood seems to be. No carpet warms the floor, no art adorns the stark white walls. An empty chair against the wall reinforces the isolation of the lone figure. Through the window on the left we see a woman dining alone, seated at a table, tossing back a glass of wine. The room is a strange combination of kitchen and office, with file cabinets and a large black armchair awkwardly placed in front of a counter. The alienation of the couple is emphasized by the separated rooms and the tree trunk strongly dividing the two halves of the house. The ebbing light of dusk and the children's lack of animation reinforce the mood of quiet desperation that settles over the scene.

The French call the period between dusk and night "entre chien et loup"—literally between the dog and the wolf—when details begin to obscure the sharp physiognomy of things and sureness yields to hesitancy and doubt. This visual ambiguity is shifted onto the narrative of *Pause,* where Moore seems to imply a loss of innocence in the painting. A green hose entwines the young boy like a snake in the garden, matching the one coiling behind the tree and slithering on the lawn

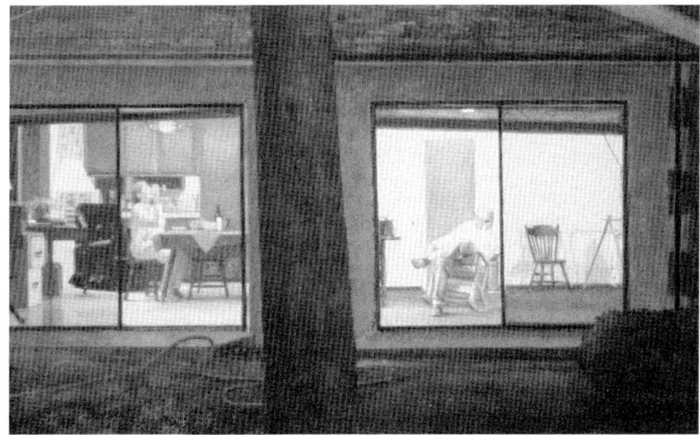

Figure 13. John Moore, *Pause,* detail.

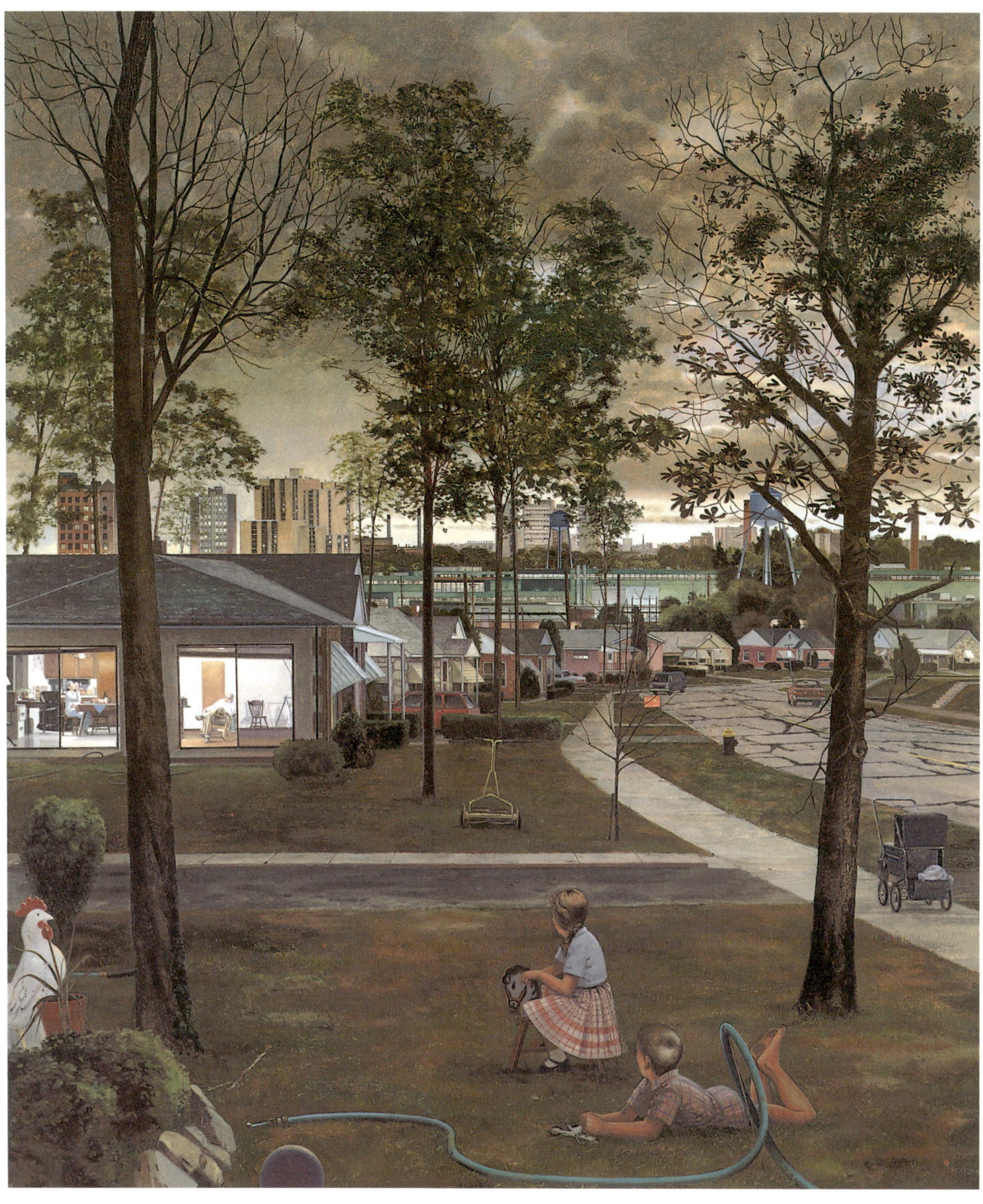

46 PAUSE, 1989–93

Oil on canvas, 72 × 62 in.
Mr. and Mrs. David Pincus.

beneath the windows of the house next door. An abandoned lawn mower in the yard and a baby carriage on the sidewalk suggest assumed parental roles interrupted and unfulfilled. A rooster perched in kitschy sentinel plasticly presides over the descent of dusk rather than announcing the hope of dawn. Childhood leisure on the lawn is played against adult languor in the house, carefree naïveté cast against torpid dejection. The transitional time of day accentuates the sense of "before" and "after" that is part of Moore's concentration on ephemerality and subjectivity. Water towers, a factory, and distant high-rise buildings express a public material power and serve as backdrops for a scene of private moral emptiness. Moore's vision in *Pause* is a paradise lost, a suburban dystopia that separates person from person, room from room, and house from house.

MOORE'S COMMITMENT to a realist style testifies to his conviction that the description of the tangible truths of the city possesses the power to reveal the ethical and cultural dimension of life within it. He creates urban images that address ordinary experience without sentimentality or parody. His aim is to be topical and descriptive about an urban area whose commonplace anonymity questions the myth of the city as a symbol of progress and modernity, yet his paintings contain neither suggestions nor reprimands. His tendency is to paint the present moment rather than the eternities, to capture the viewer's attention long enough to stimulate a curiosity that involves contemplation rather than disdain. Moore also believes that the city is a state of mind, a product of human nature, and his patiently clear record of its artifacts is his way of probing its consciousness.

Moore's cityscapes led him to believe that "the subject matter in representational painting is rarely neutral. It has important meaning, however subtle or overt."[49] His commitment to portraying the most ordinary aspects of city life—a quiet conversation on a darkened street corner, traffic weaving in and out of the city, morning or evening light transforming inert buildings into dramatic masses—is always carried out with a visual tact that avoids any appearance of technical virtuosity or excess of special pleading for a cause. He has assumed the task of taking what is marginal and reframing it as central.

Moore often employs the aerial view, which spreads the scene below for visual contemplation rather than active involvement, achieving a steadiness and cohesiveness of vision rather than suggesting movement or inviting intimacy. In his aerial views Moore resists the temptation to represent the city in a perceptual blur. His choice of an elevated position often results in a split focus or doubled gaze where the eye is invited to investigate a scene below the viewer and also one at the far horizon. This prolongs attention and slows consideration of the various realities seen in succession throughout the painting. There is an aptness to Moore's use of the aerial view; it aligns well with his historical perspective of overview as he surveys the cultural ethos of the late twentieth century, engaging the city across the traditions of other urban painters. These high vantage points might suggest a willed disconnection, a fear of social contact.

Moore capitalizes on the dichotomy between beauty and ugliness in the urban landscape, inviting the viewer to consider the implications of earlier landscape tropes—the picturesque and the sublime, the heroic and the panoramic, the pastoral and the bucolic—seen again in the contemporary age. Artists employing these modes succeeded when they invested them with the sense of time and place that correlated with the spiritual outlook of their age. Moore's cityscapes capture a particular American moment in the postindustrial age when nature and culture intersect. Unlike the bucolic and dramatic American landscapes that have celebrated steadfast values and a sense of rootedness, the cityscape in art has often expressed mobility, uncertainty, contingency, and doubt. Moore confronts the city as a product of his own moment in history; the sites he creates and the details he opts to include achieve resonance in relation to earlier traditions of city painting such as Sheeler's and Hopper's.

Moore's paintings make legible the city's diversity of building styles, variety of building materials, heterogeneity of colors, multiformity of height, distinctiveness of shape—the list seems endless. Yet Moore's cityscapes are more than an enumeration of artifacts. His city views are sites that are discovered rather than conquered. There are few dramatic surprises in his art, but many intense visual rewards for taking the time to consider them. The multifaceted aspects of urban life continue to nourish Moore's imagination as he seeks pictorial vantage points from which to view the city and investigate its complex character.

Chapter 3

Brave Old World Revisited

INDUSTRIAL LANDSCAPES AND MANUFACTURING SITES

ALONG WITH THE CITYSCAPE, the industrial image has been one of the reigning symbols of the modern era, and like the city it has evoked a conflicted response in the American psyche since the early days of the Republic.[50] Alternately celebrated in the twentieth century as a sign of hope and progress or scorned as enslaving and inhumane, industrial production has evoked widely divergent visual responses ranging from the pristine clarity of Charles Sheeler's precisionist canvases of Ford Motor Company's River Rouge plant to Jacob Riis's depressing factory photographs of oppressed laborers. Factory sites have conjured up analogies with the cathedrals of industry and the promise of progress or have been negatively associated with the crude, the repetitive, and the blighted. Nevertheless, the industrial scene has continued to fascinate artists up to the present technological age. Strongly attracted to John Kane's primitive paintings of Pittsburgh, Sheeler's precisionist factories and stacks, Lee Friedlander's gritty *Factory Valley* photographs, the German artists Hilla and Bernd Becher's deadpan shots of water towers and blast furnaces, and Rackstraw Downes's panoramic vistas of the Hackensack River and the Clairton steel works, John Moore has joined with these artists to explore the industrial image in his realist paintings. Like Kane, Moore discerns beauty in the undecorated factory exteriors that house the anonymous laborer, whose work is often as regularized and repetitive as the bricks and windows uniformly organized across the surface of the buildings themselves. Moore's factory views testify to the power of the industrial image to provide the stimulus for works of art that find a sustaining formal beauty in objects and events that allegedly deface the landscape.

Yet Moore's expression is not one of unmitigated praise. By choosing to depict the industrial landscape, Moore takes on a subject that has been shaped by cultural expectations and grounded in a specific social experience. Industry's pictorial history is complex and has been marked by ambivalence throughout the twentieth century.[51] Its imagery and the discourse surrounding it have served as markers of national history, social and political progress, as well as financial power. As the factory involves a clear economic relationship to nature based on capital, it becomes a site where issues of class and cultural relationships are embedded in its visual representation. Moore's interest in industrial imagery over the years has ranged from scenes where factory and home occupy the same terrain, to an investigation of the pictorial possibilities of the factory facade and how it interacts with modernist styles, to a series of images that invoke the precisionist paintings of the twenties and thirties.

Moore's affinity for labor sites has roots in his past. He grew up in Wellston, Missouri, a mixed residential and manufacturing district in the west end of St. Louis. Before he knew he wanted to be an artist, he often imagined his life being centered in and around the factory world. After graduating from high school he trained as a mechanical draftsman and took a job drawing planes and rocket parts for McDonnell-Douglas aircraft. Although his talents would lead him to a career in academia, his predilection for the shapes and forms of manufacturing sites never waned. He openly admired certain industrial buildings and, in his re-creation of them on canvas in an age where the shifting demands of a consumer society throw these sites into question, he invites speculation on how these forms functioned in the past, how we regard them in the present, and how our cultural values have evolved from a modernist celebration of such imaging to a revisionist view.

DURING HIS YEAR and a half at Berkeley, Moore found that the temperate climate allowed him to move outside to record sites such as *El Cerrito Vista* (pl. 47). A foreground bush holds the picture's surface and acts as a *repoussoir* to the dramatic landscape overlooking the industrial town of Richmond and the San Francisco Bay. Like Cézanne overlooking the Gulf of Marseilles from L'Estaque, Moore paints a view from on high of houses and a body of water stretching to distant hills. But instead of a sunny and serenely ordered landscape, Moore depicts a plummeting vista, multiple vanishing points, and a theatrical sunset that bathes the scene in a ceremonial purple glow. Moore's interest in light and space enters into a dialogue with time as he captures a briefly suspended moment. All is descent in this painting as the site is poised between the light at the end of the day and the night that will fall as rapidly as the telephone wires plummeting down the hill.

Moore's elevated sunset view might recall the romantic sublime of Asher B. Durand's or Frederic Church's romantic vistas if he did not pull us back to twentieth-century reality by the telephone wires and the faint glow of an electric lamp in the window of the house at the far right. It is as if the *terribilità* of Thomas Cole's vision had been checked by the technological and the domestic. That ineffable mix of the majestic and the mundane that makes up the California landscape is faithfully recorded in this painting without parody or disdain. This deliberate juxtaposition of the natural and the artificial, the pastoral and the industrial, characterizes Moore's truthfulness to the contemporary landscape.

Moore's landscape painting simultaneously develops and discovers an image of our culture and environment. Impressed by the grandeur of the California landscape, he nevertheless refuses to mine nature solely as a vein of emotional expression. Man's place in the landscape fascinated him as he worked on the painting: "It was a painting that took a while to do. I would be painting the street and the houses and began to think of the people who lived in those houses, and how they would get in a bus and stop at a mall which I was also painting. I could imagine all the types of things that were part of a place. On the right side you have the view of the house with the man reading his newspaper and his art on the wall. Painting these illusions, I felt as though I was alternately working three inches from my nose yet reaching out three miles through the distance. It was a very exhilarating painting."[52]

Moore wanted to show not just the variety but also the familiarity of the landscape. The site north of Berkeley as much as the glory of a near-cliché California sunset constitutes the subject of his canvas. Man's presence, although minimally noted, is everywhere expressed in the way he plants his bushes around his house, in the bench where he sits to wait for the bus, and in the roads that he travels to work and home. Moore divides his attention between the drama of the natural setting and the evidence of man's intervention in it.

When he returned to Philadelphia Moore found all sorts of things paintable that he had not previously considered. The truism about finding beauty in one's own backyard becomes a reality in *Standard Pressed Steel* (pl. 48), painted from the back porch of Moore's suburban Wyncote, Pennsylvania, home. The painting takes its title from the factory beneath the water tower on the horizon. Moore developed an interest in areas where suburbs abut an industrial facility. Shadowed rooftops, tilting bushes, and angular tree branches define planes and create divergent directional paths that the eye follows at different speeds, rendering a conventional suburban site into an active complex of information that convinces the viewer of season, location, and life-style. Moore pays scrupulous attention to rendering details of shingle color and brick face under the clear light of a late autumn afternoon without ever lapsing into a fussiness that would distract from the poetic mood that resonates from the scene. The inventory of particulars, from the curtained windows of the houses to the gridded facade of the factory, communicates his experience of a place and the individuality of its setting.

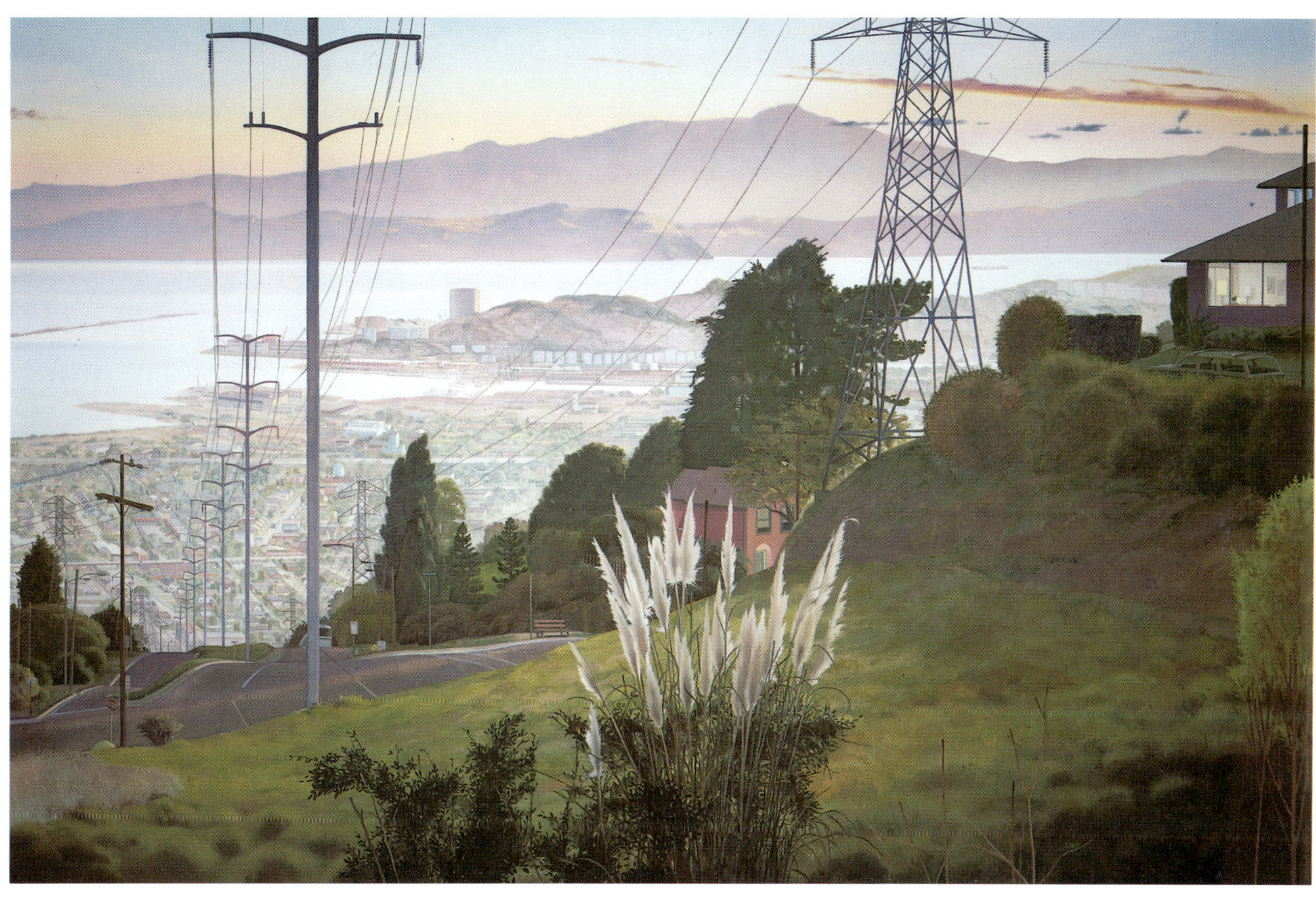

47 EL CERRITO VISTA, 1982

Oil on canvas, 90 x 139¾ in.
Private collection.

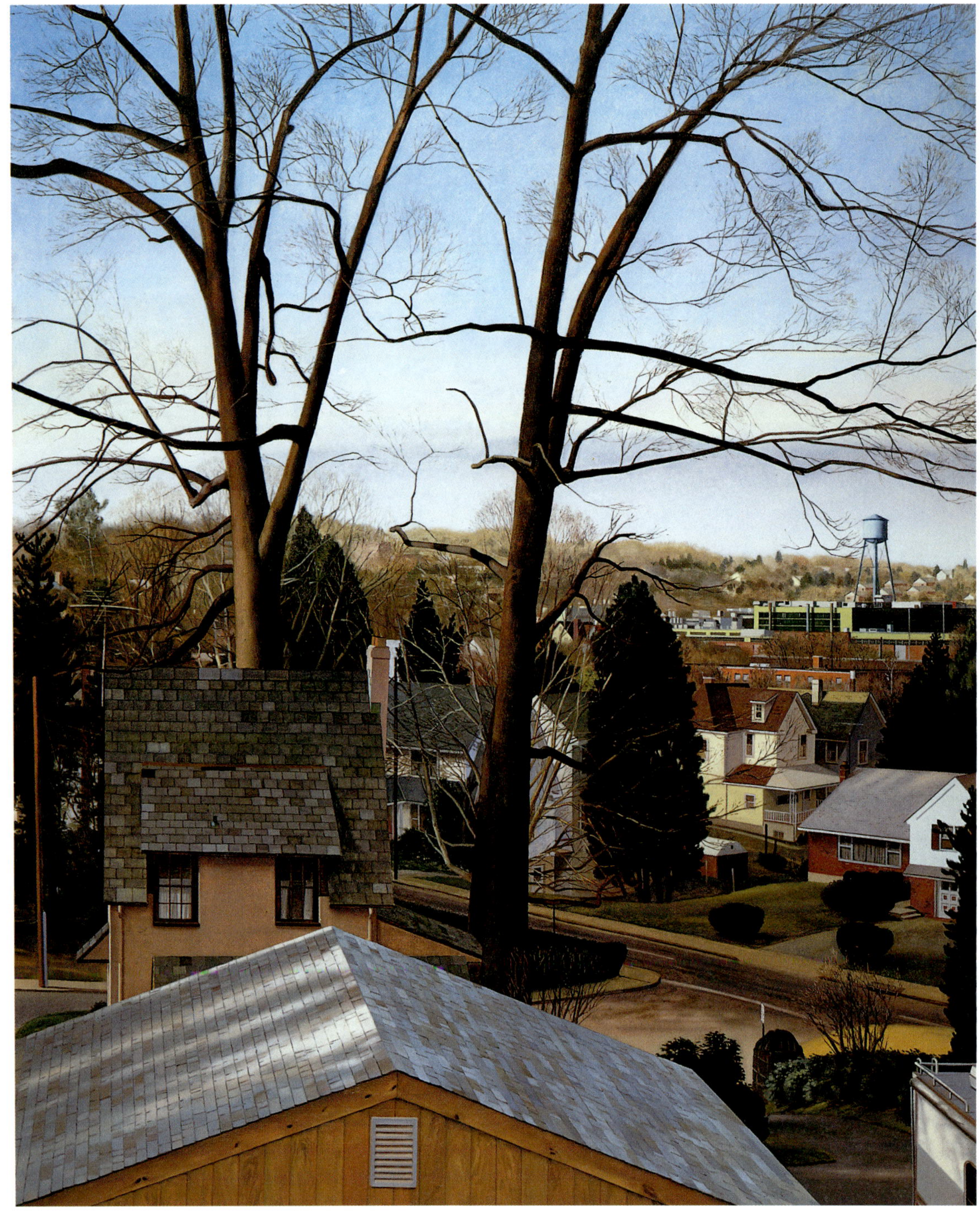

48 STANDARD PRESSED STEEL, 1983

Oil on canvas, 90 × 75 in.
CIGNA Museum and Art Collection, Philadelphia.

Charles Sheeler's painting *Clapboards* (fig. 14) crops a similar view of gables, shingles, and chimneys, but it is obvious that his precisionist interest lies in the abstract geometry of the scene. By focusing on the intersection of angles and avoiding any view of a lawn or street, Sheeler removes his scene from the domestic to dedicate it to the discovery of an architectural cubism. Moore combines a practiced hand with a candid eye to capture the sensory look of things without neglecting the conceptual spirit of the place. Water towers and trees seem to grow from the same ground, speaking clearly in this image of man's intervention rather than nature's abandon: houses have been built, shrubbery planted, roads paved, a factory erected. Nature has been harnessed and re-created in this image with clarity and restraint, allowing the poetic and the prosaic to cohabit in perfect harmony. Home and commerce blend under the fading light of a Pennsylvania sky, making us think of how the nineteenth-century rapture of Albert Bierstadt's panoramic sunsets has been domesticated and industrialized to a twentieth-century reality.

In *Light Manufacturing* and *Straight On* Moore moves up close to the factory. He plays a Hopperesque light over the facades of factories in *Light Manufacturing* (pl. 49), illustrating how light and shadow cut into the geometry of buildings, transforming their inert industrial regularity into a screen of colors and shapes momentarily animated by shifting planes of light and dark. Moore takes great care to describe the value of textures and forms that naturally occur in the industrial scene. A building fragment jutting into the lower left of the picture plane provides a field whose weathered front is a painterly surface surmounted by objects whose shapes evoke dada and minimalist sculptures. The repetition of the squares on the surface of the building in the upper left and the pattern formed by the windows on the building to the right create a grid whose axial coordinates recall the visual experience of minimalism.[53] The subtle pun contained in the title *Light Manufacturing* aptly indicates the subject of the view and the process of its achievement by the artist.

Firmly in the tradition of realism, Moore opts for the unglamorous image and finds in it his own type of beauty. What appears raw, factual, and prosaic is discovered to have an expressive pictorial content. Walker Evans once addressed this issue in an article on the American warehouse for *Architectural Forum,* stating: "If you explore the warehouse district you begin to feel the essence of these buildings. It comes out in their atmosphere of solidity and use and heavy work. The very style these structures have evolved simply by nature, could not be more fitting."[54] The forthrightness of the forms, the honesty of the structure, and the unpretentiousness of the setting are qualities that Moore has steadily admired in the industrial landscape.

Straight On (pl. 50) presents the frontal view of a warehouse beneath a strip of blue sky. Here the modular grid of the factory facade parallels the picture plane in a manner similar to

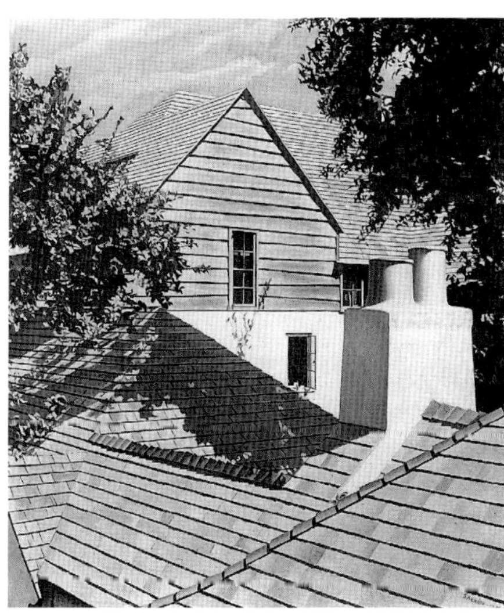

Figure 14. Charles Sheeler, *Clapboards,* 1936, oil on canvas, 21⅛ × 19½ in. Pennsylvania Academy of the Fine Arts, Philadelphia, Gift of Griffin Gribbel, R. Sturgis Ingersoll, John Frederick Lewis, Jr., William Clarke Mason, Henry T. McIlhenny, Lessing J. Rosenwald, Alfred G. B. Steel, Mrs. George F. Tyler, William L. Van Alen.

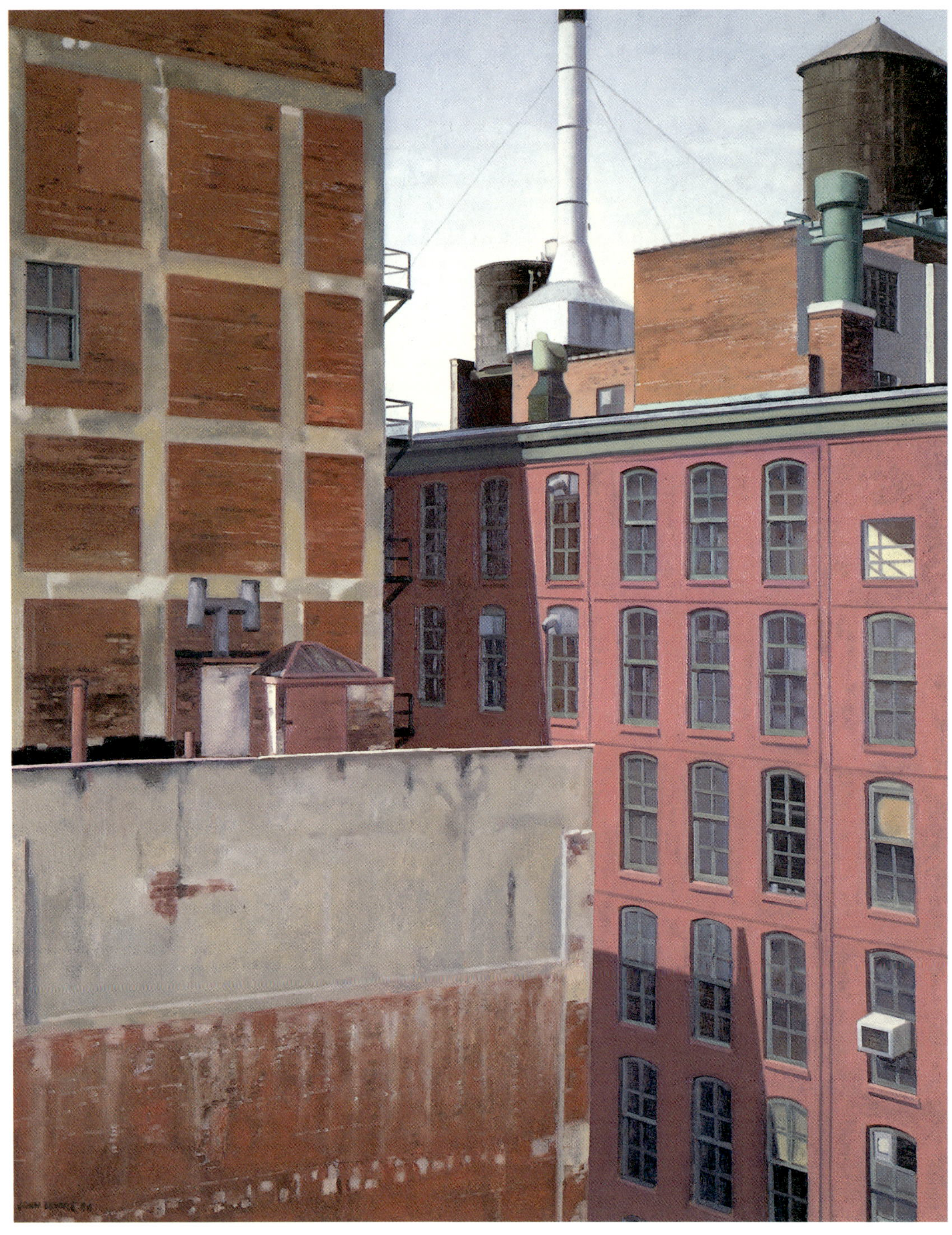

49 LIGHT MANUFACTURING, 1984

Oil on board, 30 × 24 in.
Mellon Bank Corporation, Pittsburgh.

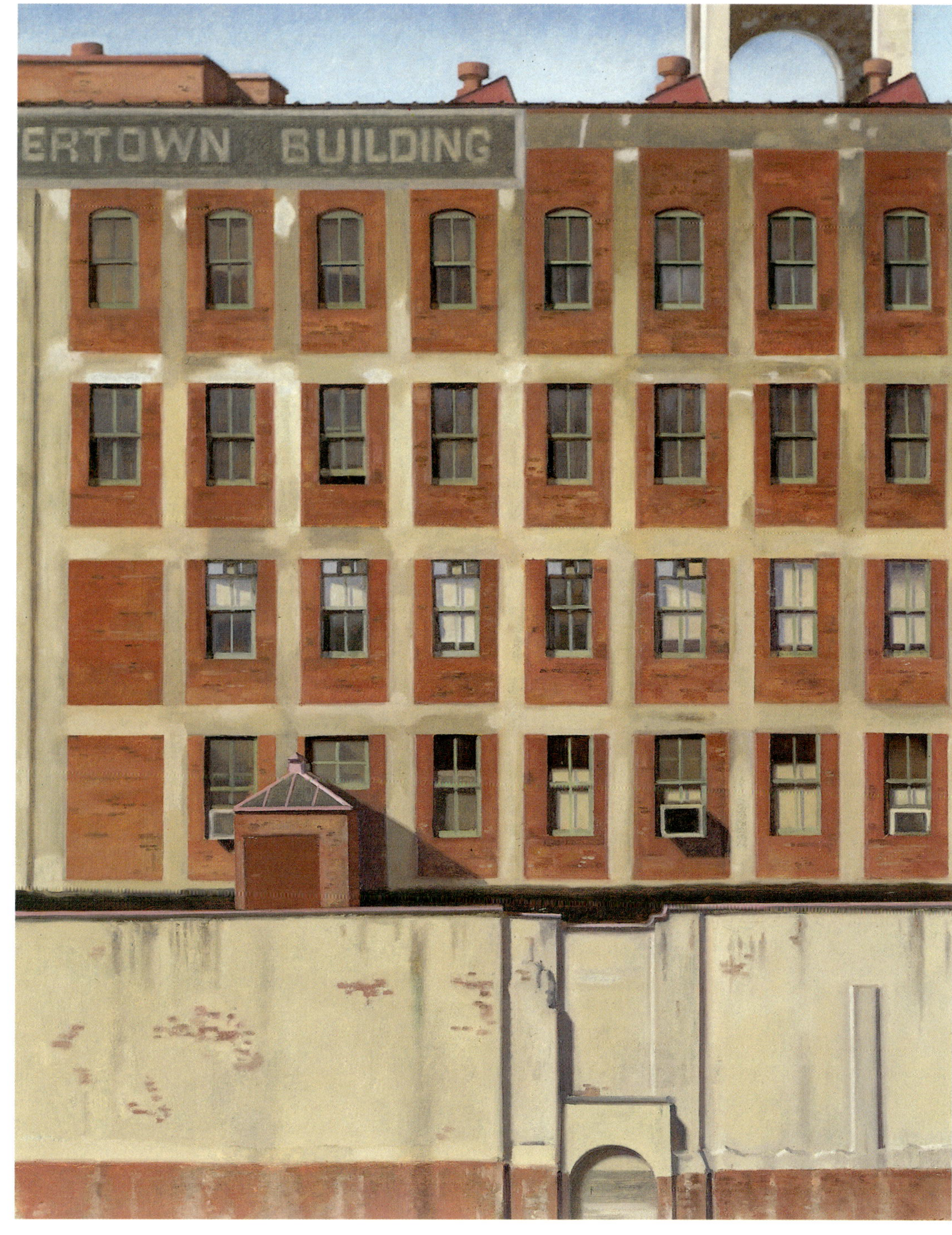

50 STRAIGHT ON, 1984

Oil on board, 30 × 24 in.
Hope Byer.

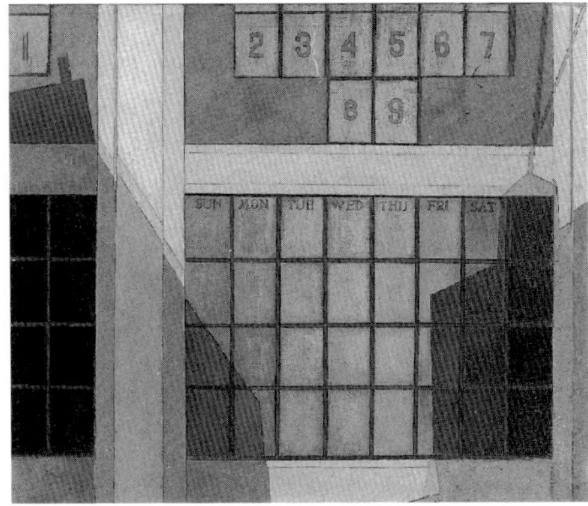

Figure 15. Charles Demuth, *Business,* 1921, oil on canvas, 20 × 24½ in. Art Institute of Chicago, Alfred Stieglitz Collection, 1949.

Charles Demuth's 1921 painting *Business* (fig. 15). Moore harnesses the language of minimalism, with its seriality, relational geometry, and evenly dispersed attention to the description of a manufacturing site, to achieve a work that combines the visual vocabulary of elemental shapes and forms of the minimalist with the pictorial candor and patient detail of the realist. Contrary to minimalism, however, Moore softens the inherent formal rigor and impersonality of the factory with painterly passages of reddish brown and ivory, romancing the stone, so to speak. He counteracts the aesthetics of boredom in the staccato pattern of the building units by the slight adjustment of window shades or by the addition of occasional air conditioners stuck into the lower part of a couple of windows.

Moore keeps the geometric vocabulary of the painting in the mind of the viewer by the constant graduation of the rectangular shape from its smallest unit as a single pane of glass, through its enlargement in the window, its repetition in the brick partition, its further elaboration in the cropped face of the factory, to its final summation in the very shape of the canvas. He invokes the aesthetic implications of precisionism, minimalism, and realism and what we know of their referents. Moore plays these various pictorial strategies against each other in a deftly balanced and visually intriguing manner, not to indulge in any shallow play of style, but to consider the richness of their pictorial and social effect in his investigation of the industrial scene.

Using a factory facade to comment on the minimalist aesthetic has its own appropriateness. Sculptors of the sixties preferred materials of industrial origin for their newness and especially for their distance from the conventional look of older art. Polyester, Plexiglas, and neon were preferred to wood, precious metals, and stone. Many artists sought to demythologize the artist's function by having their work manufactured, thus achieving the ultimate in depersonalization. Using a kind of found minimalism, Moore maintains a preference for the order and lucid structure he shared with the precisionists and minimalists, but departs from them by describing the weathered appearance of the building, detailing the distressed surfaces that are at a far remove from the industrialized regularity of the Cor-Ten steel and polished aluminum produced in such factories for sculptors of the sixties. Facture here takes precedence over manufacture as Moore works to tell us something about the scene we are viewing.

Waterville Afternoon (pl. 51) portrays a factory from across a road and a narrow band of water. As a portrait of a manufacturing site it calls to mind Sheeler's works such as *Classic Landscape* (fig. 16). Sheeler set forth his subject, with its

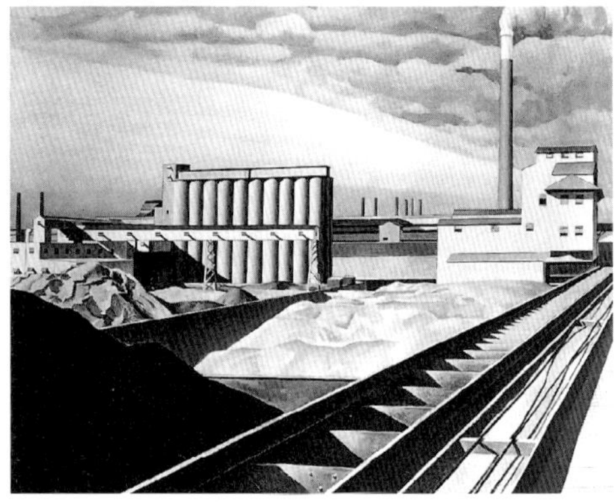

Figure 16. Charles Sheeler, *Classic Landscape,* 1931, oil on canvas, 25 × 32¼ in. Mr. and Mrs. Barney A. Ebsworth Foundation.

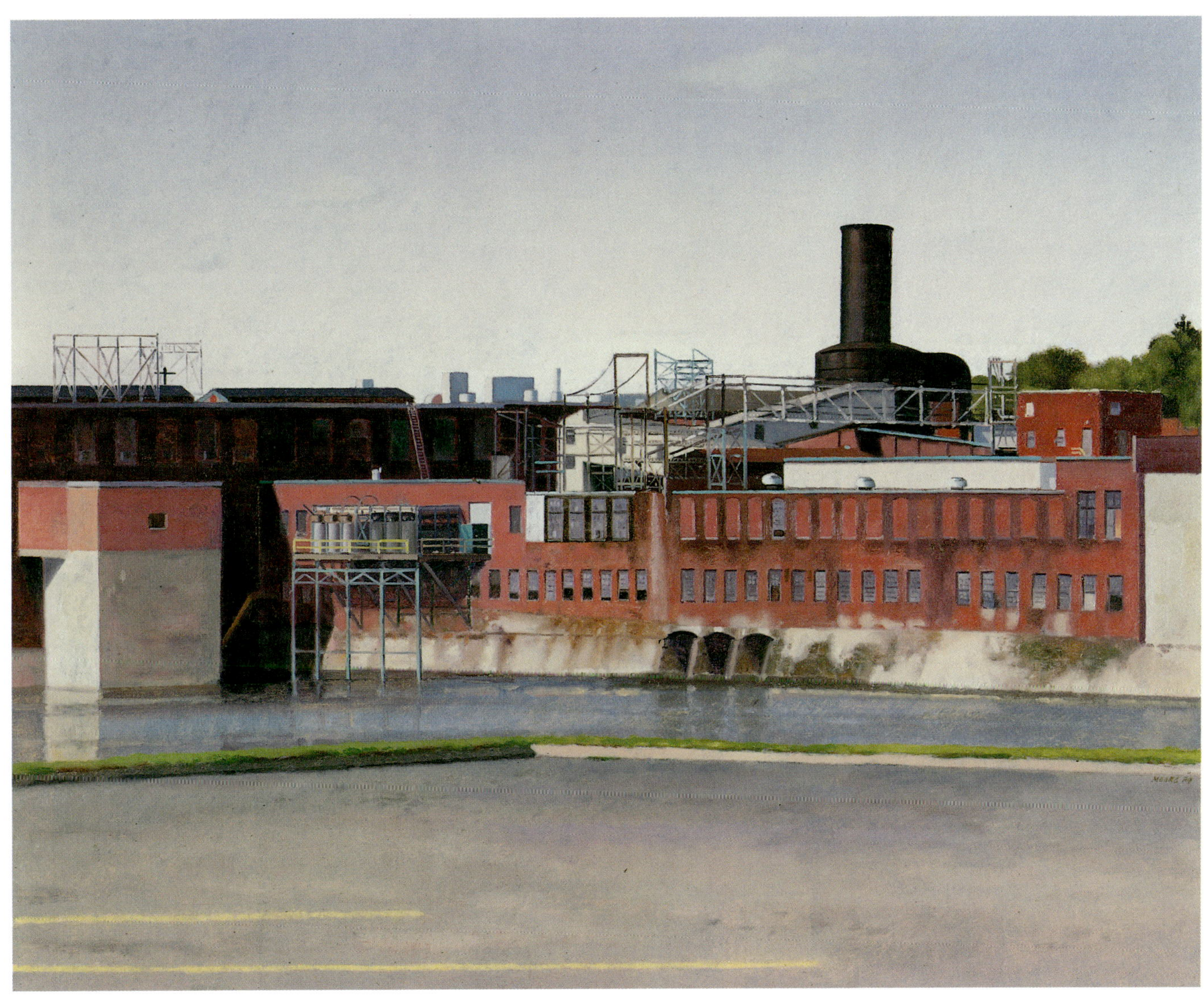

51 WATERVILLE AFTERNOON, 1984

Oil on board, 24 × 30 in.
Private collection.

impeccable surface and rigorous geometrical order, in a manner that aptly demonstrates how he earned the labels of "immaculate" and "precisionist." Clarity of form and a paring down of surfaces to essential description contribute to the crisply austere but ultimately sterile beauty of the image. Sheeler's factory scenes, at once heroic and disquieting, static and totemic, emblematize the alienation embedded in the industrial sublime.[55] Moore's factory, on the other hand, shows an exterior as weathered and textured as the facade of a Romanesque brick church. While ordered and precisely drawn, Moore's details are painterly and additive, imparting a warmth of character and suggesting human experience. Sheeler's carefully calibrated surfaces enhance the utter stillness of his scenes and, despite the working smokestacks, his images speak of absence. Moore, however, seeks out the various textures of road, water, brick, and cement, allowing them to express the effects of toil and the patina of time so that his scene appears ultimately more lived-in and humanistic despite being as depopulated as Sheeler's.

Waterville Afternoon speaks to the postindustrial age, where information and computerized technology have eclipsed manufacturing as a dominant form of production and economic power. If Sheeler's factories encoded through their formal structures those attitudes that spoke of epic power and industrial order, where man became an insignificant cipher or even nonexistent, Moore's industrial complex asks to be read against these earlier images as a visual witness to the capitalist myth of progress and power. Thus it seems appropriate that Moore's chimney stack is still and that the scene emits an aura of nostalgia and affection rather than measured restraint and sleek pictorial economy.

In *Daylight* (pl. 52) Moore portrays a view across the roofs of a poultry-processing plant overlooking Belfast, a small town in Maine. He became interested in recording the effects of a dwindling economic base in a place that sought to redefine itself when the chicken industry moved south. The patchwork roofs record the measure of time and modest economy of the town for the past fifty years. In the upper portion of the painting, land is being cleared for a parking lot to hold the cars that will bring the hoped-for tourists with their credit cards as service and leisure replace the food industry on which the town had relied.

From the edge of a corrugated tin roof, the eye is drawn across a black tar roof studded with white air vents whose gabled covers make them seem like miniaturized houses. All the elements of the typical American small town are there—the houses, the apartments, the church on the hill, the brick school buildings, even the woman and child leaving their station wagon. Nothing extraordinary occurs in the scene, no building attracts attention for long, no hidden allegory or complex symbol waits to be uncovered. The chiaroscuro of light and shade provides an element of beauty that is less dramatic in its impact than visually satisfying in its fidelity. Moore's subject is drawn from the vernacular, shunning the spectacular for the opportunity to highlight the communal aspects of American life in changing times.

The scene is humble and solid, and because it is so familiar to an American viewer it is often hard to see. As Henri Lefebvre observed, "Those things which we most take for granted as a permanent part of the nature of things are likely to be the very contingencies which distinguish our own times from those that went before and that will come after."[56] Moore's craft focuses on fixing the meaning and understanding the times of which he is a part. His work is neither apologetic nor propagandistic; what he recorded was focused, detailed, and honestly experienced. The size of the painting is neither heroic nor diminutive, just scaled to verify the moment he has chosen without prejudice or pedantry.

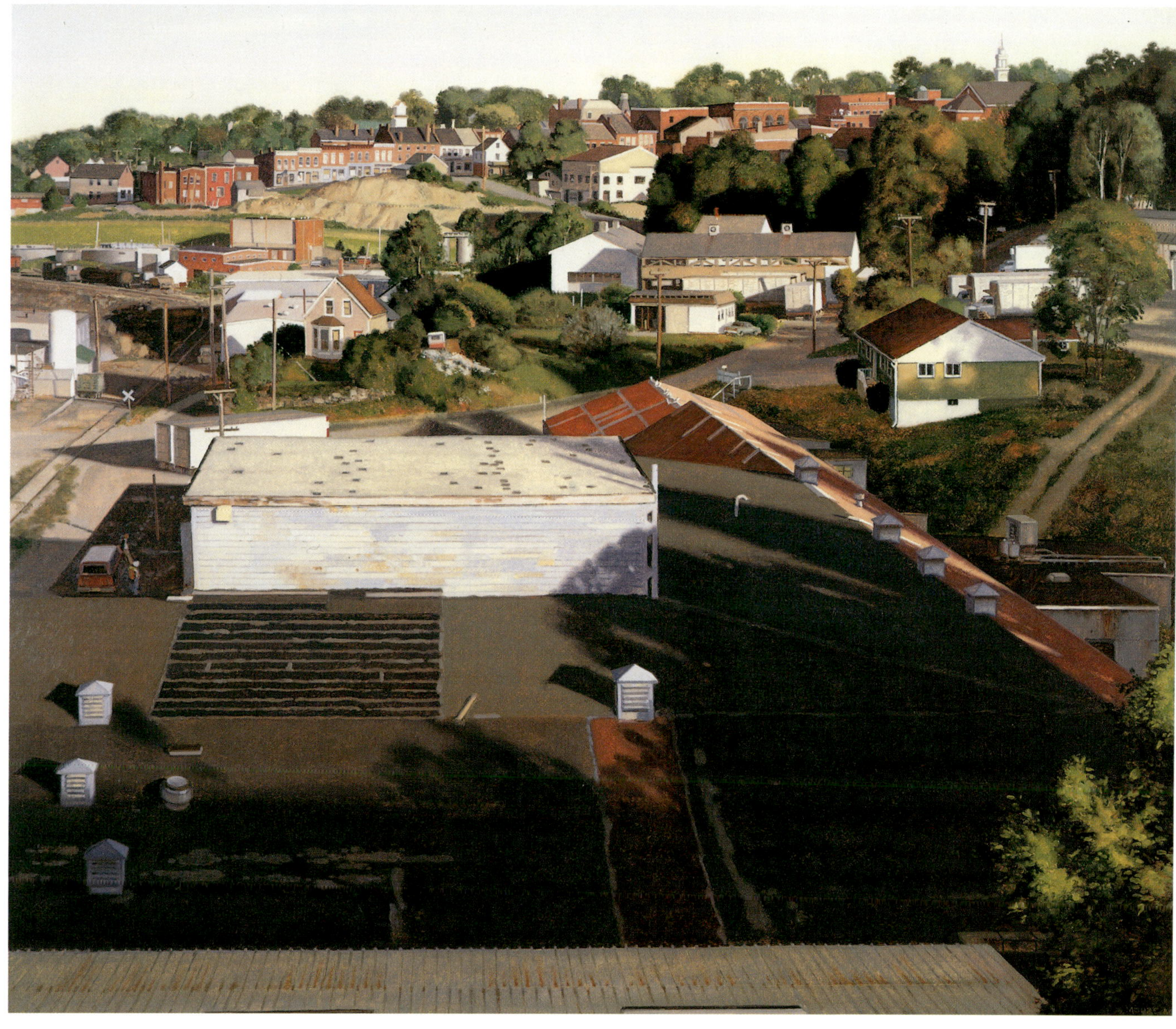

52 DAYLIGHT, 1986

Oil on canvas, 42 × 50 in.
Marshall A. Bernstein, Philadelphia.

A 1983 Charles Demuth exhibit at the Philadelphia Museum of Art and the 1985 Ralston Crawford retrospective at the Whitney Museum of American Art prompted Moore to visit Coatesville, Pennsylvania, where these two precisionists had painted the Lukens steel mill. As Moore tells it: "The fascinating thing about Coatesville is that its very center is a sprawling black mill complex surrounded by these hills. I kept driving up to get an overview and ultimately found myself standing on an abandoned tennis court amid broken glass with this incredible view of the place. The arched viaduct in the distance is where Demuth saw his view, and I found the spot where Crawford got his view. It was the most incredible sensation to find, because I was there with a reproduction of Crawford's painting, that I felt the presence of the artist. Another thing that happened was hard to believe. While I was looking over the site, an oil truck went by and lettered on the side of the truck was 'Sheeler Oil.' Something was telling me this was the place to be!"[57] Moore returned to his studio in Philadelphia, the same city where Sheeler, Demuth, and Crawford had trained as artists, and began a campaign of views of Coatesville that recorded the industrial and domestic architecture of the town.

In *Coatesville* (pl. 53) the viewer looks down at the sprawling Lukens steel plant with its chaotic jumble of buildings and projecting stacks, across to houses that look like tiny wild flowers sprouting on the distant hill. Two small patches of sky in the upper corners provide minimal relief from the complex

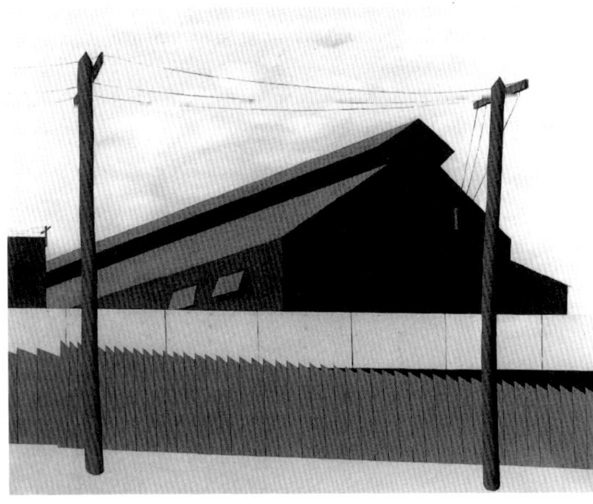

Figure 17. Ralston Crawford, *Steel Foundry, Coatesville, Pa.*, 1936–37, oil on canvas, 32 × 40 in. Whitney Museum of American Art, New York.

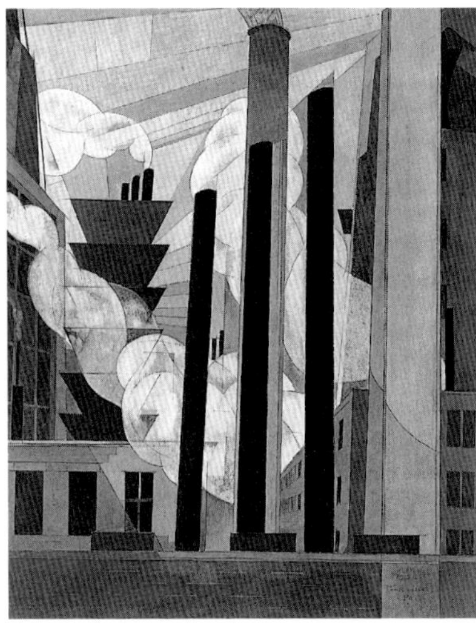

Figure 18. Charles Demuth, *End of the Parade, Coatesville, Pa.*, 1920, tempera and pencil on composition board, 19⅞ × 15¾ in. Regis Collection, Minneapolis.

detail and baroque profusion of the scene. Moore's choice of the Lukens factory places his work in the lineage of Demuth's 1920 *End of the Parade: Coatesville, Pa. (The Milltown)* (fig. 17) and Crawford's *Steel Foundry, Coatesville, Pa.* (fig. 18).

The Lukens Steel Company, originating in eighteenth-century America, is one of the oldest operating mills in Pennsylvania and has occupied the site in Coatesville since 1810. Demuth's train trips to Philadelphia and New York from nearby Lancaster familiarized him with the Coatesville landscape. His early modernist response to the industrial scene in *End of the Parade* involved flattening the volumes of the stacks and abstracting the shapes of buildings while fragmenting the sky with futurist vectors that pleat the space. He viewed the mill from below, thus emphasizing the upward thrust of the stacks and the architecture surrounded by smoke in a mythic composite of forms. Moore's *Coatesville* explores the site from an elevation, allowing him to investigate the depth of the scene and exploit the inherent geometrical nature of the buildings. The precari-

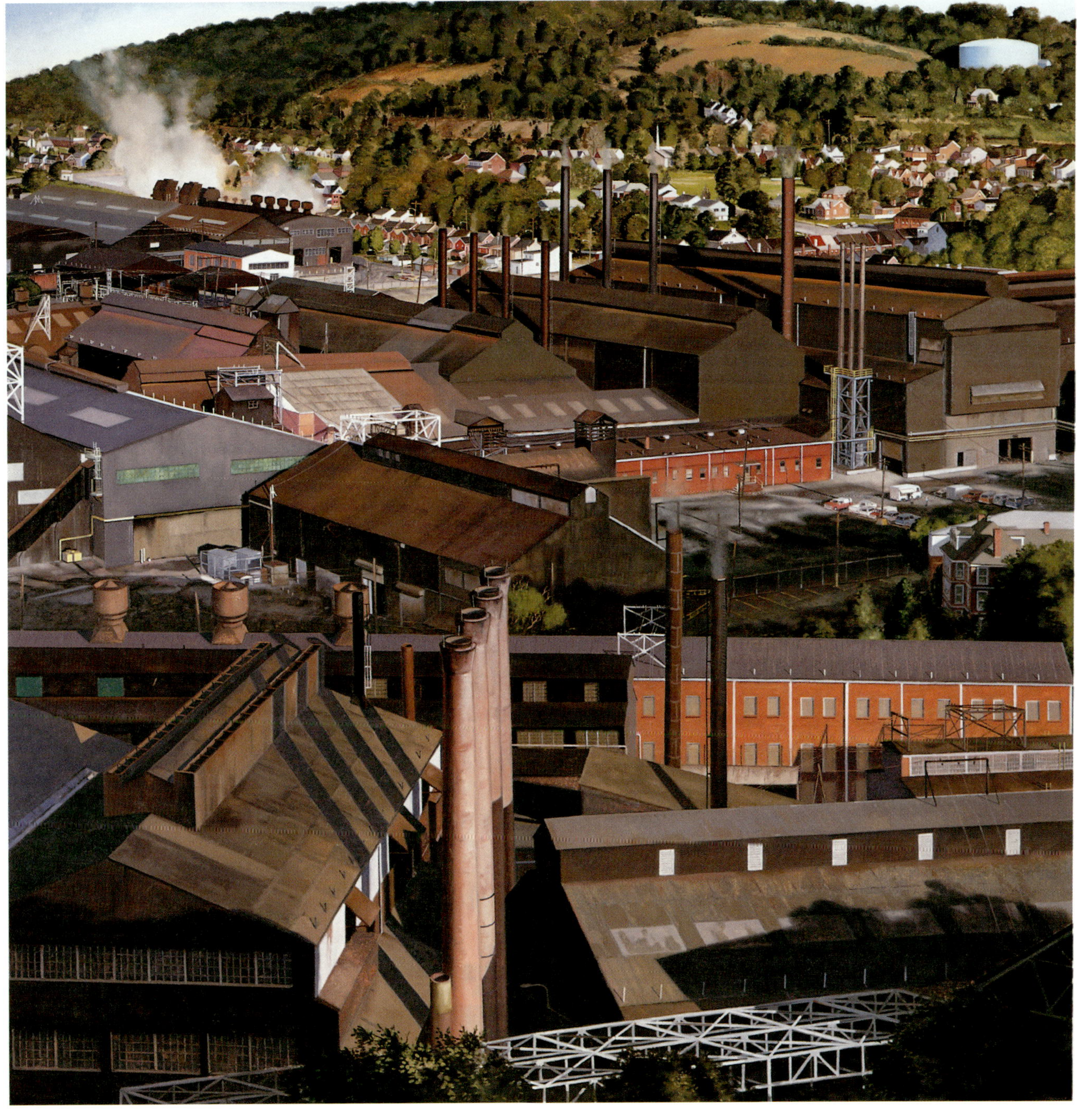

53 COATESVILLE, 1986–89

Oil on canvas, 90 × 90 in.
Becton Dickinson and Company, Franklin Lakes, New Jersey.

ous position of the viewer perched above buildings erected to perform a specific function no longer in high demand seems emblematic of the economic uncertainties associated with mill towns in late-twentieth-century America.

Crawford frames his straightforward view of *Steel Foundry, Coatesville, Pa.* between two telephone poles. The random clouds in the sky provide the only natural relief to a scene of rigidly planar and flattened forms. Despite the specificity of the title, Crawford's oil is less about the factory and its setting than it is about the modernist geometry of the design. His view is mechanistic and rational, devoid of any emotion but the pictorial. By contrast, a warm morning sun draws back over Moore's scene, creating deep pools of shadow and reiterating the staccato beat of the smokestacks. His sensitive handling of light and his color permutations enrich the factory rooftops and modulate the industrial colors of the sheds and stacks into a field that is at a distance both visually and emotionally from Crawford's impersonal paint handling and spare architectural forms.

Moore's profuse detailing of the scene enables it to be read as a powerful source of knowledge, inviting intellectual and social engagement with the subject. His commitment to this type of visual information is an index of his desire to allow more participation in the social fabric of the region. Moore's willingness to integrate the Lukens factory with the local architecture of the town is telling. In this sense he is artistically closer to the sensibility of John Kane, whose views of Pittsburgh from on high locate the steel mill within the rural landscape, replete with a regional beauty. Kane found immense dignity in labor, and his paintings resonate with deep conviction that the industrial landscape contained a beauty as lofty and lyrical as the bucolic stretches of the Hudson River valley. Moore is similarly respectful rather than iconoclastic toward the mill town. The Lukens plant visually, emotionally, and economically dominates the town, but Moore's careful notation of cars in the parking lot, factory workers buying food from a breakfast truck, and homes resting in the morning sun on the hillside recalls Gertrude Stein's words, "What they were was part of what they did, . . . " a phrase Lee Friedlander chose for the epigraph in front of his 1981 photographic study *Factory Valleys.*

This nearly-eight-foot-square canvas attests to the dominance of the man-made over the natural, to the paradoxical beauty of a landscape in which the pastoral has become the technological, soil has been replaced with brown sheds, trees have become vertical stacks, and clouds descend to become puffs of steam and gaseous exhaust. In 1923 Henry McBride praised Demuth's industrial images for their capacity "to glorify a subject that the rest of us have been taught to consider ugly."[58] Moore trades in the same type of visual oxymoron, discovering a particular type of beauty where others most often find blight. He remains aware that Coatesville offers "a view of America that's gone, or changed, or not there any- more, although the visual evidence is still there."[59] He accepts this without rancor or condescension, dedicating his skills to accepting the scene in an affirmative spirit and creating art from it.

Coatesville, West Side (pl. 54) takes us down nearly to street level, to the edge of the factory complex, where houses, a small white church or meeting hall, and outlying industrial facilities sit quietly under a late-afternoon sky. In this image Moore wants to tell us something about the community of Coatesville, what daily life might be like. He avoids the stereotypical and the extraordinary in this scene, turning instead to investigating regional existence with an honesty that is disarming.

The abstract order of the simple shapes of the various edifices alternates with the individual particularity provided by ramps, staircases, window openings, and building location to provide a sense of place that is as much an individualized portrait as it is a record of mill-town life in late-twentieth-century America. There is dignity in the small patch of lawn around the simple church and the unpretentious plainness of the facades that communicates something of the enduring character of a people whose lives are entwined with a town largely dominated by a single commodity. Unlike the previous painting, where the factory looms over the town, here the industrial structures in Coatesville coexist comfortably with domestic and ecclesiastical architecture.

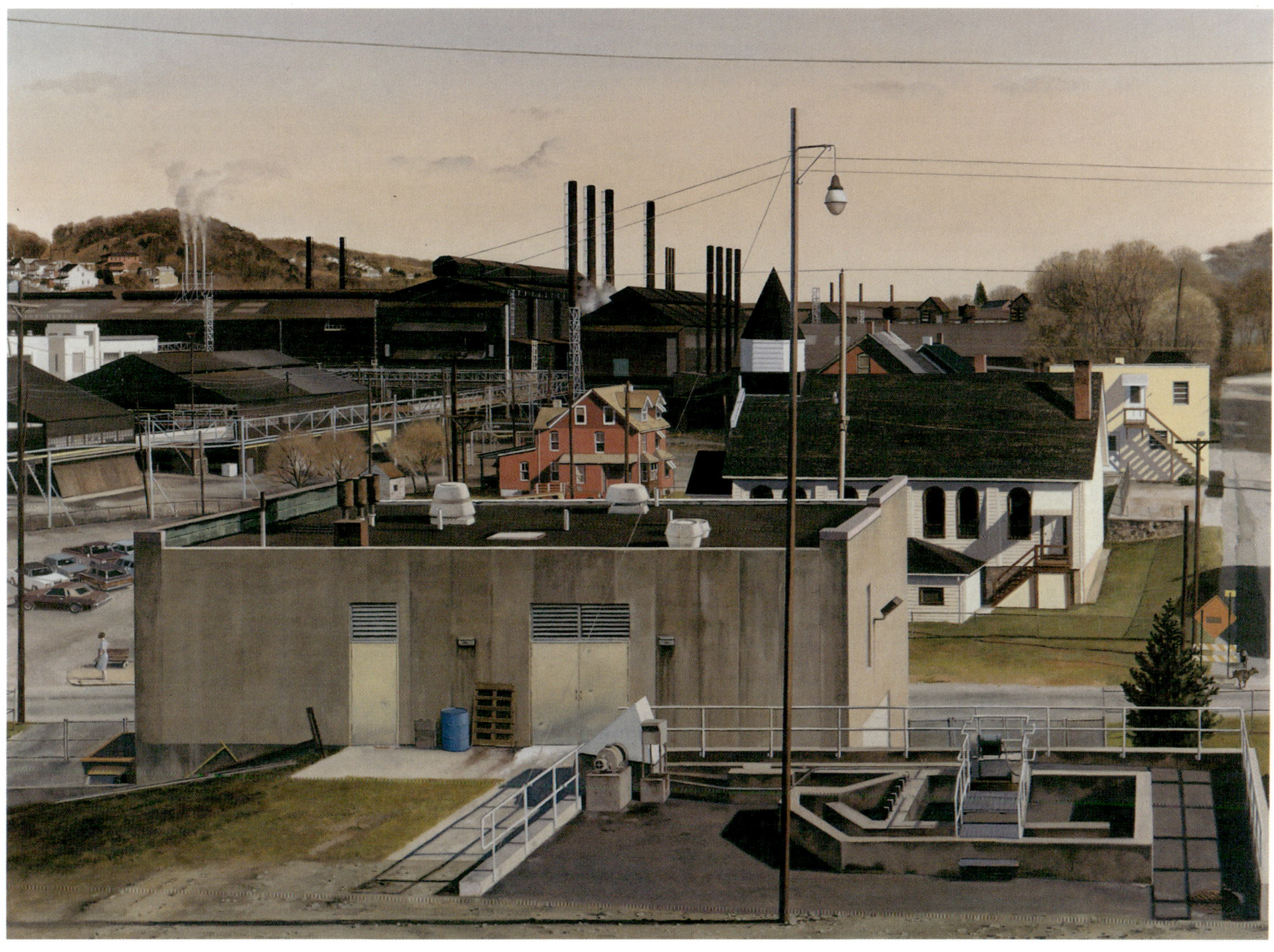

54 COATESVILLE, WEST SIDE, 1987–89

Oil on canvas, 66 × 96 in.
Alexander Moore.

Moore's inventory of this site gives us a different view of the social and economic implications of industrialism. While both scenes of Coatesville partake of an underlying abstract harmony and are rooted in a particularly American economic reality, they engage in different narratives of industrial experience. *Coatesville* is a man-made canyon of industry, its impressive bulk overwhelming the figures who labor in it. *Coatesville, West Side* contextualizes work and home, and although the almost total lack of figures might suggest the anonymity and depersonalization of labor, Moore does not show the forms in isolation or detached from their settings as he did in *Light Manufacturing* and *Straight On.* Moore's informative detail and painterly textures counteract the mechanized impersonality associated with precisionist labor sites. By avoiding a dominant or centralized focus in both scenes, Moore allows the eye and the mind to seek their own adjustments between the permanent and the ephemeral, the labored and the leisured, the heroic and the humble, the domestic and the industrial.

Near Lincoln Highway, Coatesville (pl. 55) shows a section of the Lukens factory complex from the road. Moore has chosen a view similar to Crawford's *Steel Foundry, Coatesville, Pa.* (fig. 18), but he relegates the steel mill to the background and includes stacks and other buildings behind a highway girder. For the puffy white clouds in Crawford's blue sky, Moore has substituted muted gray clouds that suggest industrial pollution more than weather. Crawford's factory is painted close up, its impassive exterior iconically presented with the repetitive fence slats and wall dividers effectively suggesting the smooth and dry mechanical operation of the foundry itself. Moore's scene is presented at a remove, with a variety of buildings pitched at different angles, their elementary volumes and tubular forms expressed in varying shades of steel grays, rusted reds, and industrial browns. Crawford's suppressed brush handling and shadowless forms make his motionless image seem to exist in a vacuum. Moore's view, while not denying the underlying abstract design inherent to such a scene, avoids such immobility by allowing the contours and silhouettes to impart a visual energy that is enhanced by the contrast of natural light with areas of artificial illumination. His scene of the factory complex conjures up images of a steel mill Parthenon or an industrial Hagia Sophia, reminding one of Sheeler's proclamation that factories were a substitute for religious expression.[60] It also recalls the promises of emancipation promoted by industry, and how faith in early-twentieth-century America was vested in economic progress. Moore neither sneers at this dream nor postures ironically at its outcome in the postindustrial age. He presents his images as updated correlates of precisionist subject matter, finding much to investigate, something to admire, and a great deal to contemplate.

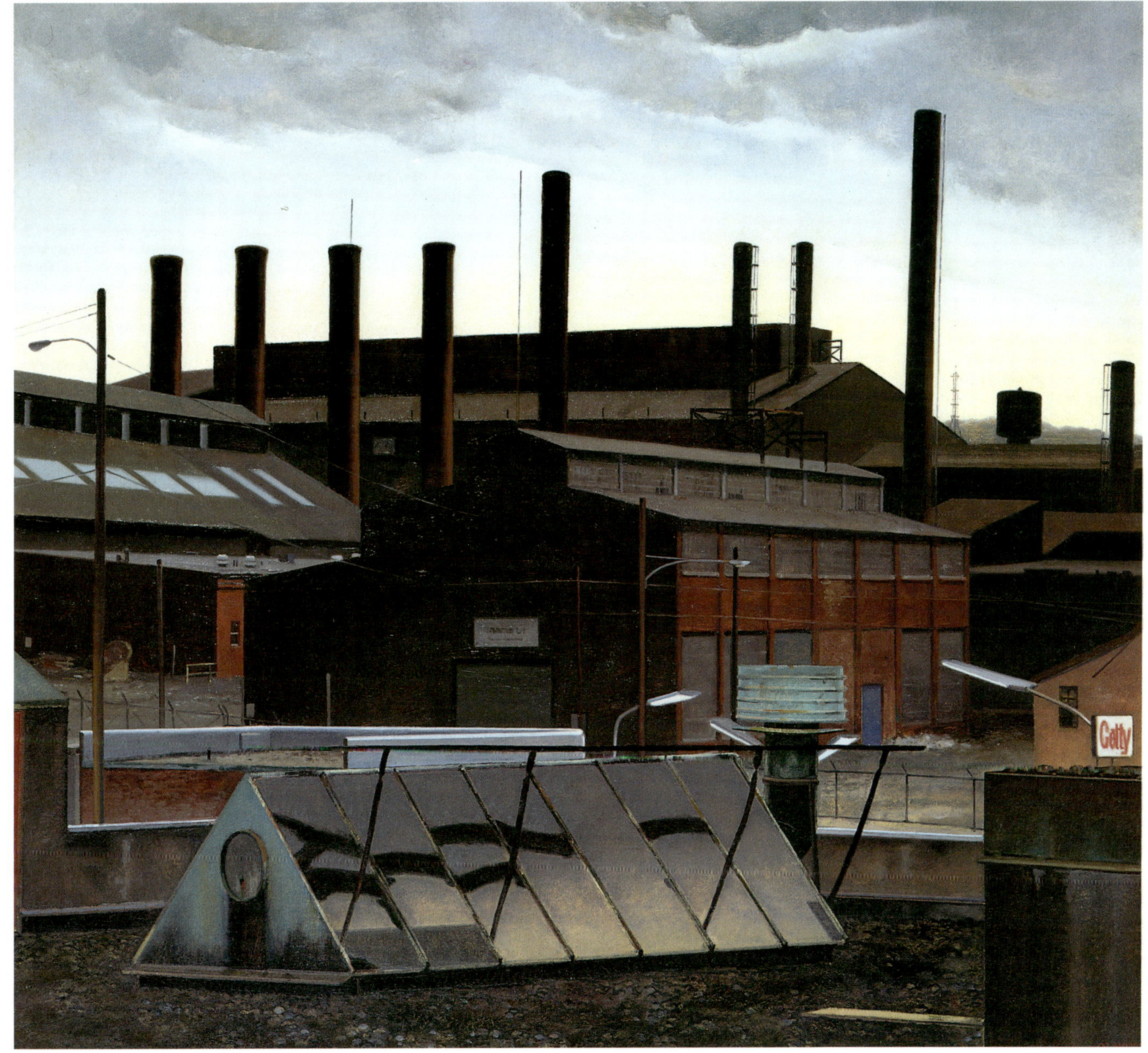

55 NEAR LINCOLN HIGHWAY, COATESVILLE, 1988

Oil on canvas, 30 × 33 in.
Courtesy Locks Gallery, Philadelphia.

Atomic (pl. 56), largely inspired by buildings in Lancaster, Pennsylvania, pays homage to Demuth's industrial scenes from his hometown. Moore's image contains the brick facades and soaring water tower familiar from several of Demuth's 1920 works such as *Lancaster* (fig. 19), *Chimney and Water Tower,* and *And the Home of the Brave.* Demuth sought to record scenes that looked quintessentially American. Drawing the indigenous factory architecture in a boldly stylized manner and casting it in shallow space, Demuth depicted what was in and of his industrial region, allowing the clean, hard edges, the primary colors, and the close-up vision to organize and define his hometown. Moore steps back from the buildings, causing the eye to traverse a road shadowed by unseen buildings on the right, to ponder the weight and density of the buildings, and to travel up the scaffolding of the water tower, whose shaded white profile holds the center of the painting.

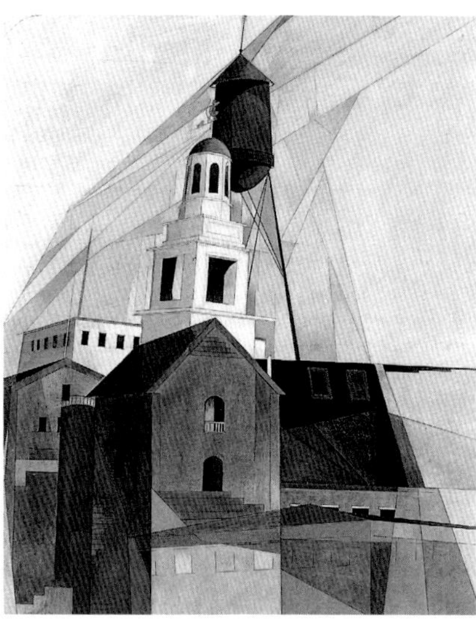

Figure 19. Charles Demuth, *Lancaster,* 1920, tempera and pencil on paper, 23 3/8 × 19 1/2 in. Philadelphia Museum of Art, Louise and Walter Arensberg Collection.

Moore counts on critical intelligence along with aesthetic sensibility to carry the meaning of his work. The water tower, poised like a rocket ready to be launched, combines with the commercial logo on the facade of the building to comment on power sources in the postindustrial age. Moore's overlaying of the older industrial architecture with the suggestion of nuclear force supplies him with a visual opportunity to combine the traditional stance of the realist as detached observer with a geography that indicates a keen awareness of the economic and political issues of the engaged activist. Grafting his image onto Demuth's precisionist sites, Moore provokes questions about the relationships of aesthetics, locale, and national pride with the realities of the eventual abandonment of such large-scale enterprises to advanced technologies and newer sources of capital. Seeing the site filtered through an older image opens a space between the subject portrayed and the meanings time has slipped over its surfaces, inviting us to consider how the paintings play off each other across the decades and develop a network of relations, repetitions, displacements, and continuities with the referents of their individual styles.

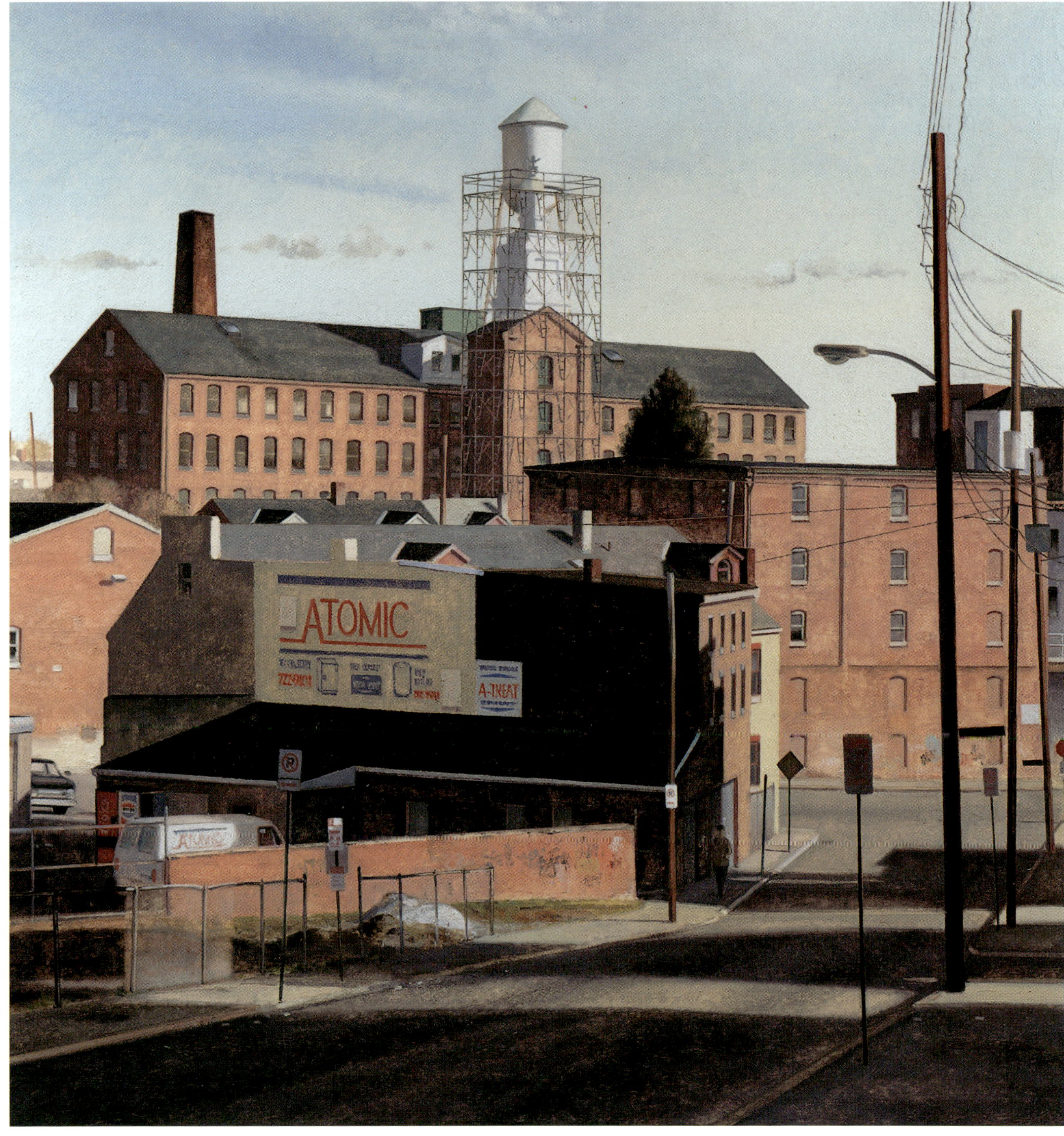

56 ATOMIC, 1992

Oil on canvas, 24 × 24 in.
Private collection.

Three Chimneys and a Dome (pl. 57) looks across the top of an industrial building over rooftops in Boston to the dome of a Christian Science church. Moore interrupts his aerial view with the repeated uprights of chimneys, establishing a vertical cadence that rhymes with other upright shapes ranging in size from a tiny discarded beer bottle and the smaller smoke vents on the roof of the foreground factory to the windows and sides of buildings and the cupola on the dome of the church. He plays rounded perpendiculars off flat strips on building facades to impart a sense of density and visual unity to the scene. The metallic cylinder on the lower foreground sets up a counter-tempo against the horizontals and verticals contained in the site. This rounded shape plays through the openings of vents to tables on a deck in the middle distance and culminates in the dome in the upper register. Sheeler's 1940 *Fugue* (fig. 20) comes to mind for its similar pulsation of stacks across the surface of the canvas and its emphasis on the geometry of the subject, but where Sheeler flattens and abstracts, Moore provides a deep perspective and textured surfaces to add complexity to his scene.

Demuth's 1921 *Incense of a New Church* (fig. 21) is also related to Moore's representation. Demuth makes an analogy between incense and factory smoke as it swirls around the pipe-organ forms of smokestacks while a chalicelike shape enmeshed in the smoke confirms the religious-industrial relationship. Demuth's painting comments on the prosperity of postwar America where business was elevated to the status of religion, recalling Calvin Coolidge's statement: "The man who builds a factory builds a temple. The man who works there worships there."[61] Moore's alliance of church and capitalism is equally compelling. He overlaps the profile of the church with the rust-colored central stack, pairing the male and female shapes like Demuth's smokestack and water tower in *Aucassin and Nicolette* (fig. 22). The relationship between religion and industry is furthered in the subtle rhyming of the dome and cupola with the boxy shape in the lower left foreground, its slightly elevated top surmounted by a cylindrical appliance, forming an industrial pun on the ecclesiastical architecture. Even nature seems to be complicit with the industrialization of the world, with the sky providing a metallic gray backdrop

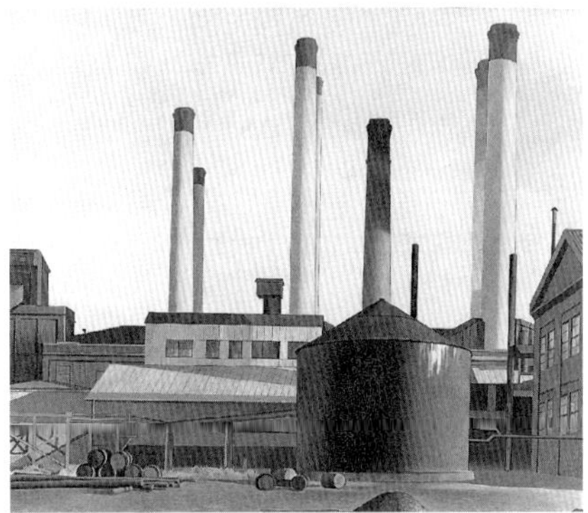

Figure 20. Charles Sheeler, *Fugue*, 1940, tempera and graphite on gessoed Masonite, 11½ × 13¼ in. Museum of Fine Arts, Boston, Arthur Mason Knapp Fund.

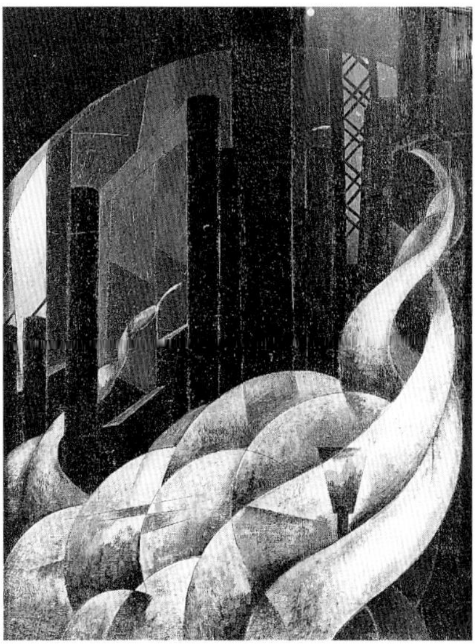

Figure 21. Charles Demuth, *Incense of a New Church*, 1921, oil on canvas, 26 × 20⅛ in. Columbus Museum of Art, Ohio, Gift of Ferdinand Howald.

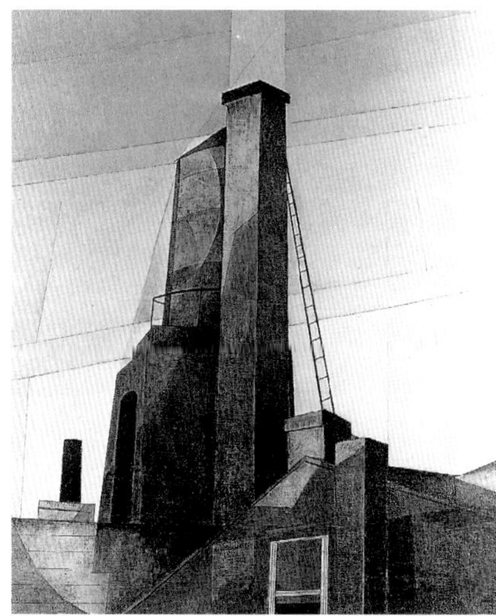

Figure 22. Charles Demuth, *Aucassin and Nicolette*, 1921, oil on canvas, 24⅛ × 20 in. Columbus Museum of Art, Ohio, Gift of Ferdinand Howald.

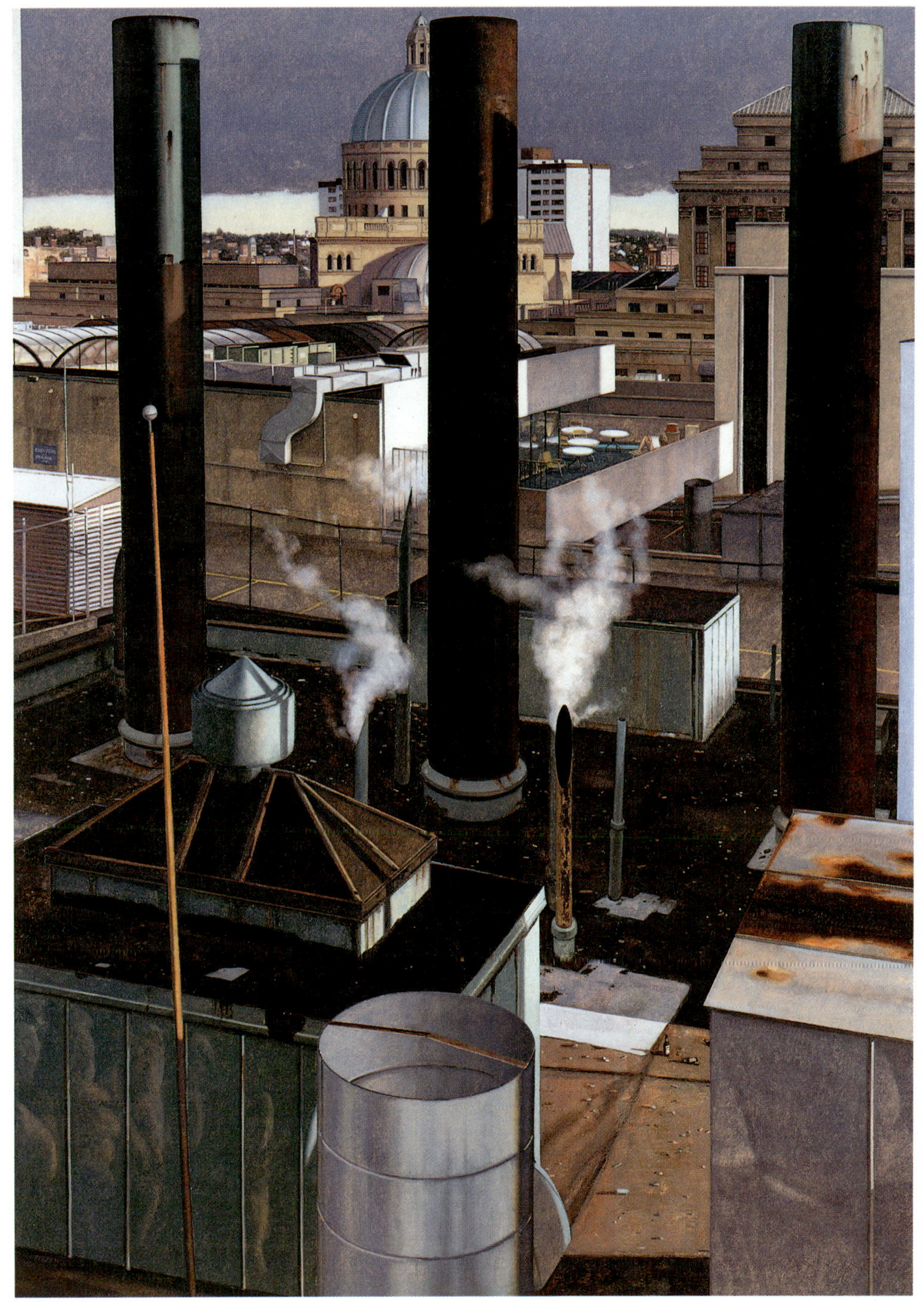

57 THREE CHIMNEYS AND A DOME, 1991–93

Oil on canvas, 66 × 48 in.
Courtesy Locks Gallery, Philadelphia.

to the scene. Moore thus particularizes the interplay of social forces through the structures that formally unite church and industry. These visual linkages allow the viewer to contemplate how America has worshipped both God and mammon in the twentieth century and how the configuration of our cities reflects this situation.

A solitary figure sits reading on the deck of the building in the middle distance and seems all the more alone for the empty tables surrounding her. This bit of humanity comes as a surprise when discovered through the thicket of hard and spiky forms in the foreground and causes one to ponder the dominance of labor over leisure. What kind of pleasure can be taken in proximity to the polluting vapors emitted from the nearby vents?

Flag Day I (pl. 58) combines views of a grain-processing plant from St. Louis in the foreground with buildings from Boston's North End in the background. Signs of technological progress such as the satellite dish, set like a metallic sun in the sky, coexist with buildings on the right and left whose facades have resisted the inroads of modernization.

The front of the grain plant holds great visual interest by its strange combination of ladders, vents, and ductwork, echoed above and to the sides by the balconies and fire escapes of the other buildings in the painting. Moore originally began the work with the dwelling behind the grain plant, intrigued by the way the building had been added onto by later generations without any stylistic regard for what was already there. It seemed to him like architecture without architects, yet it gave physical evidence of change and growth, of later generations making their mark. On a trip in 1994 to his native St. Louis he came across the grain plant, which reminded him of summer work during his teen years in similar structures. Its distressed brick facade, its almost sculptural accouterments decking the front, seemed a perfect solution to the foreground of his scene of a working-class neighborhood in Boston. Moore's attraction to the photography of Hilla and Bernd Becher becomes evident here. He shares with them an interest in a kind of archival inquiry into older, nearly extinct industrial structures seen frontally with a matter-of-fact objectivity. Like them, he is concerned less with surface styling than with an artistic logic that discovers visual intrigue in cultural artifacts that have been marginalized by postindustrial society. Moore registers the almost anthropomorphic elements of the facade of the grain plant, the green steel body of the ventilating structure on the right throwing a curved protective metal arm around the doorway and the empty blue plastic chair on the left. By its extreme clarity of presentation, the painting provides an individualized portrait of a building.

The combination of industrial and domestic architecture provides both a subject and a metaphorical construct for Moore, whose project has been to investigate and to comment through pictorial means on the way of life suggested by the architectural structures where people live and work. He brings to consciousness the traces of generations shaping their environment, be it through the whitened paint on the grain plant eroding from the red brick underneath it or the addition of gentrifying penthouse apartments accessing cable over the older tenements beneath them. Moore depicts environments that have been worked over by weather, time, and human effort. As lucidly objective as Moore's work appears, it is also deeply introspective about how America has fared; what its hopes and dreams were; how and why these took physical form through architecture; and where we think we might be today. These questions press the edges of the frame as insistently as the shadowed sides of the red brick buildings abutting the borders of *Flag Day I*.

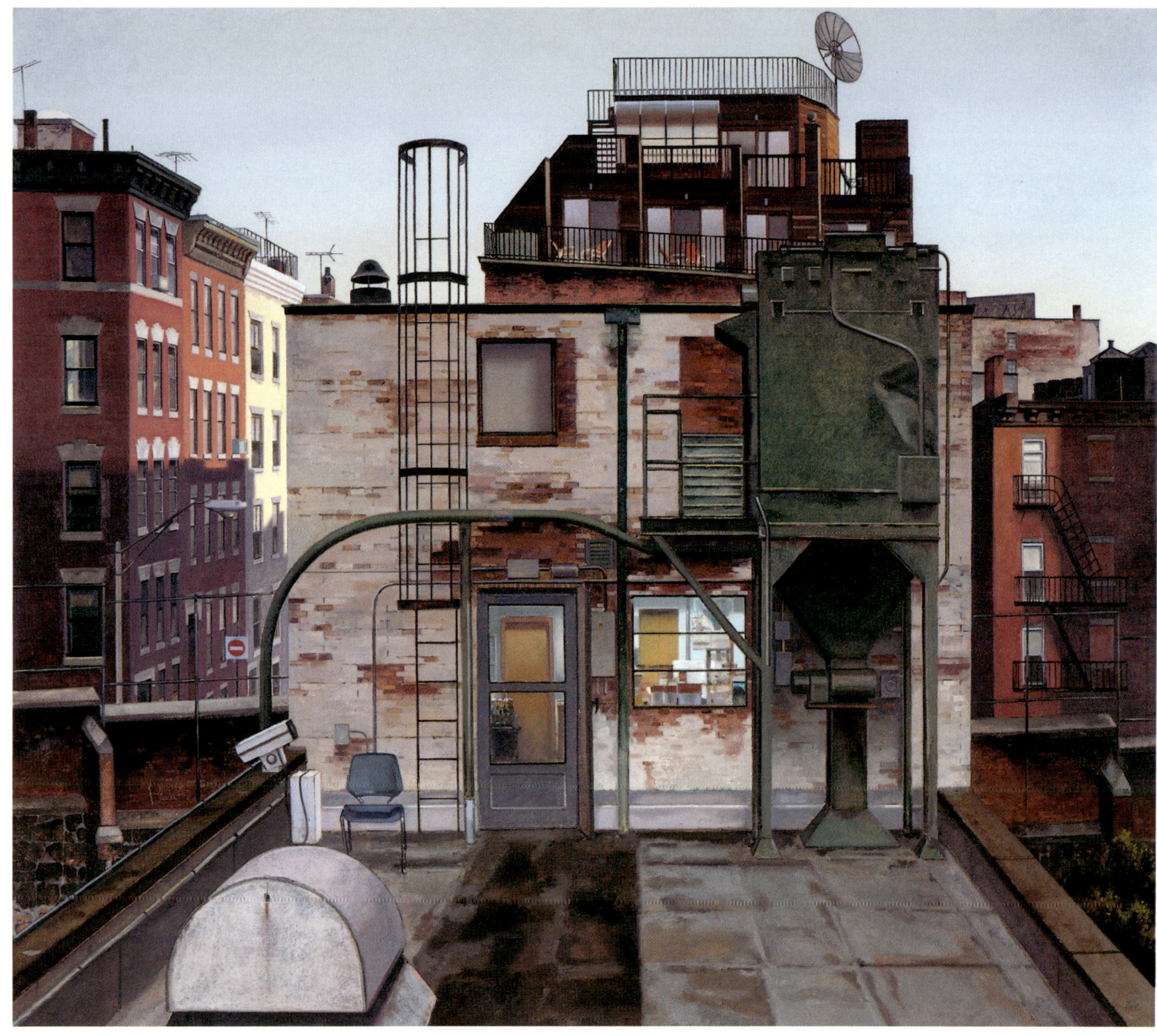

58 FLAG DAY 1, 1995

Oil on canvas, 38 × 44 in.
A. G. Rosen.

IN AN ARTICLE FOR AN EXHIBITION on precisionism and the dawn of modernism in America, William Agee wondered "if in fact there is a deeply rooted Precisionist strain in American art that goes back to the razor-sharp line of John Singleton Copley and extends through the exacting craftsmanship of the minimalist box perfected by Donald Judd in the sixties."[62] Moore's art seems to answer this in the affirmative as his industrial scenes prove him deeply attached to a particular subject matter. The majority of them are read through and against the works of the precisionists, thus testifying to Moore's consciousness of himself as an artist in a defined tradition with a desire to reflect further on imagery that held specific promise for the modern age. Moore's use of older factory paintings to reference his sites enables him to contemplate a phase of industrial capitalism that was intended to provide security for the age we live in today. The precisionists stripped their factory images of grime and ordered their industrial shapes into paragons of mathematical clarity that personified the utopian efficiency that capitalist enterprise hoped would make America a leading economic world power. Moore's records of these sites suggest a visual epitaph for a vanishing time in the American industrial economy. Environmental wear and time's eroding effects have incised their history on the surfaces of Moore's buildings. Accumulated detail slows down the reading of the image, releasing meaning gradually as the viewer is invited to compare these sites with their pristine counterparts of the 1920s and 1930s and situate them within the discursive visual and social fabric of their present situation.

As with his cityscapes, Moore often views his working-class edifices from on high and at a remove, factors that induce a sense of alienation and analogize the retrospective gaze of intervening contexts and discourses through which he prompts us to consider his images. This distance from his scenes visually suggests a view of what American industry has been in contrast to the uplifted gaze used by the precisionists that indicated what might become. Factories and steel mills, formerly icons of modern accomplishment and national prosperity, are now the symbols of a misapprehended economic well-being.

Reading Moore's industrial paintings as archives of sites endows his images with a cumulative significance that is greater than the factual record of an individual warehouse or plant seen by itself. Never allowing sentiment to undermine critical consciousness, Moore investigates the social physiognomy of the industrial landscape, seeking in idiosyncratic details, distressed surfaces, and older architectural forms some evidence of the cultural practices of modernism. If precisionism was a celebration of the industrial scene, Moore's art is an interrogation of it. How did the industrial landscape come to look this way? Why and in what ways have the ideals that motivated the building of these structures changed? How have industrialism's modern attitudes influenced our contemporary perceptions? Moore's paintings offer no easy answers, but the very act of recording such scenes in all of their complexity challenges the late-twentieth-century viewer to slow down and consider the individual, social, and historical factors that have shaped our perception of these images.

CONCLUSION

In his poem "The Wanderer: A Rococo Study," William Carlos Williams asks, "How shall I be a mirror to this modernity?"[63] As a contemporary realist painter, John Moore asks the same question and responds in canvases that express personal beliefs that he decides are worth sharing. His still lifes tell us something about the period in which they were created. His flower glasses and plastic lacquer trays, his aluminum chairs and Kleenex boxes, issue from a particular time and carry specifically American cultural memories. Their unpretentiousness allies well with Moore's own character and his intention of sharing intimately known things with a broader public. Cityscape and the industrial site share with still life the idea that the things they portray have been deliberately arranged or constructed by human hands rather than having arisen organically from nature. Moore treats his urban and industrial subjects like still-life set-ups in that he selects and rearranges buildings, often from widely divergent geographical locations, until he achieves a composition that he feels contains the spirit of place he seeks to express. Even as Moore changed his subject matter from private objects of personal use to public buildings and communal space, he retained the love of solid things fixed in measured relationships and secured with realist detail.

In essence, Moore's art has always been about depiction as an access to feeling and the diffusion of culture in material form. His work has evolved from an emphasis on formal rhythm and pattern to a profound concern for detail that describes experience. We see in Moore's art a progression toward context. The objects in his still lifes gradually came to take their place in an environment. At first isolated on tables in corners of rooms *(Spring; Summer; Red Snapper)*, they eventually were placed against windows overlooking the city *(Montrose; Downtown; Thursday)*, until the city view came to dominate the objects as the setting *(Night Studio; The Birds, 3/4, the Moon)*. He thus evolved from contemplating the beauty of the world in its simplest manifestations to embracing it in all of its inexhaustible visual density.

The realist detachment of Moore's style does not indicate the absence of emotion but testifies to a respect for the individuality of his subject. Many of his still lifes and several of his early urban views such as *San Francisco View* and *Twelfth Street* were essentially abstract subjects reluctant to abandon their nature as vital presences in a real world. Conversely, his later work, steeped as it is in the details of daily life and anchored in the material, retains enough of an abstract sense to link it with the modernist heritage from which he emerged. By rejecting abstraction as his primary expression in the late sixties, Moore did not intend to set himself apart from the mainstream. Instead, he entered into a rich dialogue with the traditions of modernism and its aesthetic heritage, and it is in terms of that dialogue that the meaning of Moore's art is best understood.

Far from being reactionary or a throwback to an earlier style, Moore's realist art actively engages the art of his time. His sensitivity to contemporary issues in the art world permeates his subject matter and expression, from the minimal colors and shapes in his early still lifes such as *Spring* and *Tiger Lilies* through the gridded repetition of visual elements in the interior of *Thursday* and the exterior of *Straight On*. Rather than ignoring earlier styles, he embraced those aspects that infiltrated his visual and theoretical consciousness, developing his art along with them. He kept one eye steadily on the latest developments in American art and the other on the traditions from which they arose, allowing both to strengthen his individuality.

To read Moore's still lifes as decorative arrangements, his cityscapes as architectural renderings, or his industrial images as merely realist reportage is to effect a closure of meaning on work that seeks to open a perspective on the wider possibilities of painting in the contemporary era. Just as Moore allows no element of narrative to confine his paintings to a single, easily grasped meaning, neither does he want his work to be locked into a system that narrowly determines its intellectual and emotional range. The genuineness of his vision reaches beyond the neat designations of stylistic schools with their casts of characters and star players on the gallery scene. Moore constructs his paintings with a sense of freedom to deal with reality and abstraction as they work for him, rather than falling lockstep into a predictable manner of producing paintings that fit a popular look or a codified critical apparatus. Moore has always followed his own instincts rather than the crowd, providing a body of work whose quality testifies to the fact that realism is neither a retrenched outpost of academic practice nor an outdated style with questionable pictorial credentials in the postmodern age.

Moore likes an observation Gore Vidal once made about Tennessee Williams's writing: "Whatever happened to him, real or imagined, he turned into prose. Except for occasional excursions into fantasy, he sticks pretty close to life as he experienced or imagined it. He could not possess his own life until he had written about it. The desire to occupy a larger space than that which is afforded would produce reveries. The reveries would be written down as a story. He could thus make a play of the story, and have the play produced so that he could, at relative leisure, like God, arrange his original experience into something that was no longer God's—an impossessible—but his."[64] The affinity with Moore's own artistic practice is obvious as he has sought to record on canvas a sensibility fully conscious of twentieth-century American art and life.

NOTES

1 Irving Sandler, *Alex Katz.* New York: Harry N. Abrams, Inc., 1979, 58.

2 Fairfield Porter, *Art in Its Own Terms. Selected Criticism, 1935–1975,* edited and with an introduction by Rackstraw Downes. New York: Taplinger, 1979, 69–73. For a history of the contemporary realist movement see Frank H. Goodyear, Jr., *Contemporary American Realism since 1960.* Boston: New York Graphic Society, 1981; and John L. Ward, *American Realist Painting: 1945–1980.* Ann Arbor: Michigan: UMI Research Press, 1989.

3 Linda Nochlin, *Realism Now.* New York: Vassar College Art Gallery, 1968, 8.

4 A few examples are Udo Kultermann, *New Realism.* Greenwich, Connecticut: New York Graphic Society, 1970, 8; Cindy Nemser, "Representational Painting in 1971. A New Synthesis," *Arts,* December 1971/January 1972, 41–46; Gerrit Henry, "The Real Thing," *Art International,* Summer 1972, 87–91, 144; John Perreault, "Light Rays Caught and Bent," *Village Voice,* October 12, 1972, 27–28; Lawrence Alloway, "Art," *The Nation,* November 6, 1972, 445–46; Peter Schjeldahl, "Realism—A Retreat to the Fundamentals?," *New York Times,* December 24, 1972, D25–26, Peter Frank, "John Moore," *Art News,* January 1976, 122–23; Anne d'Harnoncourt, "John Moore," in *Philadelphia: Three Centuries of American Art.* Philadelphia: Philadelphia Museum of Art, 1976, 633 –34; John Russell, "The Many Faces of Naturalism," *New York Times,* August 10, 1980, D25.

5 A sampling of these are *New Realism,* State University of New York at Potsdam, 1971; *The Realist Revival,* American Federation of Arts Traveling Exhibition, 1973; *New Images: Figuration in American Painting,* Queens Museum, New York, 1974; *The Big Still Life,* Alan Frumkin Gallery, New York, 1979; *Realism/Photorealism,* Tulsa, Oklahoma, 1980; *Real, Really Real, Super Real,* San Antonio, Texas, 1981; *Contemporary American Realism since 1960,* Pennsylvania Academy of the Fine Arts, Philadelphia, 1982; *Aspects of the City,* Metropolitan Museum of Art, New York, 1983; *American Realism: The Precise Image,* Isetan Museum, Tokyo, 1985; *American Landscape,* Minnesota Museum of Art, St. Paul, 1989.

6 Scott Burton, *Direct Representation.* New York: Fischbach Gallery, 1969, unpaginated.

7 Twelve years later *Direct Representation* was seen as a landmark in the turn to new realism. If critics disagreed with Burton on his definition of the term, it was nonetheless acknowledged that the show initiated a discussion of the issues. See Lawrence Alloway, "The Renewal of Realist Criticism," *Art in America,* September 1981, 109.

8 Peter Schjeldahl, "New York," *Art International* 13, November 1969, 70.

9 Robert Pincus-Witten, "Direct Representation, Fischbach Gallery," *Artforum* 8, November 1969, 80.

10 Cindy Nemser, "Representational Painting in 1971. A New Synthesis," *Arts,* December 1971/ January 1972, 46.

11 John Perreault, "Light Rays Caught and Bent," *Village Voice,* October 12, 1972, 28.

12 Letter to the author, August 7, 1993.

13 Rackstraw Downes in Alvin Martin et al., *Real, Really Real, Super Real.* San Antonio, Texas: San Antonio Museum, 1981, 70.

14 Robert Pinsky, interview with Adam J. Sorkin in *Contemporary Literature,* 1984, 3.

15 Rosalind Constable, "Style of the Year: The Inhumanists," *New York,* December 16, 1968, 44.

16 James Mellow, "New York Letter," *Art International,* April 1969, 34.

17 Barry Lord, "The Eleven O'Clock News in Color," *Artscanada,* June 1970, 9.

18 See, for example, Frank H. Goodyear, Jr., *Contemporary American Realism since 1960.* Boston: New York Graphic Society in association with the Pennsylvania Academy of the Fine Arts, 1981; and John L. Ward, *American Realist Painting 1945–1980.* Michigan: U.M.I. Research Press, 1989.

19 José Ortega y Gasset, *Meditations on Quixote.* New York: Norton, 1961, 41.

20 For the role of Philadelphia in early American still life, see William H. Gerdts, *Painters of the Humble Truth. Masterpieces of American Still Life 1801–1939.* Columbia, Missouri: University of Missouri Press, 1981; and Nicolai Cikovsky, Jr., *Raphaelle Peale Still Lifes.* New York: Harry N. Abrams, Inc., 1988.

21 William Carlos Williams, "Still Lifes," *Hudson Review* 16, Winter 1963, 515.

22 Laurie Anderson, "Group—Fischbach," *Arts,* November 1972, 70.

23 Wallace Stevens, *Collected Poetry.* New York: Alfred A. Knopf, 1954, 295.

24 Ibid.

25 Carol Zemel, *Still Life and City View: Realist Paintings by John Moore.* New York: Buscaglia-Castellani Art Gallery, 1983, 10 –11.

26 Ibid., 11.

27 For the role of the window as a symbol of the spectacle of vision and as an empirical structure of perception, see Steven Z. Levine, "The Window Metaphor and Monet's Windows," *Arts,* November 1979, 98–104; Carla Gottlieb, *The Window in Art.* New York: Abaris Books, 1981; Suzanne Delehanty, *The Window in Twentieth Century Art.* Purchase, New York: Neuberger Museum, 1986.

28 See Sheldon Nodelman, "Roman Illusionism," *Art News Annual,* 1971, 27–38.

29 Stevens, 467.

30 Octavio Paz, "San Idelfonso Nocturne," in *The Collected Poems of Octavio Paz 1957–1987,* edited and translated by Eliot Weinberger. New York: New Directions Books, 1987, 411.

31 Joan Miró, quoted in Arthur Danto, "Miró's Little Miracles," *Art News,* October 1993, 141.

32 Stevens, 397–98.

33 John Moore, lecture at Tyler School of Art, Temple University, November 1994.

34 Donald Kuspit, "Individual and Mass Identity in Urban Art: The New York Case," *Art in America,* September–October 1977, 67.

35 Moore, quoted in Susan Meyer, *Twenty Oil Painters and How They Work.* New York: Watson-Guptill Publications, 1978.

36 Charles Le Clair, *Color in Contemporary Painting.* New York: Watson-Guptill Publications, 1991, 17–20.

37 Moore, as quoted in Anne Schultes, "City Scenes," *Montgomery County Record,* Pennsylvania, June 28, 1987, C1.

38 Rackstraw Downes, quoted in Alvin Martin et al., *Real, Really Real, Super Real,* 35.

39 Edward Hopper, quoted in Lloyd Goodrich, *Edward Hopper.* New York: Whitney Museum of American Art, 1964, 30.

40 Letter to the author, June 1995.

41 Telephone conversation with author, August 1994.

42 Hamlin Garland, "Local Color," in *Crumbling Idols.* Cambridge: Harvard University Press, 1960, 54.

43 Robert Henri. "A Practical Talk to Those Who Study Art," *Philadelphia Press,* May 12, 1901, reprinted in Robert Henri, *The Art Spirit,* edited by Margery Ryerson. Philadelphia: J. B. Lippincott Co., 1923, 274–75.

44 Nathaniel Hawthorne, "Sights from a Steeple," in *The Works of Nathaniel Hawthorne,* vol. 1. Boston: Houghton Mifflin, 1851, 218.

45 Childe Hassam, *The New York Sun.* February 23, 1913, 16.

46 Georg Simmel, "The Metropolis and Mental Life," in *On Individuality and Social Forms: Selected Writings.* Chicago: Chicago University Press, 1971, 329–30.

47 Rosanna Warren, "Music for Railroad, Telephone Wire, and Easter," in *Each Leaf Shines Separate.* New York: W. W. Norton, 1984, 45.

48 Stevens, 529.

49 Moore, quoted in Alvin Martin et al., *Real, Really Real, Super Real,* 84.

50 See Leo Marx, *The Machine in the Garden.* New York: Oxford University Press, 1964.

51 See Gail Stavitsky, "Reordering Reality: Precisionist Directions in American Art, 1915–1941," in *Precisionism in America: Reordering Reality.* New York: Harry N. Abrams, Inc., in association with the Montclair Art Museum, 1994, 12–39.

52 Moore, quoted from taped transcript of the Distinguished Faculty Lecture, Samuel Paley Library, Temple University, Philadelphia, Pa., November 4, 1987.

53 On the grid in modern art, see Rosalind Krauss, "Grids," in *The Originality of the Avant-Garde and Other Modernist Myths.* Cambridge: M.I.T. Press, 1985.

54 Walker Evans, "The American Warehouse," *Architectural Forum* 116, April 1962, 94.

55 On the ambivalent messages of Sheeler's industrial scenes, see Carol Troyen and Erica E. Hirshler, *Charles Sheeler: Paintings and Drawings.* Boston: Little, Brown and Company, 1987; and Karen Lucic, *Charles Sheeler and the Cult of the Machine.* London: Reaktion Books, 1991.

56 Henri Lefebvre, *Everyday Life in the Modern World,* translated by Sacha Rabinovitch. London: Allen Lane, 1971, 24.

57 Moore, Distinguished Faculty Lecture, November 4, 1987.

58 Henry McBride, "Modern Art," *Dial* 74, February 1923, 218.

59 Moore, quoted in Laura Rath, *Uncommon Vistas. Urban, Suburban, and Industrial Views.* Boston: Boston University Art Gallery, 1989, 4.

60 Karen Tsujimoto, *Images of America.* San Francisco: Museum of Modern Art, 1982, 85.

61 Calvin Coolidge, quoted in William E. Leuchtenberg, *The Perils of Prosperity.* Chicago: University of Chicago Press, 1958, 188.

62 William Agee, "Precisionism and the Dawn of American Modernism," *New Criterion,* May 1995, 47.

63 William Carlos Williams, "The Wanderer: A Rococo Study," in *The Collected Poems of William Carlos Williams,* edited by A. William Litz and Christopher MacGowan. New York: New Directions Books, 1982, 28.

64 Gore Vidal, *At Home.* New York: Viking Books, 1988, 52–53.

CHRONOLOGY

1941
Born April 25 in St. Louis, Missouri, to John Moore and Catherine Hurley Moore, the first of four children.

1958
Graduates from high school, studies mechanical drafting at David Rankin, Jr. School of Mechanical Trades, St. Louis, and is hired as a draftsman–technical illustrator at McDonnell-Douglas in St. Louis. Takes painting lessons from a local artist and attends evening classes at Washington University.

1962
Attends Washington University full time. Graduates in 1966.

1964
Studies at Chautauqua Institution, Chautauqua, New York.

1965
Studies at Yale Summer School, Norfolk, Connecticut. Marries Sandra Rosenfeld.

1966
Attends Yale University and works part-time as a graphic designer for the New Haven Redevelopment Agency. Studies with Lester Johnson, Jack Tworkov, Lennart Andersen, and Richard Lindner. Jack Tworkov moderates panel on realism with panelists Alex Katz, Philip Pearlstein, John Button. Moore receives National Foundation on the Arts and Humanities grant.

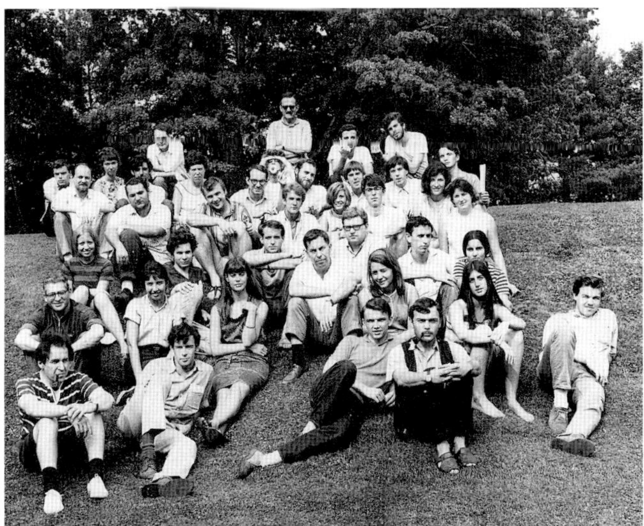

Yale Summer School, Norfolk Connecticut, Class of 1965. John Moore, extreme right. Faculty included William Bailey, fifth row left; Bernard Chaet, center top; Richard Ziemann, front row left; Al Blaustein, second row left; and George Wardaw, second row center.

1968
Receives MFA from Yale with the Ely Harwood Schless Memorial Prize. Artist-in-residence at Yale Summer School. Meets Robert and Sylvia Plimack Mangold, Vincent Longo, and Mel Bochner. Hired by David Pease to teach at Tyler School of Art, Temple University, in Philadelphia. Through David Pease meets Larry Day and Sidney Goodman, two Philadelphia realist painters, and Chuck Close.

1969
Son Aaron is born. Exhibits in *Direct Representation,* Fischbach Gallery, New York, with Sylvia Plimack Mangold, Yvonne Jacquette, Bruno Civitico, and Robert Bechtle. First New York show for all but Bechtle.

1970
Travels in Italy, France, and Spain. Special attraction to elegant perspectival architecture in works of Paolo Uccello and Piero della Francesca and to the clarity and simplicity of Fra Angelico. Commitment to still life reinforced after seeing Spanish still-life masters.

1971
Attends discussion group of figurative painters at the New York apartment of Nancy Grilhkes; other attendees include Gabriel Laderman, Sidney Tillim, William Bailey, Larry Day, Donald Perlis, Milet Andrejevic, Natalie Charkow.

1972
Son Alex is born.

1973
Receives the Childe Hassam Award, American Academy of Arts and Letters. First solo exhibitions at Fischbach Gallery and the Pennsylvania Academy of the Fine Arts, Philadelphia. Work included in *The Realist Revival,* American Federation of Arts traveling group exhibition. Meets Martha and Walter Erlebacher, and Elizabeth Osborne in Philadelphia.

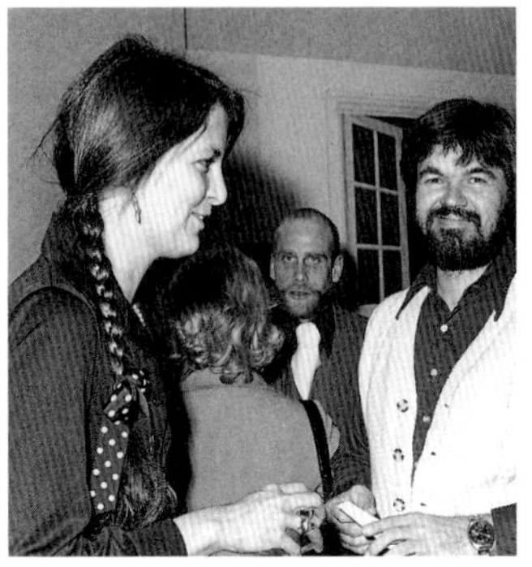

Anne D'Harnoncourt, Aladar Marburger, John Moore, Pennsylvania Academy of the Fine Arts opening, 1973.

1974
Teaches at Skowhegan School of Painting and Sculpture, where he meets Janet Fish, Rackstraw Downes, Leland Bell, and Fairfield Porter. Meets Neil Welliver and Altoon Sultan at Fischbach.

1976
Participates in a panel on realism and photorealism moderated by Cindy Nemser with Gregory Battcock, Chuck Close, Janet Fish, and Diane Burko at the Alliance of Figurative Artists meeting in New York, which he attended with Frank Galuszka over a four-year period and called his consciousness-raising support group for figurative artists.

1978–80
Chairman of Painting, Drawing, and Sculpture Department at Tyler School of Art. Hires Jillian Denby and Bruno Civitico.

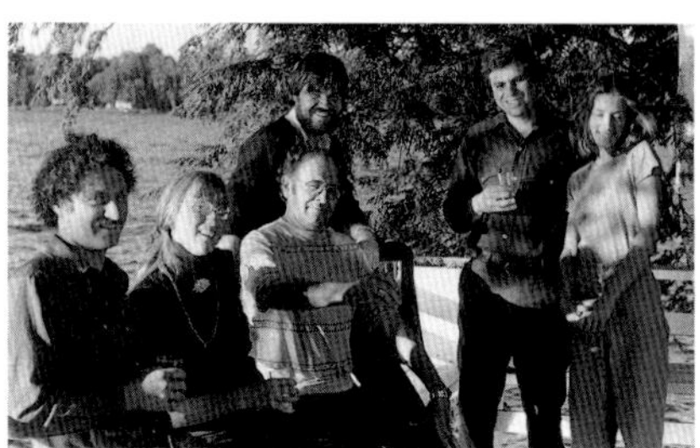

Fred Brandes, Janet Fish, Aldo Casanova, John Moore, Herb Schiffren, Robin Schiffren, Skowhegan, 1974.

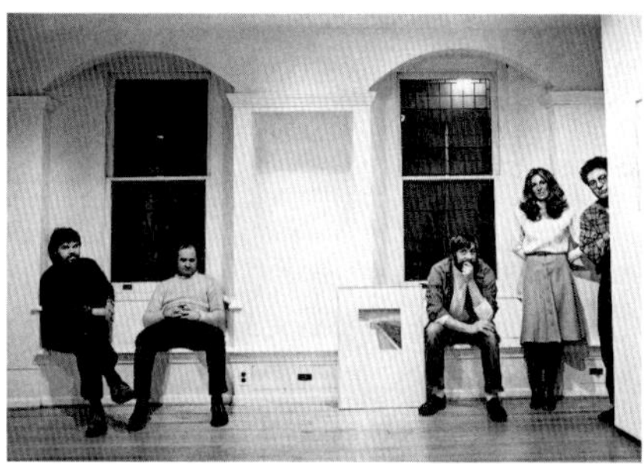

John Moore, Sidney Goodman, David Pease, Connie Vick, Italo Scanga, Philadelphia, 1974.

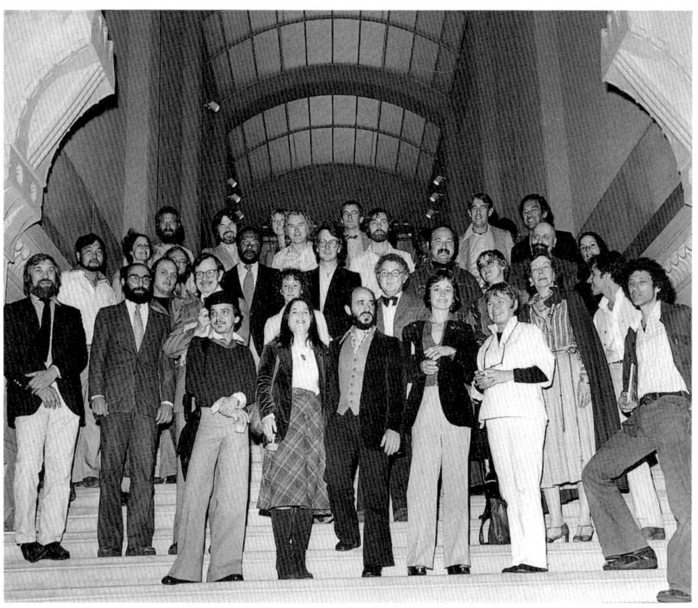

Artists of Philadelphia at opening of exhibition *Contemporary Drawings: Philadelphia*. Furness Building, Pennsylvania Academy of the Fine Arts, 1978.

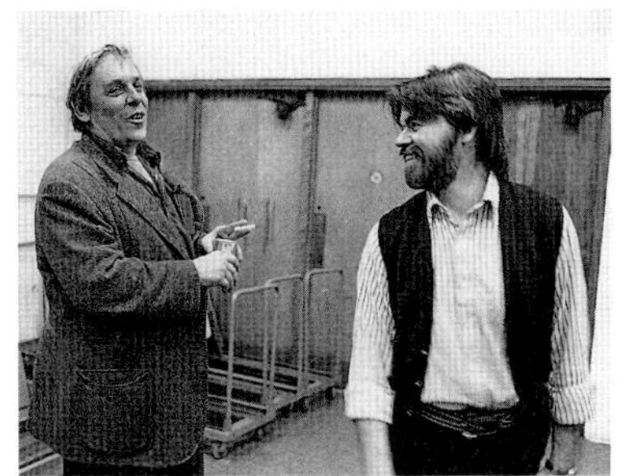
Jack Beal, John Moore, Tyler School of Art, 1979.

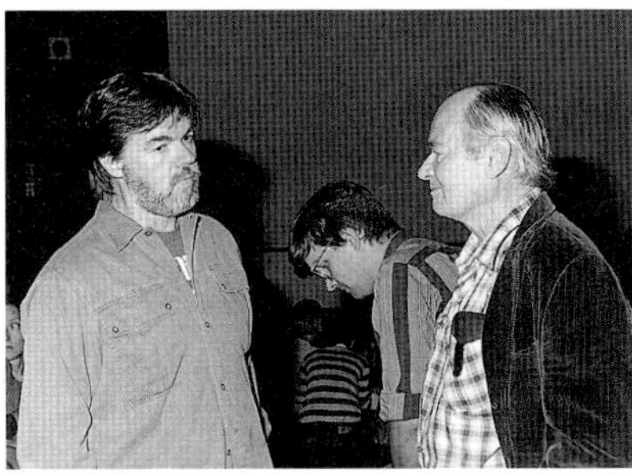
John Moore, Elmer Bischoff, Berkeley, 1982

1979
The Big Still Life show at Frumkin. Meets Jack Beal and Alfred Leslie.

1980
Meets Jackie Winsor, Howardena Pindell, George Schneeman, Susan Hall at Skowhegan. Joan Brown invites him to teach at Berkeley. Travels in Italy, France, and Spain.

1981–82
Teaches at University of California at Berkeley. Moves outdoors to larger vistas. Moves to Hirschl & Adler Modern gallery in New York. Becomes friends with Bay Area figurative artists Elmer Bischoff, Paul Wonner, and William Theo Brown, as well as Robert Yarber, Christopher Brown, and Anne Healy.

1982
Receives National Endowment for the Arts Visual Arts Fellowship in painting.

1984
Teaches at Skowhegan with Stuart Diamond, Frank Lobdell, Richard Haas, Frank Bowling, and Barbara Zucker.

1987
Is awarded the Creative Achievement Award by Temple University and delivers a lecture titled "The Past and Present: Painting at the End of the Eighties" in the Distinguished Faculty Lecture Series at Paley Library, Temple University.

1988
Moves to Boston to teach at Boston University. Meets George Nick. Advocates faculty appointments of Harriet Shorr, Katherine Porter, Graham Nickson, John Walker, and Alfred Leslie.

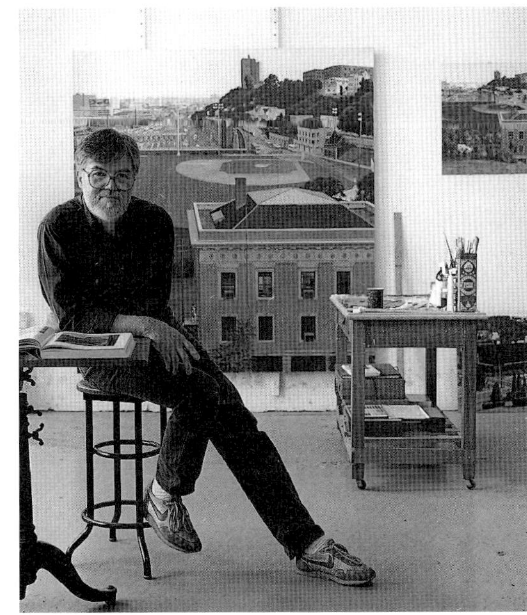
John Moore, Boston, 1990.

1990
Travels to Barcelona, Spain, in conjunction with solo exhibition; reaffirms interest in Miró. Moved by Spanish polychrome sculptures at Marees Museum.

1991
Receives National Endowment for the Arts Visual Arts Fellowship in painting.

1992
Visits Paris for six weeks. Composition studies after Derain at the Orangerie and Corot at the Louvre.

1994
Solo exhibitions with Alpha Gallery in Boston, Hirschl & Adler Modern in New York, and Marian Locks Gallery in Philadelphia.

1996
Is awarded 1996 Academy Award in Art, American Academy of Arts and Letters.

EXHIBITIONS

Selected Solo Exhibitions

1973
Fischbach Gallery, New York; Pennsylvania Academy of the Fine Arts

1974
Alpha Gallery, Boston; Vick, Klaus and Rosen Gallery, Philadelphia

1975
Fischbach Gallery, New York

1977
Dart Gallery, Chicago

1978
Fischbach Gallery, New York; University of Missouri, St. Louis

1979
Marian Locks Gallery, Philadelphia

1980
Fischbach Gallery, New York

1981
Capricorn Gallery, Washington, D.C.; College of William and Mary, Williamsburg, Virginia

1983
Hirschl & Adler Modern, New York; Buscaglia-Castellani Art Gallery, Niagara University, Niagara, New York

1985
Hirschl & Adler Modern, New York

1987
Marian Locks Gallery, Philadelphia

1989
Boston University Art Gallery

1990
Hirschl & Adler Modern, New York; Sala Nonell, Barcelona, Spain

1994
Alpha Gallery, Boston; Hirschl & Adler, New York; Marian Locks Gallery, Philadelphia

1995
Boston College Museum of Art, *Urban Landscapes*

Selected Group Exhibitions

1969
Fischbach Gallery, New York, *Direct Representation*; Phyllis Kind Gallery, Chicago; London Arts Gallery, Detroit

1971
State University of New York, Potsdam Gallery, *New Realism;* University of Rhode Island Art Gallery, Kingston, *From Life*

1972
Fischbach Gallery, New York, *Jacquette, Mangold, Moore, and Shatter*

1973
American Federation of Arts traveling exhibition, *The Realist Revival*

1973–74
American Academy of Arts and Letters, New York, *Hassam Exhibition*

1974
Queens Museum, Flushing, New York, *New Images: Figuration in American Painting;* Krannert Art Museum, Champaign-Urbana, Illinois, *Contemporary American Painting and Sculpture*

1975
Minnesota Museum of Art, St. Paul, *Drawings U.S.A.*

1976
Marian Locks Gallery, Philadelphia, *Philadelphia: A Decade;* Pennsylvania Academy of the Fine Arts, Philadelphia, *In This Academy;* Philadelphia Museum of Art, *Philadelphia: Three Centuries of American Art*

1977
Kennedy Gallery, New York, *Artists Salute Skowhegan;* Boston University Art Gallery, *Still Life*; Art Institute of Chicago, *Drawings of the Seventies*; Institute of Contemporary Art, Boston, *Collectors Collect Contemporary*

1978
Butler Institute of American Art, Youngstown, Ohio, *Forty-First Annual Exhibition*; Forum Gallery, New York, *Still Life: A New Sensibility*; College of William and Mary, Williamsburg, Virginia, *American Realism*; Pennsylvania Academy of the Fine Arts, Philadelphia, *Three Hundred and Fifty Masterpieces of American Painting*

1979
Alan Frumkin Gallery, New York, *The Big Still Life*; Boston University Art Gallery; University of Virginia Art Gallery, Charlottesville

1980
Thorpe Intermedia Gallery, Sparkhill, New York, *New York Realists 1980;* Nassau County Museum of Art, New York, *Contemporary Naturalism;* Philbrook Art Center, Tulsa, Oklahoma, *Realism/ Photorealism*

1981
San Antonio Museum of Art, San Antonio, Texas, *Real, Really Real, Super Real: Directions in Contemporary Realism;* Indianapolis Museum of Art; Tucson Museum, Arizona

1982
Pennsylvania Academy of the Fine Arts, Philadelphia, *Contemporary American Realism since 1960;* Virginia Museum of Fine Arts, Richmond; Oakland Museum, California

1983
Pennsylvania Academy of the Fine Arts, Philadelphia, *Perspectives on Contemporary American Realism: Works on Paper from the Collection of Jalane and Richard Davidson;* The Art Institute of Chicago; Joseloff Gallery, Hartford Art School, Connecticut, *Watercolor in America;* Metropolitan Museum of Art, New York, *Aspects of the City;* Fort Lauderdale Museum of Art, Florida, *New Narrative Painting;* Charles More Gallery, Philadelphia, *City Visions;* Waterville, Maine, *Homage to Skowhegan;* Colby College Art Museum, Rockport, Maine, *Maine Coast Artists*

1985
Hirschl & Adler Galleries, New York, *American Still Lifes from the Hirschl & Adler Collection;* Isetan Museum, Tokyo, *American Realism: The Precise Image;* Osaka, Japan, Daiman Museum; Yokohama, Japan, Takashimaya Gallery; Koplin Gallery, Los Angeles, *Interior/ Exterior*

1986
Philadelphia Museum of Art, *Philadelphia Collects*

1989
Minnesota Museum of Art, St. Paul, *American Landscape;* Fitchburg Art Museum, Massachusetts, *Monocular Vision*

1990
Miyagi Museum of Art, Sendai, Japan, *American Realism and Figurative Art: 1952–1990;* Sogo Museum of Art, Yokohama, Japan; Tokushima Modern Art Museum, Tokushima, Japan; Museum of Modern Art, Shiga, Japan; Kochi Prefectural Museum of Folk Art; Tokyo, Japan

1991
Boston Center for the Arts, *12th Annual Boston Drawing Show;* Levinson Kane Gallery, Boston, *Inclusion/Exclusion: City Life;* Orlando Museum of Art, Florida, *Exquisite Paintings*

1993
Gerald Peters Gallery, Santa Fe, *Still Life 1963–1993;* Maine Coast Artists, Rockport, Maine, *Looking at the Land;* Yale University Art Gallery, New Haven, Connecticut, *Yale Collects Yale*

1995
Florida International University Art Museum, Miami, *American Art Today: Night Paintings;* Wright State University Art Galleries, Dayton, Ohio, *Urban Landscape: Rackstraw Downes, Yvonne Jacquette, John Moore*; Gerald Wunderlich & Co., New York, *The Urban Landscape*; The Murray Collection, Scranton, Pennsylvania

1996
Hirschl & Adler Modern, New York, *Picturing Gotham;* American Academy of Arts and Letters, *Annual Awards and Exhibition;* Library of the Boston Athenaeum, *The Future of the Past;* Museum of Fine Arts, Boston, *Corkscrew to Collage: Still Life*

PUBLIC COLLECTIONS

American Can Corporation, New York

American Telephone and Telegraph Corporation, New York

Art Institute of Chicago

Balis and Company, New York

Chase Manhattan Bank, N.A., New York

CIGNA Corporation, Philadelphia

Colby College Museum of Art, Waterville, Maine

Commerce Bancshares of Kansas City, Missouri

Dartmouth College, Hanover, New Hampshire

First International Bank, Houston, Texas

L. B. Foster Corporation, Pennsylvania

Hallmark Cards, Kansas City, Missouri

John Hancock Mutual Life Insurance Company, Boston

IBM Corporation, New York

McNay Art Institute, San Antonio, Texas

Mellon Bank, Pittsburgh

Metropolitan Museum of Art, New York

Minnesota Museum of Art, St. Paul

Museum of Art, Rhode Island School of Design, Providence

Museum of Fine Arts, Boston

Neuberger Museum of Art, State University of New York, Purchase

Pennsylvania Academy of the Fine Arts, Philadelphia

Philadelphia Museum of Art

San Francisco Museum of Modern Art

Shearson Lehman Brothers Incorporated, New York

Smith College Art Museum, Northampton, Massachusetts

University of Massachusetts, Amherst

Wellington Management, Boston

Yale University Art Gallery, New Haven, Connecticut

SELECT BIBLIOGRAPHY

Acconci, Vito H. "John Moore." *Art News,* November 1969.

Alloway, Lawrence. "Art." *The Nation,* November 6, 1972.

Anderson, Laurie. "Group: Fischbach." *Arts,* November 1972, 70.

Arthur, John. *American Realism and Figurative Art: 1952–1990.* Miyagi, Japan: The Miyagi Museum of Art, 1991.

———. *American Realism: The Precise Image.* Tokyo: Isetan Museum of Art, 1985.

———. *Realism/Photorealism.* Tulsa, Oklahoma: Philbrook Art Center, October, 1980.

———. *Spirit of Place.* Boston: Bullfinch Press, 1989.

———. *Still Life 1963–1993.* Santa Fe, New Mexico: Gerald Peters Gallery, 1993.

"Artist John Moore: The Commonplace Becomes the Extraordinary." *Boston University Today,* September 11, 1989.

"Artist Moore Visits Campus, Discusses Student Paintings." *Second Front,* West Georgia State College, Carrollton, 1974.

"Art Listings." *Boston Phoenix,* September 29, 1989, 37.

"Art of Tyler Faculty Illustrates Calendar." *Times Chronicle,* Montgomery County, Pa., December 27, 1984.

"At the Museum." *Providence Journal Bulletin,* November 3, 1973.

Battcock, Gregory. *Super Realism: A Critical Anthology.* New York: E. P. Dutton, Inc., 1975.

Bowles, Jerry. "Review and Previews: John Moore." *Art News,* December 1971, 18.

Burke, Bobbye. "Artists as Humanists." *Women's Caucus for the Arts Newsletter,* April 1977, 51.

Burton, Scott. *Direct Representation.* New York: Fischbach Gallery, 1969.

———. *The Realist Revival.* New York: American Federation of Arts, 1972.

Cohen, Ronny. "John Moore." *Artforum* 24, February 1986, 106–7.

Contemporary American Painting and Sculpture. Champaign, Illinois: Krannert Art Museum, 1974.

Day, Meredith Fife. "Boston University Art Gallery/Boston. Boston University School for the Arts: Visual Arts Faculty Exhibition." *Art New England,* April/May 1993, 57.

———. "John Moore Exhibits Urban Landscapes at Alpha Gallery." *Newbury Street Guide,* Boston, January 21, 1994, 9.

Degener, Patricia. "Print Workshop Shows Itself Off." *St. Louis Post-Dispatch,* February 25, 1982, 8E.

Derfner, Phyllis. "New York Letter." *Art International* 17, November 1973, 50–52.

Di Niscemi, Margherita. "Mayor Likes Modern Art." *Art World,* April 15, 1978, 17.

Donohoe, Victoria. "Academy Show Strives to Foster Dynamic Image." *Philadelphia Inquirer,* April 25, 1976, 1D.

———. "A Comeback for Landscapes." *Philadelphia Inquirer,* March 28, 1975, 3D.

———. "Behind Every Work, There's a Story." *Philadelphia Inquirer,* July 1, 1973, 43.

———. "Dutch Master Flying on a 747 Jet Lands at Home. *Philadelphia Inquirer,* March 2, 1979, 27.

———. "Realist Painter John Moore Brings Traditional Still-Life up to Date." *Philadelphia Inquirer,* March 1977, 17.

———. "Temple's John Moore Adds Variety to Realism." *Philadelphia Inquirer,* November 16, 1973, 14.

———. "The Work of Eleven Artists, 'Celebrating Philadelphia.'" *Philadelphia Inquirer,* May 10, 1986, 21.

Evett, Kenneth. "On Art." *New Republic,* February 3, 1973, 25–26.

Forman, Nessa. "Piero Updated (or What Moore Does)." *Philadelphia Sunday Bulletin,* November 25, 1973, 8.

———. "Three Shows of Note." *Philadelphia Bulletin,* March, 1977, 14.

Frackman, Noel. "Hugh Kepets/John Moore." *Arts* 50, January 1976, 21–22.

Frank, Peter. "A Broad Spectrum." *Art News,* February 1974, 78.

———. "John Moore." *Art News* 75, January 1976, 122–23.

Gaston, Michael. "Introduction." *Art as Likeness.* Bethlehem, Pa.: Moravian College, 1976.

Gilbert-Rolfe, Jeremy. "John Moore: Fischbach." *Artforum* 12, December 1973, 88.

Giuliano, Charles. "Alpha Gallery/Boston. John Moore: Recent Paintings." *Art New England,* March/April 1994, 20.

Godfrey, Robert. *The Figure in Recent American Painting.* New Wilmington, Pa.: Westminster College, 1974.

Goldman, Susanne. "Gallery 210 Hosts Moore." *University of Missouri Current,* November 16, 1978.

Goldsmith, Benedict I. *New Realism.* Potsdam, New York: Brainerd Hall Art Museum, 1971.

Goodyear, Frank H., Jr. *Contemporary American Realism.* Boston: New York Graphic Society, 1981.

———. *Perspectives on Contemporary American Realism. Works of Art on Paper from the Collection of Jalane and Richard Davidson.* Philadelphia: Pennsylvania Academy of the Fine Arts, 1982.

d'Harnoncourt, Anne. "John Moore," in *Philadelphia: Three Centuries of American Art.* Philadelphia: Philadelphia Museum of Art, 1976.

Henry, Gerrit. "John Moore." *Art News* 71, November 1972, 83.

———. *John Moore. Cityscapes–New Paintings.* Philadelphia: Locks Gallery, 1994.

———. "A Realist Twin Bill." *Art News* 72, January 1973, 26–28.

———. *Realist Watercolors.* Miami: Florida International University, 1983.

———. "The Real Thing." *Art International* 16, Summer 1972, 87–91, 144.

———. "Reviews and Previews: John Moore." *Art News* 71, November 1972, 83.

Henry, Shannon. "Uncommon Perception." *Muse,* September 21, 1989, 1–12.

Howrigan, Roger. Introduction to *New York Realists.* Sparkhill, N.Y.: Thorpe Intermedia Gallery, 1980.

"John Moore." *New Yorker,* February 6, 1978, 16.

"John Moore." *New York Times,* February 3, 1978, 15.

"John Moore. *Glass Table.*" *Illinois University College,* 1974, 84.

Kay, Jane Holtz. "New Editions." *Art News* 76, March 1977, 116.

King, Mary. "Artists Guild Show of Prints, Drawings." *St. Louis Post-Dispatch,* December 20, 1965, 3B.

———. "Guild Has Show of Young Talent." *St. Louis Post-Dispatch,* February 23, 1966, 3C.

———. "Moore, Rosen Exhibits." *St. Louis Post-Dispatch,* November 8, 1978, 4H.

———. "'Print Makers': A Surprise Show." *St. Louis Post-Dispatch,* June 17, 1966, 3B.

Kingsley, April. "Review. John Moore." *Artforum* 11, December 1972, 83.

Kramer, Hilton. "Art: Five-Gallery Realist Show." *New York Times,* September 12, 1980, C20.

———. "Art: Worthy Variety of Local Debuts." *New York Times,* September 22, 1973, 27.

Kultermann, Udo. *New Realism.* Greenwich, Conn.: New York Graphic Society, 1970.

Le Clair, Charles. *The Art of Watercolor.* Englewood Cliffs, N.J.: Prentice Hall, 1985.

———. *Color in Contemporary Painting.* New York: Watson-Guptill Publications, 1991.

Lieberman, William S. *"Thursday,"* in Phillipe de Montebello, *Notable Acquisitions.* New York: Metropolitan Museum of Art, 1983–84.

Mannheimer, Marc. "Boston University Art Gallery/Boston. John Moore: Uncommon Vistas." *Art New England,* December 1989/January 1990, 39.

Marandel, J. Patrice. *Albert Pilavin Collection: Twentieth-Century American Art.* Providence: Museum of Art, Rhode Island School of Design, 1973.

"Marian Locks Gallery Show." *Philadelphia Inquirer,* June 7, 1985, 1C.

Marter, Joan M. *In This Academy.* Philadelphia: Pennsylvania Academy of the Fine Arts, 1976, 255.

Martin, Alvin. *American Realism. Twentieth-Century Drawings and Watercolors from the Glenn C. Janns Collection.* San Francisco: San Francisco Museum of Modern Art, 1986.

Martin, Alvin, et al. *Real, Really Real, Super Real.* San Antonio, Texas: San Antonio Museum, 1981.

McFadden, Sarah. "Report from Philadelphia." *Art in America* 67, May–June 1979, 21–31.

McGill, Douglas C. "Personal Art and the Skowhegan Experience." *New York Times,* August 17, 1982, 14.

McManus, Otile. "Portraits of the City's Soul." *Boston Globe,* October 20, 1989, 79.

Medoff, Eve. "John Moore," in Susan Meyer, *Twenty Oil Painters and How They Work.* New York: Watson-Guptill Publications, 1978.

———. "John Moore—Realism Reinvented." *American Artist* 42, March 1987, 36–72.

Nemser, Cindy. "Representational Painting in 1971. A New Synthesis." *Arts* 46, December 1971/January 1972, 41–46.

Osborn, Florence. "A. T. Gallery Show." *New Haven Register,* May 12, 1968, 17.

Perreault, John. "Airplane Art in a Head Wind." *Village Voice,* October 4, 1973, 24.

———. "Light Rays Caught and Bent." *Village Voice,* October 12, 1972, 27–28.

Pincus-Witten, Robert. "*Direct Representation,* Fischbach Gallery." *Artforum* 8, November 1969, 78–80.

Rath, Laura J. *John Moore. Uncommon Vistas.* Boston: Boston University Art Gallery, 1989.

"Research and Creativity Cited." *Temple Times* 17, May 28, 1987.

Russell, John. "Critic's Choices. Art." *New York Times,* November 10, 1985, G2.

———. "The Many Faces of Naturalism." *New York Times,* August 10, 1980, D25.

Sachs, Sid. "Art and Architecture in Philadelphia." *New Art Examiner,* October 1980, 15.

Schad, Tennyson, ed. *Research and Development Art Collection.* Philadelphia: Smith Kline, 1988.

Schjeldahl, Peter. "New York." *Art International* 13, December 1969, 70.

———. "Realism—A Retreat to the Fundamentals?" *New York Times,* December 24, 1972, 25–26.

Schwartz, Ellen. "The Big Still Life." *Art News* 78, May 1979, 168–70.

Shultes, Anne. "City Scenes." *Montgomery County Record,* Jenkintown, Pa., June 28, 1987, C1–2.

Smith, Corinna, and Brian Wallis. "The Big Still Life." *Arts* 53, May 1979, 95.

Sozanski, Edward. "Locks Gallery." *Philadelphia Inquirer,* October 7, 1994, 38.

Speigel, Olga. "Moore: La Ilusion de realidad del paisaje industrial." *La Vanguardia–Barcelona,* March 22, 1990, 38.

Stapen, Nancy. "BU Still Keeps the Faith with Figurative Art." *Boston Globe,* February 9, 1993, 1.

Stein, Judith. "Portrait: Philadelphia." *Portfolio,* November/December 1980.

Temin, Christine. "A Strong Show of Drawings." *Boston Globe,* September 6, 1991, 1, 34.

"Temple Recognizes Artist's Naturalistic Works." *Times Chronicle,* Jenkintown, Pa., July 1, 1987, 4.

Ward, John L. *American Realist Painting 1945–80.* Ann Arbor, Mich.: UMI Research Press, 1989.

Welish, Marjorie. "New York Letter." *Art International* 16, December 1972, 70.

Yau, John. "John Moore: An Introduction," in *John Moore.* New York: Hirschl & Adler Modern, 1983.

Zelnick, Steve. "The Romance of Realism." *Faculty Herald. Temple University* 17, November 23, 1987, 5–6.

Zemel, Carol. *Still-Life and City View: Realist Paintings by John Moore.* New York: Buscaglia-Castellani Art Gallery, 1983.

Zimmer, William. "Yale Celebrates Its Artists and Its Collectors since 1950." *New York Times,* June 27, 1993, 14.

INDEX

PHOTOGRAPH CREDITS

Del Bogart Plate 3

Will Brown Plates 10, 12, 13, 14, 15, 16, 17, 23, 25, 26, 28, 29, 30, 34, 49, 50, 51, 52, 53, 55, 57

Eeva-inkeri Plates 21, 22

Courtesy of Fischbach Gallery Plate 11

Michael Lavin Flower Plate 58

Greg Heins Plates 19, 20, 31, 32, 33, 35, 36, 37, 38, 39, 40, 41, 42, 43, 44, 45, 46, 54

Robert E. Mates Figures 5 and 8

Joseph Painter Plate 48

Len Rubenstein Frontispiece